Quick & Easy

Quick
& Easy

p

This is a Parragon Publishing Book
First printed in 2000

Parragon Publishing
Queen Street House
4 Queen Street
Bath BA1 1HE, UK

ISBN: 0-75253-963-9

Printed in Indonesia

NOTE

Cup measurements in this book are for American cups.
Tablespoons are assumed to be 15ml. Unless otherwise stated,
milk is assumed to be full fat, eggs are medium
and pepper is freshly ground black pepper.

Recipes using uncooked eggs should be
avoided by infants, the elderly, pregnant women and anyone
suffering from an illness.

Contents

Introduction   8

Soups

Appetizers & Snacks

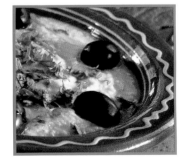

Fish & Seafood

Meat Dishes

Chicken & Poultry

Pasta & Rice

Desserts

Index   254

Introduction

This book is designed to appeal to anyone who wants a wholesome, but quick and easy diet, and includes many recipes suitable for vegetarians and vegans. Its main aim is to show people that, with a little forethought, it is possible to spend very little time in the kitchen while still enjoying good food.

Appetizing Food

The recipes collected here come from all over the world; some of the Indian and barbecue dishes featured require marinating, often overnight, but it is worth remembering that their actual cooking time is very short once the marinade has been absorbed. The more exotic dishes on offer are balanced by some traditional dishes that are sure to be firm family favorites. If you want fast food for everyday meals, or you are short on time and want to prepare a delicious dinner party treat, there is something for everybody in this book.

To save time in the kitchen, always make sure that you have the requisite basics in your cupboard. By keeping a stock of staple foodstuffs, such as rice, pasta, spices, and herbs, you can easily turn your hand to any number of these recipes.

KEEPING A FULL PANTRY CUPBOARD

Flour

You will need to keep a selection of flour: Self-rising and wholewheat are the most useful. You may also like to keep some rice flour and cornstarch for thickening sauces and to add to cakes, cookies and puddings. Buckwheat, garbanzo-bean, and soy flours are also worth stocking. These are useful for combining with other flours to vary flavors and textures.

Grains and Rices

A good variety of grains is essential. For rice, choose from long-grain, basmati, Italian arborio, short-grain, and wild rice. Also look for fragrant Thai rice, jasmine rice, and combinations of different varieties to add color and texture to your dishes. When choosing your rice, remember that brown rice is a better source of vitamin B1 and fiber than white rice.

Other grains and cereals that are useful include barley, millet, bulgur wheat, polenta, oats, semolina, sago, and tapioca.

Pasta

Pasta is very popular nowadays, and there are many types and shapes to choose from. Keep a good selection, such as basic lasagne sheets, tagliatelle or fettuccine (flat ribbons), and spaghetti. For a change, sample some of the many fresh pastas now available. Better still, make your own — handrolling pasta can be very satisfying, and you can buy a machine for rolling the dough and cutting certain shapes.

Legumes

Legumes are a valuable source of protein, vitamins, and minerals. Stock up on dried soy beans, navy beans, red kidney beans, cannellini beans, garbanzo beans, lentils, split peas, and butter beans. Buy dried legumes for soaking and cooking yourself, or canned varieties for speed and convenience.

Herbs

A good selection of herbs is important for adding extra flavors to your cooking. Fresh herbs are preferable to dried varieties, but it is essential to have dried ones in stock as a useful backup. Store dried basil, thyme, bay leaves, oregano, rosemary, Italian seasoning and bundles of bouquet garni.

Chilies

These come both fresh and dried and in many colors. The "hotness" varies so use with caution. The seeds are hottest and are usually discarded. Ground red chilis should also be used sparingly. Check whether the powder is pure chili or a chili seasoning or blend, which should be milder.

Nuts and Seeds

As well as adding protein, vitamins, and useful fats to the diet, nuts and seeds add important flavor and texture to vegetarian meals. Make sure you keep a good supply of nuts such as hazelnuts, pine nuts, and walnuts. Coconut is useful, too.

For your seed collection, have sesame, sunflower, pumpkin, and poppy. Pumpkin seeds in particular are a good source of zinc.

Dried Fruit

Currants, raisins, golden raisins, dates, apples, apricots, figs, pears, peaches, prunes, papayas, mangoes, figs, bananas and pineapples can all be bought dried and can be used in many sweet and savory recipes. When buying dried fruit, look for untreated varieties: for example, buy figs that have not been rolled in sugar, and choose unsulfured apricots, if they are available.

Oils and Fats

Oils are useful for adding subtle flavorings to foods, so it is a good idea to have a selection in your cupboard. Use a light olive oil for cooking and extra-virgin olive oil for salad dressings. Use sunflower oil as a good general-purpose oil. Sesame oil is wonderful in stir-fries; hazelnut and walnut oils are superb in salad dressings. Oils and fats

Ragù Sauce

3 tbsp olive oil

3 tbsp butter

2 large onions, chopped

4 celery stalks, thinly sliced

1 cup chopped bacon

2 garlic cloves, chopped

1 lb 2 oz ground lean beef

2 tbsp tomato paste

1 tbsp all-purpose flour

14-oz can chopped tomatoes

⅔ cup beef stock

⅔ cup red wine

2 tsp dried oregano

½ tsp freshly grated nutmeg

salt and pepper

1 Heat the oil and butter in a pan over a medium heat. Add the onions, celery, and bacon and fry for 5 minutes, stirring.

2 Stir in the garlic and ground beef and cook, stirring until the meat has lost its redness. Lower the heat and cook for 10 minutes, stirring.

3 Increase the heat to medium, stir in the tomato paste and the flour, and cook for 1-2 minutes. Stir in the tomatoes, stock, and wine and bring to a boil, stirring. Season and stir in the oregano and nutmeg. Cover and simmer for 45 minutes, stirring. The sauce is now ready to use.

Introduction

contain the important fat-soluble vitamins A, D, E, and K. Remember all fats and oils are high in calories, although some contain less saturated fat (believed to increase the risk of heart disease) than others.

Vinegars

Choose three or four vinegars – red or white wine, cider, distilled, tarragon, sherry, or balsamic, to name just a few. Each will add its own character to your recipes.

Mustards

Mustards are made from black, brown, or white mustard seeds that are ground and mixed with spices. Meaux mustard is made from mixed mustard seeds and has a grainy texture with a warm, taste. Dijon mustard, made from husked and ground mustard seeds, has a sharp flavor. Its versatility in salads and with barbecue dishes makes it ideal for the vegetarian. German mustard is mild and is best used in Scandinavian and German dishes.

Bottled Sauces

Soy sauce is widely used in oriental cooking and is made from fermented yellow soy beans mixed with wheat, salt, yeast, and sugar. Light soy sauce tends to be salty, whereas dark soy sauce tends to be sweeter. Teriyaki sauce gives an authentic Japanese flavoring to stir-fries. Black bean and yellow bean sauces add an instant authentic Chinese flavor to stir-fries.

Storing Spices

Your basic stock of spices should include fresh ginger and garlic, ground red chilis, turmeric, paprika, cloves, cardamom, black pepper, ground coriander, and ground cumin. The powdered spices should be kept in airtight containers to preserve their flavors, while the fresh ginger and garlic will keep for 7 to 10 days in the refrigerator.

Other useful items, to be acquired as your repertoire increases, are cumin seeds (black as well as white), onion seeds, mustard seeds, cloves, cinnamon, dried red chilies, fenugreek, and garam masala (a mixture of spices that can either be bought ready-made, or home made in quantity for use whenever required).

Using Spices

You can use spices whole, ground, roasted, fried, or mixed with yogurt as part of a marinade for meat and poultry. One spice can alter the flavor of a dish and a combination of several can produce different colors and textures. The quantities of spices shown in the recipes are simply guides. Increase or decrease them as you wish, especially in the cases of salt and ground red chilis, which are a matter of taste.

Many of the recipes in this book call for ground spices, which are available in supermarkets as well as in ethnic grocers. In India, where spices are an important ingredient in everyday cooking, whole spices are ground at home, and there is no doubt that freshly ground spices do make a noticeable difference to the taste of a dish.

Introduction

Some recipes specify roasted spices. In India, this is done on a *thawa*, but you can use a heavy, ideally cast-iron skillet. No water or oil is needed: the spices are simply dry-roasted whole while the pan is shaken to stop them burning on the bottom of the pan.

Remember that long cooking over a low heat improves the taste of the food as it allows the spices to be absorbed. This is why reheating dishes the following day is no problem for most Indian food.

USEFUL ORIENTAL INGREDIENTS

Bamboo Shoots

These are added for texture, as they have very little flavor. Available in cans, they are a common ingredient in Chinese cooking.

Beansprouts

These are mung bean shoots, which are very nutritious, containing many vitamins. They add crunch to a recipe and are widely available. Do not overcook them, because they wilt and do not add texture to the dish.

Black Beans

These are soybeans and are very salty. They can be bought and crushed with salt and then rinsed or used in the form of a bottled sauce for convenience.

Chinese Beans

These long beans can be eaten whole and are very tender. Green beans make an acceptable substitute.

Chinese Five-Spice Powder

An aromatic blend of cinnamon, cloves, star anise, fennel, and brown peppercorns that is often used in marinades.

Chinese Leaves

A light green leaf with a sweet flavor. It is found readily in most supermarkets.

Hoisin Sauce

A dark brown, sweet, thick sauce that is widely available bottled. Made from spices, soy sauce, garlic, and chili, it is often served as a dipping sauce.

Lychees

These are worth buying fresh because they are easy to prepare. Inside the inedible skin is a fragrant white fruit. Available canned, lychees are a classic ingredient of many Chinese dishes.

Mango

Choose a ripe mango for its sweet, scented flesh. If a mango is under-ripe when bought, leave it in a sunny place for a few days before using.

Noodles

The Chinese use several varieties of noodle. You will probably find it easiest to use the dried varieties, such as egg noodles, which are yellow; rice stick noodles, which are white and very fine; or transparent noodles, which are opaque when dry and turn transparent while cooking. However, cellophane or rice noodles can also be used.

Oyster Sauce

Readily available in jars, this brown sauce is made from oysters, salt, seasonings, and cornstarch. It adds a rich, savory flavor to dishes.

Bok Choi

Also known as Chinese cabbage, this has a mild, slightly bitter flavor.

Rice Vinegar

This has a mild, sweet taste that is very delicate. It is available in some supermarkets, but if not available use cider vinegar instead.

Rice Wine

This is similar to dry sherry in color, alcohol content, and smell, but it is worth buying rice wine for its distinctive flavor.

Sesame Oil

This is made from roasted sesame seeds and has an intense flavor. It burns easily and is therefore added at the end of cooking for flavor, and is not used for frying.

Soy Sauce

This is widely available, but it is worth buying a good grade of sauce. It is produced in both light and dark varieties — the former is used with fish and vegetables for a lighter color and flavor, while the latter, being darker, richer, saltier, and more intense, is used as a dipping sauce or with strongly flavored meats.

Star Anise

This is an eight-pointed, star-shaped pod with a strong anise flavor. The spice is also available ground. If a pod is added to a dish, it should be removed before serving.

Szechuan Pepper

This is hot and spicy and should be used sparingly. It is red in color and is readily available.

Tofu

This soy bean paste is available in several forms. The cake variety, which is soft and spongy and a white-gray color, is used in this book. It is very bland, but adds texture to dishes and is perfect for absorbing all the other flavors in the dish.

Water Chestnuts

These are flat and round and can usually only be purchased in cans, already peeled. They add a delicious crunch to dishes and have a slightly sweet flavor.

Yellow Beans

Again a soybean and very salty. Use a variety that is chunky rather than smooth.

Basic Recipes

These recipes form the basis of several of the dishes contained throughout this book. Many of these basic recipes can be made in advance and stored in the refrigerator until required, so cooking a dish that includes them is even quicker to prepare!

Basic Tomato Sauce

2 tbsp olive oil

1 small onion, chopped

1 garlic clove, chopped

14-oz can chopped tomatoes

2 tbsp chopped parsley

1 tsp dried oregano

2 bay leaves

2 tbsp tomato paste

1 tsp sugar

salt and pepper

1 Heat the oil in a pan over a medium heat and fry the onion for 2-3 minutes, or until translucent. Add the garlic and fry for 1 minute.

2 Stir in the chopped tomatoes, parsley, oregano, bay leaves, tomato paste, sugar, and salt and pepper to taste.

3 Bring the sauce to a boil, then simmer, uncovered, for 15–20 minutes, or until the sauce has reduced by half. Taste the sauce and adjust the seasoning if necessary. Discard the bay leaves just before serving.

Béchamel Sauce

1¼ cups milk

2 bay leaves

3 cloves

1 small onion

4 tbsp butter, plus extra for greasing

6 tbsp all-purpose flour

1¼ cups light cream

large pinch of freshly grated nutmeg

salt and pepper

1 Pour the milk into a small pan and add the bay leaves. Press the cloves into the onion, add to the pan, and bring the milk to a boil. Remove the pan from the heat and set aside to cool.

2 Strain the milk into a measuring jug and rinse the pan. Melt the butter in the pan and stir in the flour. Stir for 1 minute, then gradually pour in the milk, stirring constantly. Cook the sauce for 3 minutes, then pour in the cream and bring it to a boil. Remove from the heat and season with nutmeg, and salt and pepper to taste.

Lamb Sauce

2 tbsp olive oil

1 large onion, sliced

2 celery stalks, thinly sliced

1 lb 2 oz lean lamb, ground

3 tbsp tomato paste

5 oz bottled sun-dried tomatoes, drained and chopped

1 tsp dried oregano

1 tbsp red-wine vinegar

⅔ cup chicken stock

salt and pepper

1 Heat the oil in a skillet over a medium heat and fry the onion and celery until the onion is translucent, about 3 minutes. Add the lamb and fry, stirring frequently, until it browns.

2 Stir in the tomato paste, sun-dried tomatoes, oregano, vinegar, and stock. Season with salt and pepper to taste.

3 Bring to a boil and cook, uncovered, for 20 minutes, or until the meat has absorbed the stock. Taste and adjust the seasoning if necessary.

Cheese Sauce

2 tbsp butter

1 tbsp all-purpose flour

1 cup milk

2 tbsp light cream

pinch of freshly grated nutmeg

⅓ cup sharp Cheddar, grated

1 tbsp freshly grated Parmesan

salt and pepper

1 Melt the butter in a pan. Stir in the flour and cook for 1 minute. Gradually pour in the milk, stirring all the time. Stir in the cream and season the sauce with nutmeg, and salt and pepper to taste.

2 Simmer the sauce for 5 minutes to reduce, then remove it from the heat and stir in the cheeses. Stir until the cheeses have melted and blended into the sauce.

Espagnole Sauce

2 tbsp butter

¼ cup all-purpose flour

1 tsp tomato paste

1 cup plus 2 tbsp veal stock, hot

1 tbsp Madeira wine

1½ tsp white-wine vinegar

2 tbsp olive oil

2 tbsp diced bacon

2 tbsp diced carrot

2 tbsp diced onion

1 tbsp diced celery

1 tbsp chopped leek

1 tbsp chopped fennel

1 fresh thyme sprig

1 bay leaf

1 Melt the butter in a pan. Add the flour and cook, stirring, until lightly colored. Add the tomato paste, then stir in the hot veal stock, Madeira, and white-wine vinegar and cook for 2 minutes.

2 Heat the oil in a separate pan. Add the bacon, carrot, onion, celery, leek, fennel, thyme sprig, and bay leaf and fry until the vegetables have softened. Remove the vegetables from the pan with a draining spoon and drain thoroughly. Add the vegetables to the sauce and leave to simmer for 4 hours, stirring occasionally. Strain the sauce before using.

Italian Red Wine Sauce

⅔ cup brown stock

⅔ cup Espagnole Sauce (see left)

½ cup red wine

2 tbsp red-wine vinegar

4 tbsp chopped shallots

1 bay leaf

1 thyme sprig

pepper

1 First make a demiglace sauce. Put the Brown Stock and Espagnole Sauce in a pan and heat for 10 minutes, stirring occasionally.

2 Meanwhile, put the red wine, red-wine vinegar, shallots, bay leaf, and thyme in a pan, bring to a boil, and reduce by three-quarters.

3 Strain the demiglace sauce and add to the pan containing the red wine sauce and leave to simmer for 20 minutes, stirring occasionally. Season with pepper to taste and strain the sauce before using.

How to Use This Book

Each recipe contains a wealth of useful information, including a breakdown of nutritional quantities, preparation and cooking times, and level of difficulty. All of this information is explained in detail below.

This amount of time represents the actual cooking time.

The nutritional information provided for each recipe is per serving or per portion. Optional ingredients, variations or serving suggestions have not been included in the calculations.

The number of chef's hats represents the difficulty of each recipe, ranging from easy (1 chef's hat) to difficult (5 chef's hats).

This amount of time represents the preparation of ingredients, including cooling, chilling, and soaking times.

The ingredients for each recipe are listed in the order that they are used.

The method is clearly explained with step-by-step directions that are easy to follow.

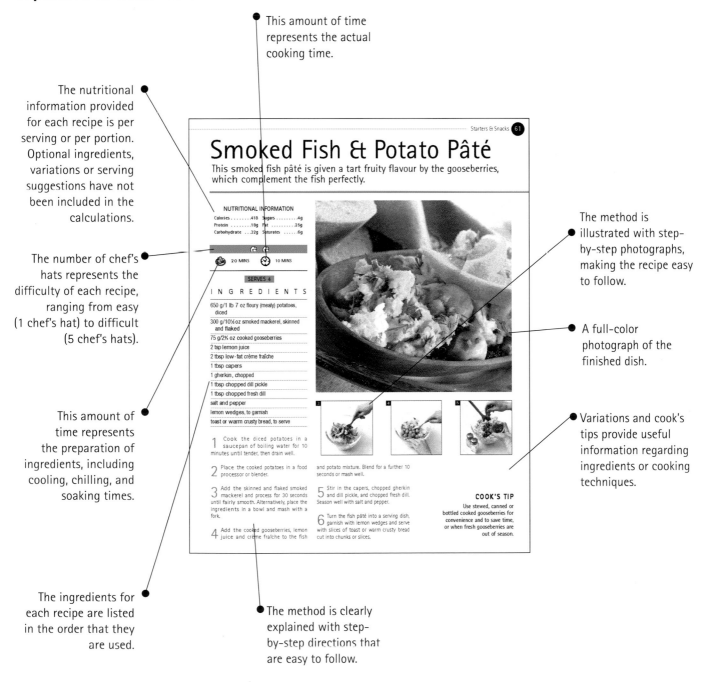

The method is illustrated with step-by-step photographs, making the recipe easy to follow.

A full-color photograph of the finished dish.

Variations and cook's tips provide useful information regarding ingredients or cooking techniques.

Starters & Snacks 61

Smoked Fish & Potato Pâté

This smoked fish pâté is given a tart fruity flavour by the gooseberries, which complement the fish perfectly.

NUTRITIONAL INFORMATION

Calories . . . . .418 Sugars 4g
Protein . . . . .18g Fat 25g
Carbohydrate . . .32g Saturates 6g

20 MINS   10 MINS

SERVES 4

INGREDIENTS

650 g/1 lb 7 oz floury (mealy) potatoes, diced

300 g/10½ oz smoked mackerel, skinned and flaked

75 g/2¾ oz cooked gooseberries

2 tsp lemon juice

2 tbsp low-fat crème fraîche

1 tbsp capers

1 gherkin, chopped

1 tbsp chopped dill pickle

1 tbsp chopped fresh dill

salt and pepper

lemon wedges, to garnish

toast or warm crusty bread, to serve

1 Cook the diced potatoes in a saucepan of boiling water for 10 minutes until tender, then drain well.

2 Place the cooked potatoes in a food processor or blender.

3 Add the skinned and flaked smoked mackerel and process for 30 seconds until fairly smooth. Alternatively, place the ingredients in a bowl and mash with a fork.

4 Add the cooked gooseberries, lemon juice and crème fraîche to the fish and potato mixture. Blend for a further 10 seconds or mash well.

5 Stir in the capers, chopped gherkin and dill pickle, and chopped fresh dill. Season well with salt and pepper.

6 Turn the fish pâté into a serving dish, garnish with lemon wedges and serve with slices of toast or warm crusty bread cut into chunks or slices.

COOK'S TIP

Use stewed, canned or bottled cooked gooseberries for convenience and to save time, or when fresh gooseberries are out of season.

Soups

The soups in this chapter combine a variety of flavors and textures from all around the world: there are thick soups, thin clear consommés, and soups to appeal to vegetarians. The range of soups include thick and creamy winter warmers and light and spicy oriental recipes. Many have

been chosen because of their nutritional content and may be eaten as part of a low-fat diet. All, however, can be eaten as a first course or as a light meal with fresh bread. This interesting mix of recipes has a special emphasis on Mediterranean, Indian, and oriental soups — something to please everybody.

Tuscan Onion Soup

This soup is best made with white onions, which have a mild flavor. If you cannot get hold of them, use large Spanish onions instead.

NUTRITIONAL INFORMATION

Calories 390	Sugars 0g
Protein 9g	Fat 33g
Carbohydrate ...15g	Saturates 14g

5–10 MINS   40–45 MINS

SERVES 4

I N G R E D I E N T S

⅓ cup diced pancetta ham

1 tbsp olive oil

4 large white onions, thinly sliced
  into rings

3 garlic cloves, chopped

3½ cups chicken or ham stock, hot

4 slices ciabatta or other Italian bread

3 tbsp butter

2¾ oz Gruyère or cheddar

salt and pepper

1 Dry fry the pancetta in a large saucepan for 3–4 minutes until it begins to brown. Remove the pancetta from the pan and set aside until required.

2 Add the oil to the pan and cook the onions and garlic over a high heat for 4 minutes. Reduce the heat, cover, and cook for 15 minutes, or until the onions are lightly caramelized.

3 Add the stock to the saucepan and bring to a boil. Reduce the heat and leave the mixture to simmer, covered, for about 10 minutes.

4 Toast the slices of ciabatta on both sides under a preheated broiler, for 2–3 minutes, or until golden. Spread the ciabatta with butter and top with the Gruyère or cheddar cheese. Cut the bread into bite-size pieces.

5 Add the reserved pancetta to the soup and season with salt and pepper to taste.

6 Pour into 4 soup bowls and top with the toasted bread.

COOK'S TIP

Pancetta is similar to bacon, but it is air-dried and salt-cured for about 6 months. Pancetta is available from Italian delicatessens and supermarkets. If you cannot find pancetta use unsmoked slab bacon instead.

Pumpkin Soup

This thick, creamy soup has a wonderful, warming golden color.
It is flavored with orange and thyme.

NUTRITIONAL INFORMATION

Calories	111	Sugars	........4g
Protein	.........2g	Fat	..........6g
Carbohydrate	....5g	Saturates	.......2g

 10 MINS   35–40 MINS

SERVES 4

I N G R E D I E N T S

2 tbsp olive oil

2 onions, chopped

2 garlic cloves, chopped

2 lb pumpkin, peeled and cut into
   1-inch chunks

1 ½ quarts vegetable or chicken
   stock, boiling

finely grated peel and juice of 1 orange

3 tbsp fresh thyme, stems removed

⅔ cup milk

salt and pepper

crusty bread, to serve

1 Heat the olive oil in a large saucepan. Add the onions to the pan and cook for 3–4 minutes, or until softened. Add the garlic and pumpkin and cook for a further 2 minutes, stirring well.

2 Add the boiling vegetable or chicken stock, orange peel and juice, and 2 tablespoons of the thyme to the pan. Leave to simmer, covered, for 20 minutes, or until the pumpkin is tender.

3 Place the mixture in a food processor and blend until smooth. Alternatively, mash the mixture with a potato masher until smooth. Season to taste.

4 Return the soup to the saucepan and add the milk. Reheat the soup for 3–4 minutes, or until it is piping hot but not boiling.

5 Sprinkle with the remaining fresh thyme just before serving.

6 Divide the soup among 4 warm soup bowls and serve with lots of fresh crusty bread.

COOK'S TIP

If you can't find fresh pumpkin, substitute butternut squash.

Artichoke Soup

This refreshing chilled soup is ideal for *al fresco* dining. Bear in mind that this soup needs to be chilled for 3-4 hours, so allow plenty of time.

NUTRITIONAL INFORMATION

Calories 159	Sugars 2g	
Protein 2g	Fat 15	
Carbohydrate 5g	Saturates 6g	

 5 MINS   15 MINS

SERVES 4

INGREDIENTS

1 tbsp olive oil

1 onion, chopped

1 garlic clove, crushed

2 x 14-oz can artichoke hearts, drained

2 ½ cups vegetable stock, hot

⅔ cup light cream

2 tbsp fresh thyme, stalks removed

2 sun-dried tomatoes, cut into strips

fresh, crusty bread, to serve

1 Heat the oil in a large saucepan and fry the chopped onion and crushed garlic, stirring, for 2–3 minutes, or until just softened.

2 Using a sharp knife, roughly chop the artichoke hearts. Add the artichoke pieces to the onion and garlic mixture in the pan. Pour in the hot vegetable stock, stirring well.

3 Bring the mixture to a boil, then reduce the heat and leave to simmer, covered, for about 3 minutes.

4 Place the mixture into a food processor and blend until smooth. Alternatively, push the mixture through a strainer to remove any lumps.

5 Return the soup to the saucepan. Stir the light cream and fresh thyme into the soup.

6 Transfer the soup to a large bowl, cover, and leave to chill in the refrigerator for about 3–4 hours.

7 Transfer the chilled soup to individual soup bowls and garnish with strips of sun dried tomato. Serve with crusty bread.

VARIATION

Try adding 2 tablespoons of dry vermouth to the soup in step 5, if you wish.

Vegetable & Bean Soup

This wonderful combination of cannellini beans, vegetables, and vermicelli is made even richer by the addition of pesto and dried mushrooms.

NUTRITIONAL INFORMATION

Calories . . . . . . .294 Sugars 2g
Protein . . . . .11g Fat 16g
Carbohydrate . . .30g Saturates 2g

  30 MINS 30 MINS

SERVES 4

I N G R E D I E N T S

1 small eggplant

2 large tomatoes

1 potato, peeled

1 carrot, peeled

1 leek

15-oz can cannellini beans

3 ¾ cups vegetable or chicken stock, hot

2 tsp dried basil

½ oz dried porcini mushrooms,
    soaked for 10 minutes in enough warm
    water to cover

1 ¾ oz vermicelli

3 tbsp pesto

freshly grated Parmesan cheese, to serve
    (optional)

1 Slice the eggplant into rings about ½ inch thick, then cut each ring into quarters.

2 Cut the tomatoes and potato into small dice. Cut the carrot into sticks, about 1 inch long and slice the leek into rings.

3 Place the cannellini beans and their liquid in a large saucepan. Add the eggplant, tomatoes, potatoes, carrot, and leek, stirring to mix.

4 Add the stock to the pan and bring to a boil. Reduce the heat and leave to simmer for 15 minutes.

5 Add the basil, dried mushrooms and their soaking liquid, and the vermicelli and simmer for 5 minutes, or until all of the vegetables are tender.

6 Remove the pan from the heat and stir in the pesto.

7 Serve with freshly grated Parmesan cheese, if using.

Garbanzo Bean Soup

A thick vegetable soup that is a delicious meal in itself. Serve with Parmesan cheese and sun-dried tomato-flavored ciabatta bread.

NUTRITIONAL INFORMATION

Calories 297	Sugars 0g
Protein 11g	Fat 18g
Carbohydrate ...24g	Saturates 2g

 5 MINS   15 MINS

SERVES 4

INGREDIENTS

2 tbsp olive oil

2 leeks, sliced

2 zucchini, diced

2 garlic cloves, crushed

2 x 14-oz cans chopped tomatoes

1 tbsp tomato paste

1 fresh bay leaf

3¾ cups chicken stock

14-oz can garbanzo beans, drained
   and rinsed

8 oz spinach

salt and pepper

TO SERVE

Parmesan cheese

sun-dried tomato bread

1 Heat the oil in a large saucepan. Add the leeks and zucchini and cook briskly for 5 minutes, stirring constantly.

2 Add the garlic, tomatoes, tomato paste, bay leaf, stock, and garbanzo beans. Bring to a boil and simmer for 5 minutes.

3 Shred the spinach finely, add to the soup, and cook for 2 minutes. Season.

4 Remove the bay leaf from the soup and discard.

5 Serve the soup with freshly grated Parmesan cheese and sun-dried tomato bread.

COOK'S TIP

Garbanzo beans are used extensively in North African cuisine and are also found in Italian, Spanish, Middle Eastern, and Indian dishes. They have a deliciously nutty flavor with a firm texture and are an excellent canned ingredient to keep in your cupboard.

Spinach & Mascarpone Soup

Spinach is the basis for this delicious soup, but use sorrel or watercress instead for a pleasant change.

NUTRITIONAL INFORMATION

Calories	537	Sugars	.........2g
Protein	.........6g	Fat	..........53g
Carbohydrate	....9g	Saturates	......29g

5 MINS   35 MINS

SERVES 4

INGREDIENTS

4 tbsp butter

1 bunch scallions, trimmed and chopped

2 celery stalks, chopped

3 cups spinach or sorrel, or
  3 bunches watercress

3 ½ cups vegetable stock

1 cup mascarpone cheese

1 tbsp olive oil

2 slices thick-cut bread, cut into cubes

½ tsp caraway seeds

salt and pepper

sesame bread sticks, to serve

1 Melt half the butter in a very large saucepan. Add the scallions and celery and cook gently for about 5 minutes, or until softened.

2 Pack the spinach, sorrel, or watercress into the saucepan. Add the vegetable stock and bring to a boil. Reduce the heat and simmer, covered, for 15–20 minutes.

3 Transfer the soup to a blender or food processor and blend until smooth, or pass through a strainer; return to the saucepan.

4 Add the mascarpone cheese to the soup and heat gently, stirring, until smooth and blended. Taste and season with salt and pepper.

5 Melt the remaining butter with the oil in a skillet. Add the bread cubes and fry in the hot oil until golden brown, adding the caraway seeds toward the end of cooking so they do not burn.

6 Ladle the soup into 4 warmed bowls. Sprinkle with the croutons and serve at once, accompanied by the sesame bread sticks.

VARIATIONS

Any leafy vegetable can be used to make this soup to give variations to the flavor. For anyone who grows their own vegetables, it is the perfect recipe for experimenting with a glut of produce. Try young beet leaves or surplus lettuces for a change.

Calabrian Mushroom Soup

The Calabrian Mountains in southern Italy provide large amounts of wild mushrooms that are rich in flavor and color.

NUTRITIONAL INFORMATION

Calories . . . . . . .452 Sugars 5g
Protein . . . . .15g Fat 26g
Carbohydrate . . .42g Saturates 12g

 5 MINS   25–30 MINS

SERVES 4

INGREDIENTS

2 tbsp olive oil

1 onion, chopped

1 lb mixed mushrooms, such as ceps,
    oyster, and button

1¼ cups milk

3¾ cups vegetable stock, hot

8 slices of rustic bread or French stick

2 garlic cloves, crushed

3 tbsp butter, melted

½ cup finely grated Gruyère cheese

salt and pepper

1 Heat the oil in a large skillet and cook the onion for 3–4 minutes, or until soft and golden.

2 Wipe each mushroom with a damp cloth and cut any large mushrooms into smaller, bite-size pieces.

3 Add the mushrooms to the pan, stirring quickly to coat them in the oil.

4 Add the milk to the pan and bring to a boil. Cover and leave to simmer for about 5 minutes. Gradually stir in the hot vegetable stock and season with salt and pepper to taste.

5 Under a preheated broiler, toast the bread on both sides until golden.

6 Mix together the garlic and butter and spoon generously over the toast.

7 Place the toast in the bottom of a large tureen or divide it among 4 individual serving bowls and pour the hot soup over. Top with the grated Gruyère cheese and serve at once.

COOK'S TIP

Mushrooms absorb liquid, which can lessen the flavor and affect cooking properties. Therefore, carefully wipe them with a damp cloth rather than rinsing them in water.

Tomato & Pasta Soup

Plum tomatoes are ideal for making soups and sauces because they have denser, less watery flesh than rounder varieties.

NUTRITIONAL INFORMATION

Calories . . . . . . .503 Sugars 16g
Protein . . . . .9g Fat 28g
Carbohydrate . . .59g Saturates 17g

5 MINS   50–55 MINS

SERVES 4

INGREDIENTS

4 tbsp unsalted butter

1 large onion, chopped

2 ½ cups vegetable stock

2 lb Italian plum tomatoes, skinned
   and roughly chopped

pinch of baking soda

8 oz dried fusilli

1 tbsp sugar

⅔ cup heavy cream

salt and pepper

fresh basil leaves, to garnish

1 Melt the butter in a large pan. Add the onion and fry for 3 minutes, stirring. Add 1¼ cups vegetable stock to the pan, with the chopped tomatoes and baking soda. Bring the soup to a boil,

reduce the heat and simmer for 20 minutes.

2 Remove the pan from the heat and set aside to cool. Purée the soup in a blender or food processor and pour through a fine strainer back into the saucepan.

3 Add the remaining vegetable stock and the fusilli to the pan, then season to taste with salt and pepper.

4 Add the sugar to the pan and bring to a boil. Reduce the heat and simmer for about 15 minutes.

5 Pour the soup into a warm tureen, swirl the heavy cream around the surface of the soup and garnish with fresh basil leaves. Serve immediately.

VARIATION

To make orange and tomato soup, simply use half the quantity of vegetable stock, topped up with the same amount of fresh orange juice and garnish the soup with orange peel.

Lettuce & Tofu Soup

This is a delicate, clear soup of shredded lettuce and small chunks of tofu with sliced carrot and scallions.

NUTRITIONAL INFORMATION

Calories 113	Sugars 2g	
Protein 5g	Fat 8g	
Carbohydrate 3g	Saturates 1g	

 5 MINS   15 MINS

SERVES 4

I N G R E D I E N T S

7 oz tofu

2 tbsp vegetable oil

1 carrot, sliced thinly

½-inch piece gingerroot,
    cut into thin shreds

3 scallions, sliced diagonally

5 cups vegetable stock

2 tbsp soy sauce

2 tbsp dry sherry

1 tsp sugar

1½ cups shredded romaine lettuce

salt and pepper

1 Using a sharp knife, cut the tofu into small cubes.

2 Heat the vegetable oil in a preheated wok or large saucepan. Add the tofu and stir-fry until browned. Remove with a draining spoon and drain on paper towels.

3 Add the carrot, gingerroot and scallions to the wok or saucepan and stir-fry for 2 minutes.

4 Add the vegetable stock, soy sauce, sherry, and sugar. Stir well to mix all the ingredients. Bring to a boil and simmer for 1 minute.

5 Add the romaine lettuce to the wok or saucepan and stir until it has just wilted.

6 Return the tofu to the pan to reheat. Season with salt and pepper to taste and serve the soup immediately in warm bowls.

COOK'S TIP

For a prettier effect, score grooves along the length of the carrot with a sharp knife before slicing. This will create a flower effect as the carrot is sliced. You can also slice the carrot on the diagonal to make longer slices.

Clear Chicken & Egg Soup

This tasty chicken soup has the addition of poached eggs, making it both delicious and filling. Use fresh, homemade stock for the best flavor.

NUTRITIONAL INFORMATION

Calories 138	Sugars 1g
Protein 16g	Fat 7g
Carbohydrate 1g	Saturates 2g

🍲 5 MINS   🕐 35 MINS

SERVES 4

INGREDIENTS

1 tsp salt

1 tbsp rice wine vinegar

4 eggs

3¾ cups chicken stock

1 leek, sliced

1 cup broccoli flowerets

1 cup shredded cooked chicken

2 open-cap mushrooms, sliced

1 tbsp dry sherry

dash of chili sauce

ground red chilis, to garnish

VARIATION

Use 4 dried Chinese mushrooms, rehydrated according to the package directions, instead of the open-cap mushrooms, if you prefer, for a deeper flavor.

1 Bring a large saucepan of water to a boil and add the salt and rice wine vinegar.

2 Reduce the heat so it is just simmering and carefully break the eggs into the water, one at a time. Poach the eggs for 1 minute.

3 Remove the poached eggs with a draining spoon and set aside.

4 Bring the chicken stock to a boil in a separate pan and add the leek, broccoli, chicken, mushrooms, and sherry and season with chili sauce to taste. Cook for 10–15 minutes.

5 Add the poached eggs to the soup and cook for a further 2 minutes. Carefully transfer the soup and poached eggs to 4 soup bowls. Dust with a little ground red chilis and serve immediately.

Lamb & Rice Soup

This is a very filling soup, because it contains rice and tender pieces of lamb. Serve before a light main course.

NUTRITIONAL INFORMATION

Calories 116   Sugars 0.2g
Protein . . . . .9g   Fat 4g
Carbohydrate . . .12g   Saturates 2g

 5 MINS   🕐 35 MINS

SERVES 4

I N G R E D I E N T S

5 oz lean lamb

¼ cup long-grain rice

3¾ cups lamb stock

1 leek, sliced

1 garlic clove, thinly sliced

2 tsp light soy sauce

1 tsp rice wine vinegar

1 medium open-cap mushroom, thinly sliced

salt

1 Using a sharp knife, trim any fat from the lamb and cut the meat into thin strips; set aside until required.

2 Bring a large pan of lightly salted water to a boil and add the rice. Bring back to a boil, stir once, reduce the heat, and cook for 10–15 minutes until tender.

3 Drain the rice, rinse under cold running water, drain again, and set aside until required.

4 Meanwhile, put the lamb stock in a large saucepan and bring to a boil.

5 Add the lamb strips, leek, garlic, soy sauce, and rice wine vinegar to the stock in the pan. Reduce the heat, cover, and leave to simmer for 10 minutes, or until the lamb is tender and cooked through.

6 Add the mushroom slices and the rice to the pan and cook for a further 2–3 minutes, or until the mushroom is completely cooked through.

7 Ladle the soup into 4 individual warmed soup bowls and serve immediately.

VARIATION

Use a few dried Chinese mushrooms, rehydrated according to the package directions and chopped, as an alternative to the open-cap mushroom for a deeper flavor. Add the Chinese mushrooms with the lamb in step 4.

Chili Fish Soup

Chinese mushrooms add an intense flavor to this unique soup. If they are unavailable, use sliced open-cap mushrooms.

NUTRITIONAL INFORMATION

Calories 166	Sugars 1g	
Protein 23g	Fat 7g	
Carbohydrate 4g	Saturates 1g	

 15 MINS   15 MINS

SERVES 4

INGREDIENTS

½ oz Chinese dried mushrooms

2 tbsp sunflower oil

1 onion, sliced

1½ cups snow peas

1½ cups bamboo shoots

3 tbsp sweet chili sauce

5 cups fish or vegetable stock

3 tbsp light soy sauce

2 tbsp fresh cilantro, plus extra to garnish

1 lb cod fillet, skinned and cubed

COOK'S TIP

Cod is used in this recipe because it is a meaty white fish. For luxury, use monkfish instead.

There are many different varieties of dried mushrooms, but shiitake are best. They are not cheap, but a small amount will go a long way.

 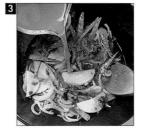 

1 Place the mushrooms in a large bowl. Pour enough boiling water over to cover and leave to stand for 5 minutes. Drain the mushrooms thoroughly in a colander. Using a sharp knife, roughly chop the mushrooms.

2 Heat the sunflower oil in a preheated wok or large skillet. Add the sliced onion to the wok and stir-fry for 5 minutes, or until softened.

3 Add the snow peas, bamboo shoots, chili sauce, stock, and soy sauce to the wok and bring to a boil.

4 Add the cilantro and cod and leave to simmer for 5 minutes, or until the fish is cooked through.

5 Transfer the soup to warm bowls, garnish with extra cilantro, if wished, and serve hot.

Crab & Ginger Soup

Two classic ingredients in Chinese cooking are blended together in this recipe for a fragrant and flavorful soup.

NUTRITIONAL INFORMATION

Calories	32	Sugars 1g
Protein	.........6g	Fat 0.4g
Carbohydrate	....1g	Saturates 0g

10 MINS   25 MINS

SERVES 4

INGREDIENTS

1 carrot

1 leek

1 bay leaf

3¾ cups fish stock

2 cooked crabs

1-inch piece fresh gingerroot, grated

1 tsp light soy sauce

½ tsp ground star anise

salt and pepper

1 Using a sharp knife, chop the carrot and leek into small pieces and place in a large saucepan with the bay leaf and fish stock.

2 Bring the mixture in the saucepan to a boil.

3 Reduce the heat, cover, and leave to simmer for about 10 minutes, or until the vegetables are nearly tender.

4 Remove all of the meat from the cooked crabs. Break off and reserve the claws; break the joints and remove the meat, using a fork or skewer.

5 Add the crabmeat to the pan of fish stock, together with the ginger, soy sauce, and star anise and bring to a boil. Leave to simmer for about 10 minutes, or until the vegetables are tender and the crab is heated through.

6 Season the soup then ladle into a warmed soup tureen or individual serving bowls and garnish with crab claws. Serve immediately.

VARIATION

If fresh crabmeat is unavailable, use drained canned crabmeat or thawed frozen crabmeat instead.

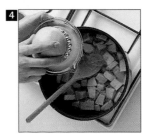

Mushroom Noodle Soup

A light, refreshing clear soup of mushrooms, cucumber, and small pieces of rice noodles, flavored with soy sauce and a touch of garlic.

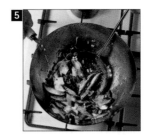

NUTRITIONAL INFORMATION

Calories	84	Sugars 1g
Protein	.........1g	Fat 8g
Carbohydrate	....3g	Saturates 1g

5 MINS   10 MINS

SERVES 4

INGREDIENTS

4 oz flat or open-cap mushrooms

½ cucumber

2 scallions

1 garlic clove

2 tbsp vegetable oil

1 oz Chinese rice noodles

¾ tsp salt

1 tbsp soy sauce

1 Wash the mushrooms and pat dry on paper towels; slice thinly. Do not remove the peel because this adds flavor.

2 Halve the cucumber lengthways. Scoop out the seeds, using a teaspoon, and slice the cucumber thinly.

3 Chop the scallions finely and cut the garlic clove into thin strips.

4 Heat the vegetable oil in a large saucepan or wok.

5 Add the scallions and garlic to the pan or wok and stir-fry for 30 seconds. Add the mushrooms and stir-fry for 2–3 minutes.

6 Stir in 2½ cups water. Break the noodles into short pieces and add to the soup. Bring to a boil, stirring occasionally.

7 Add the cucumber slices, salt, and soy sauce, and simmer for 2–3 minutes.

8 Serve the mushroom noodle soup in warmed bowls, distributing the noodles and vegetables evenly.

COOK'S TIP

Scooping the seeds out from the cucumber gives it a prettier effect when sliced, and also helps to reduce any bitterness. You can, however, leave the seeds in if you like.

Curried Chicken & Corn Soup

Tender cooked chicken strips and baby corn cobs are the main flavors in this delicious clear soup, flavored with just a hint of ginger.

NUTRITIONAL INFORMATION

Calories 206	Sugars 5g	
Protein 29g	Fat 5g	
Carbohydrate ...13g	Saturates 1g	

5 MINS   30 MINS

SERVES 4

INGREDIENTS

6-oz can corn kernels, drained

3¾ cups chicken stock

2½ cups cooked, lean chicken,
    cut into strips

16 baby corn cobs

1 tsp Chinese curry powder

½-inch piece fresh gingerroot, grated

3 tbsp light soy sauce

2 tbsp chopped chives

1 Place the canned corn in a food processor, together with ⅔ cup of the chicken stock and process until the mixture forms a purée.

2 Pass the corn purée through a fine strainer, pressing with the back of a spoon to remove any husks.

3 Pour the remaining chicken stock into a large saucepan and add the strips of cooked chicken. Stir in the corn purée.

4 Add the baby corn cobs and bring the soup to a boil. Boil the soup for 10 minutes.

5 Add the Chinese curry powder, grated fresh gingerroot, and light soy sauce and stir well to combine. Cook for a further 10–15 minutes.

6 Stir the chopped chives into the soup. Transfer the curried chicken and corn soup to warm soup bowls and serve immediately.

COOK'S TIP

Prepare the soup up to 24 hours in advance without adding the chicken, cool, cover, and store in the refrigerator. Add the chicken and heat the soup through thoroughly before serving.

Shrimp Soup

This soup is an interesting mix of colors and textures. The egg may be made into a flat omelet and added as thin strips if preferred.

NUTRITIONAL INFORMATION

Calories	123	Sugars	.......0.2g
Protein	........13g	Fat	...........8g
Carbohydrate	....1g	Saturates	.......1g

5 MINS   20 MINS

SERVES 4

INGREDIENTS

2 tbsp sunflower oil

2 scallions, thinly sliced diagonally

1 carrot, coarsely grated

1½ cups thinly sliced large closed cap mushrooms

1 quart fish or vegetable stock

½ tsp Chinese five-spice powder

1 tbsp light soy sauce

4 oz large peeled shrimp, or peeled tiger prawns, defrosted if frozen

½ bunch watercress, trimmed and roughly chopped

1 egg, well beaten

salt and pepper

4 large shrimp in shells, to garnish (optional)

1 Heat the oil in a wok, swirling it around until really hot. Add the scallions and stir-fry for 1 minute. Add the carrots and mushrooms and continue to cook for about 2 minutes.

2 Add the stock and bring to a boil. Season to taste with salt and pepper, five-spice powder, and soy sauce and simmer for 5 minutes.

3 If the shrimp are really large, cut them in half before adding to the wok and simmer for 3-4 minutes.

4 Add the watercress to the wok and mix well. Slowly pour in the beaten egg in a circular movement so it cooks in threads in the soup. Adjust the seasoning and serve each portion topped with a whole shrimp.

COOK'S TIP

The large open mushrooms with black gills give the best flavor but they tend to spoil the color of the soup, making it very dark. Oyster mushrooms can also be used.

Chicken & Pasta Broth

This satisfying soup makes a good lunch or supper dish and you can use any vegetables you have at hand to make it seasonal.

NUTRITIONAL INFORMATION

Calories	295	Sugar	.........8g
Protein	........25g	Fats	..........10g
Carbohydrates	...29g	Saturates	......2g

5 MINS   20 MINS

SERVES 4

INGREDIENTS

12 oz boneless chicken breast meat

2 tbsp sunflower oil

1 onion, diced

1½ cups diced carrots

1½ cups cauliflower flowerets

3¾ cups chicken stock

2 tsp Italian seasoning

4 oz small pasta shapes

salt and pepper

Parmesan cheese (optional) and crusty
   bread, to serve

1 Finely dice the chicken, discarding any skin.

2 Heat the oil and quickly sauté the chicken and vegetables until they are lightly colored.

3 Stir in the stock and herbs. Bring to a boil and add the pasta. Return to the boil, cover, and simmer for 10 minutes.

4 Season to taste and sprinkle with Parmesan cheese, if using. Serve with crusty bread.

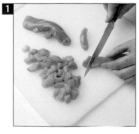

Lemon & Chicken Soup

This delicately flavored summer soup is surprisingly easy to make, and tastes delicious.

NUTRITIONAL INFORMATION

Calories	506	Sugars	.........4g
Protein	........19g	Fat	..........31g
Carbohydrate	...41g	Saturates	......19g

5–10 MINS   1¼ HOURS

SERVES 4

I N G R E D I E N T S

4 tbsp butter

8 shallots, thinly sliced

2 carrots, thinly sliced

2 celery stalks, thinly sliced

1½ cups finely chopped boned chicken breasts

3 lemons

1¼ quarts chicken stock

8 oz dried spaghetti, broken into small pieces

⅔ cup heavy cream

salt and white pepper

TO GARNISH

fresh parsley sprig

3 lemon slices, halved

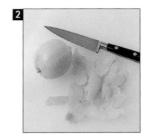

COOK'S TIP

You can prepare this soup up to the end of step 3 in advance, so all you need do before serving is heat it through before adding the pasta and the finishing touches.

1 Melt the butter in a large saucepan. Add the shallots, carrots, celery, and chicken and cook over a low heat, stirring occasionally, for 8 minutes.

2 Thinly pare the lemons and blanch the lemon peel in boiling water for 3 minutes; squeeze the juice from the lemons.

3 Add the lemon peel and juice to the pan, together with the chicken stock. Bring slowly to a boil over a low heat and simmer for 40 minutes, stirring occasionally.

4 Add the spaghetti to the pan and cook for 15 minutes. Season to taste with salt and white pepper and add the cream. Heat through, but do not allow the soup to boil or it will curdle.

5 Pour the soup into a tureen or individual bowls and garnish with the parsley and half slices of lemon. Serve immediately.

Chicken & Leek Soup

This satisfying soup can be served as a main course. You can add rice and bell peppers to make it even more hearty, as well as colorful.

NUTRITIONAL INFORMATION

Calories	183	Sugar	.........4g
Protein	........21g	Fats	..........9g
Carbohydrates	....4g	Saturates	......5g

5 MINS   1¼ HOURS

SERVES 4–6

INGREDIENTS

2 tbsp butter

12 oz boneless chicken

2½ cups leeks, skinned and chopped into 1-inch pieces

1¼ quarts chicken stock

1 bouquet garni

8 pitted prunes, halved

salt and white pepper

cooked rice and diced bell peppers (optional)

1 Melt the butter in a large saucepan over a medium heat.

2 Add the chicken and leeks to the saucepan and fry for 8 minutes.

3 Add the chicken stock and bouquet garni and stir well.

4 Season well with salt and pepper to taste.

5 Bring the soup to a boil and simmer for 45 minutes.

6 Add the prunes to the saucepan with some cooked rice and diced bell peppers, if using, and simmer for about 20 minutes.

7 Remove the bouquet garni from the soup and discard. Serve the chicken and leek soup immediately.

VARIATION

Instead of the bouquet garni sachet, you can use a bunch of fresh mixed herbs, tied together with string. Choose herbs such as parsley, thyme and rosemary.

Red Bell Pepper Soup

This soup has a real Mediterranean flavor, using sweet red bell peppers, tomato, chili and basil. It is great served with a warm olive bread.

NUTRITIONAL INFORMATION

Calories 55	Sugar 10g
Protein 2g	Fats 0.5g
Carbohydrates . . .11g	Saturates 0.1g

 5 MINS   25 MINS

SERVES 4

INGREDIENTS

1½ cups seeded and sliced red bell peppers

1 onion, sliced

2 garlic cloves, crushed

1 green chili, chopped

1¼ cups strained puréed tomatoes

2½ cups vegetable stock

2 tbsp chopped basil

fresh basil sprigs, to garnish

1 Put the bell peppers in a large saucepan with the onion, garlic, and chili. Add the tomatoes and vegetable stock and bring to a boil, stirring well.

2 Reduce the heat to a simmer and cook for 20 minutes, or until the bell peppers have softened. Drain, reserving the liquid and vegetables separately.

3 Purée the vegetables by pressing through a strainer with the back of a spoon. Alternatively, blend in a food processor until smooth.

4 Return the vegetable purée to a clean saucepan with the reserved cooking liquid. Add the basil and heat through until hot. Garnish the soup with fresh basil sprigs and serve.

VARIATION

This soup is also delicious served chilled with ⅔ cup plain yogurt swirled into it.

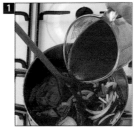

Partan Bree

This traditional Scottish soup is thickened with a purée of rice and crabmeat cooked in milk. Add sour cream, if liked, at the end of cooking.

NUTRITIONAL INFORMATION

Calories 112	Sugars 5g	
Protein 7g	Fat 2g	
Carbohydrate ...18g	Saturates 0.3g	

 1 HOUR   35 MINS

SERVES 6

INGREDIENTS

1 boiled crab

scant ½ cup long-grain rice

2½ cups skim milk

2½ cups fish stock

1 tbsp anchovy paste

2 tsp lime or lemon juice

1 tbsp chopped fresh parsley, or I tsp chopped fresh thyme

3–4 tbsp sour cream (optional)

salt and pepper

snipped chives, to garnish

COOK'S TIP

If you are unable to buy a whole crab, use about 175 g/6 oz frozen crab meat and thaw thoroughly before use; or a 175 g/6 oz can of crab meat which just needs thorough draining.

1 Remove and reserve all the brown and white meat from the crab, then crack the claws and remove and chop that meat; reserve the claw meat.

2 Put the rice and milk into a saucepan and bring slowly to a boil. Cover and simmer gently for about 20 minutes.

3 Add the reserved white and brown crabmeat and seasoning and simmer for a further 5 minutes.

4 Cool a little, then press through a strainer, or blend in a food processor or blender until smooth.

5 Pour the soup into a clean saucepan and add the fish stock and the reserved claw meat. Bring slowly to a boil, then add the anchovy paste and lime or lemon juice and adjust the seasoning.

6 Simmer for a further 2–3 minutes. Stir in the parsley or thyme and then swirl sour cream, if using, through each serving. Garnish with snipped chives.

Smoked Haddock Soup

Smoked haddock gives this soup a wonderfully rich flavor, while the mashed potatoes and cream thicken and enrich the stock.

NUTRITIONAL INFORMATION

Calories	169	Sugars	........8g
Protein	........16g	Fat	...........5g
Carbohydrate	...16g	Saturates	......3g

25 MINS   40 MINS

SERVES 4–6

I N G R E D I E N T S

8 oz smoked haddock fillet

1 onion, finely chopped

1 garlic clove, crushed

2½ cups water

2½ cups skim milk

1–1½ cups mashed potatoes, hot

2 tbsp butter

about 1 tbsp lemon juice

6 tbsp low-fat plain fromage blanc

4 tbsp chopped fresh parsley

salt and pepper

1 Put the fish, onion, garlic, and water into a saucepan. Bring to a boil, cover, and simmer for 15–20 minutes.

2 Remove the fish from the pan, strip off the skin, and remove all the bones. Flake the flesh finely.

3 Return the skin and bones to the cooking liquid and simmer for 10 minutes. Strain, discarding the skin and bone. Pour the liquid into a clean pan.

4 Add the milk, flaked fish, and seasoning to the pan. Bring to the boil and simmer for about 3 minutes.

5 Gradually whisk in sufficient mashed potato to make a fairly thick soup, then stir in the butter and sharpen to taste with lemon juice.

6 Add the fromage blanc and 3 tablespoons of the chopped parsley. Reheat gently and adjust the seasoning. Sprinkle with the remaining parsley and serve immediately.

COOK'S TIP

Undyed smoked haddock can be used in place of the bright yellow fish; it gives a paler color but just as much flavor. Alternatively, use smoked cod or smoked whiting.

Bacon, Bean & Garlic Soup

A mouthwatering vegetable, bean, and bacon soup with a garlic flavor to make in the microwave. Serve with wholewheat bread.

NUTRITIONAL INFORMATION

Calories 261	Sugars 5g	
Protein 23g	Fat 8g	
Carbohydrate ...25g	Saturates 2g	

5 MINS   20 MINS

SERVES 4

INGREDIENTS

8 oz lean smoked slab bacon slices

1 carrot, thinly sliced

1 celery stalk, thinly sliced

1 onion, chopped

1 tbsp oil

3 garlic cloves, sliced

3 cups vegetable stock, hot

7-oz can chopped tomatoes

1 tbsp chopped fresh thyme

about 14 oz canned cannellini beans, drained

1 tbsp tomato paste

salt and pepper

grated cheddar cheese, to garnish

COOK'S TIP

For a more substantial soup, add 2 oz small pasta shapes or short pieces of spaghetti when you add the stock and tomatoes. You will also need to add an extra ⅔ cup vegetable stock.

1 Chop 2 slices of the bacon and place in a bowl. Cook on HIGH power for 3–4 minutes until the fat runs out and the bacon is well cooked. Stir the bacon halfway through cooking to separate the pieces. Transfer to a plate lined with paper towels and leave to cool; when cool, the bacon pieces should be crisp and dry. Place the carrot, celery, onion, and oil in a large bowl. Cover and cook on HIGH power for 4 minutes.

2 Chop the remaining bacon and add to the bowl with the garlic. Cover and cook on HIGH power for 2 minutes.

3 Add the stock, the contents of the can of tomatoes, the thyme, beans, and tomato paste. Cover and cook on HIGH power for 8 minutes, stirring halfway through; season to taste. Ladle the soup into warmed bowls and sprinkle with the crisp bacon and grated cheese.

Spicy Dhal & Carrot Soup

This delicious, warming, and nutritious soup includes a selection of spices to give it a "kick". It is simple to make and extremely good to eat.

NUTRITIONAL INFORMATION

Calories 173	Sugars 11g
Protein 9g	Fat 5g
Carbohydrate ...24g	Saturates 1g

⌚ 10 MINS   🕐 50 MINS

SERVES 6

INGREDIENTS

½ cup split red lentils

1¼ cups vegetable stock

2 cups peeled and sliced carrots

2 onions, chopped

1½ x 7-oz can chopped tomatoes

2 garlic cloves, chopped

2 tbsp vegetable ghee or oil

1 tsp ground cumin

1 tsp ground coriander

1 fresh green chili, seeded and chopped, or 1 tsp minced chili from a jar

½ tsp ground turmeric

1 tbsp lemon juice

salt

1¼ cups skim milk

2 tbsp chopped fresh cilantro

plain yogurt, to serve

1 Place the lentils in a strainer and wash well under cold running water. Drain and place in a large saucepan with 3½ cups of the vegetable stock, the carrots, onions, tomatoes, and garlic. Bring the mixture to a boil, reduce the heat, cover, and simmer for 30 minutes.

2 Meanwhile, heat the ghee or oil in a small pan. Add the cumin, coriander, chili and turmeric and fry gently for 1 minute.

3 Remove from the heat and stir in the lemon juice and salt to taste.

4 Purée the soup in batches in a blender or food processor. Return the soup to the saucepan. Add the spice mixture and the remaining 1¼ cups stock or water and simmer for 10 minutes.

5 Add the milk to the soup and adjust the seasoning according to taste.

6 Stir in the chopped cilantro and reheat gently. Serve hot, with a swirl of yogurt.

Spicy Lentil Soup

For a warming, satisfying meal on a cold day, this lentil dish is packed full of taste and goodness.

NUTRITIONAL INFORMATION

Calories 155   Sugars 4g
Protein ....11g   Fat 3g
Carbohydrate ...22g   Saturates 0.4g

1 HOUR   1¼ HOURS

SERVES 4

INGREDIENTS

½ cup red lentils

2 tsp vegetable oil

1 large onion, chopped finely

2 garlic cloves, crushed

1 tsp ground cumin

1 tsp ground coriander

1 tsp garam masala

2 tbsp tomato paste

4½ cups vegetable stock

about 2 cups canned corn kernels, drained

salt and pepper

TO SERVE

low-fat plain yogurt

chopped fresh parsley

warmed pita bread

1 Rinse the red lentils in cold water. Drain the lentils well and set aside.

2 Heat the oil in a large nonstick saucepan and fry the onion and garlic gently until softened, but not browned.

3 Stir in the cumin, coriander, garam masala, tomato paste, and 4 tablespoons of the stock. Mix well and simmer gently for 2 minutes.

4 Add the lentils and pour in the remaining stock. Bring to a boil, reduce the heat, and simmer, covered, for 1 hour until the lentils are tender and the soup thickened. Stir in the corn and heat through for 5 minutes; season well.

5 Ladle into warmed soup bowls and top each with a spoonful of yogurt and a sprinkling of parsley. Serve with warmed pita bread.

COOK'S TIP

Many of the variety of breads available today either contain fat or are brushed with oil before baking. Always check the ingredients list for fat content.

Chunky Potato & Beef Soup

This is a real winter warmer — pieces of tender beef and chunky mixed vegetables are cooked in a liquid flavored with sherry.

NUTRITIONAL INFORMATION

Calories	187	Sugars	........3g
Protein	........14g	Fat	..........9g
Carbohydrate	...12g	Saturates	......2g

5 MINS

35 MINS

SERVES 4

INGREDIENTS

2 tbsp vegetable oil

8 oz lean braising or frying steak, cut into strips

8 oz new potatoes, halved

1 carrot, diced

2 celery stalks, sliced

2 leeks, sliced

3¾ cups beef stock

8 baby corn cobs, sliced

1 bouquet garni

2 tbsp dry sherry

salt and pepper

chopped fresh parsley, to garnish

1 Heat the vegetable oil in a large saucepan.

2 Add the strips of meat to the saucepan and cook for 3 minutes, turning constantly.

3 Add the halved potatoes, diced carrot and sliced celery and leeks. Cook for a further 5 minutes, stirring.

4 Pour the beef stock into the saucepan and bring to a boil. Reduce the heat until the liquid is simmering, then add the sliced baby corn cobs and the bouquet garni.

5 Cook the soup for a further 20 minutes, or until cooked through.

6 Remove the bouquet garni from the saucepan and discard. Stir the dry sherry into the soup and season to taste with salt and pepper.

7 Pour the soup into warmed bowls and garnish with the chopped fresh parsley. Serve at once with crusty bread.

COOK'S TIP

Make double the quantity of soup and freeze the remainder in a rigid container for later use. When ready to use, leave in the refrigerator to defrost thoroughly, then reheat until piping hot.

Mushroom & Ginger Soup

Thai soups are very quickly and easily put together, and are cooked so each ingredient is still identifiable in the finished dish.

NUTRITIONAL INFORMATION

Calories 74   Sugars 1g
Protein . . . . .3g   Fat 3g
Carbohydrate . . . .9g   Saturates 0.4g

1½ HOURS   15 MINS

SERVES 4

I N G R E D I E N T S

½ oz dried Chinese mushrooms, or
   1⅓ cups field or crimini mushrooms

1 quart vegetable stock, hot

4 oz thread egg noodles

2 tsp sunflower oil

3 garlic cloves, crushed

1-inch piece gingerroot, finely shredded

½ tsp mushroom catsup

1 tsp light soy sauce

2 cups bean sprouts

cilantro leaves, to garnish

1 Soak the dried Chinese mushrooms, if using, for at least 30 minutes in 1¼ cups of the hot vegetable stock. Remove the stems and discard, then slice the mushrooms; reserve the stock.

2 Cook the noodles for 2–3 minutes in boiling water. Drain and rinse and set aside.

3 Heat the oil over a high heat in a wok or large, heavy skillet. Add the garlic and ginger, stir, and add the mushrooms. Stir over a high heat for 2 minutes.

4 Add the remaining vegetable stock with the reserved stock and bring to a boil. Add the mushroom catsup and soy sauce.

5 Stir in the bean sprouts and cook until tender. Put some noodles in each bowl and ladle the soup on top. Garnish with cilantro leaves and serve immediately.

COOK'S TIP

Rice noodles contain no fat and are ideal for for anyone on a low-fat diet.

Yogurt & Spinach Soup

Whole young spinach leaves add vibrant color to this unusual soup.
Serve with hot, crusty bread for a nutritious, light meal.

NUTRITIONAL INFORMATION

Calories 227	Sugars 13g	
Protein 14g	Fat 7g	
Carbohydrate ...29g	Saturates 2g	

15 MINS   30 MINS

SERVES 4

INGREDIENTS

2½ cups chicken stock

4 tbsp long-grain rice, rinsed and drained

4 tbsp water

1 tbsp cornstarch

2½ cups low-fat plain yogurt

juice of 1 lemon

3 egg yolks, lightly beaten

12 oz young spinach leaves, washed and drained

salt and pepper

1 Pour the stock into a large pan, season, and bring to the boil. Add the rice and simmer for 10 minutes until barely cooked. Remove from the heat.

2 Combine the water and cornstarch to make a smooth paste.

3 Pour the yogurt into a second pan and stir in the cornstarch mixture. Set the pan over a low heat and bring the yogurt slowly to a boil, stirring with a wooden spoon in one direction only: this will stabilize the yogurt and prevent it from separating or curdling on contact with the hot stock. When the yogurt has reached boiling point, stand the pan on a heat diffuser and leave to simmer slowly for 10 minutes. Remove the pan from the heat and allow the mixture to cool slightly before stirring in the beaten egg yolks.

4 Pour the yogurt mixture into the stock, stir in the lemon juice, and stir to blend thoroughly. Keep the soup warm, but do not allow it to boil.

5 Blanch the spinach leaves in a large pan of boiling, salted water for 2–3 minutes until they begin to soften but have not wilted. Tip the spinach into a colander, drain well, and stir it into the soup; let the spinach warm through. Taste the soup and adjust the seasoning if necessary. Serve in wide shallow soup plates, with hot, fresh crusty bread.

Red Lentil Soup with Yogurt

Tasty red lentil soup flavored with chopped cilantro. The yogurt adds a light piquancy to the soup, made in a microwave.

NUTRITIONAL INFORMATION

Calories 280	Sugars 6g
Protein 17g	Fat 7g
Carbohydrate ...40g	Saturates 4g

5 MINS   30 MINS

SERVES 4

INGREDIENTS

2 tbsp butter

1 onion, finely chopped

1 celery stalk, finely chopped

1 large carrot, grated

1 dried bay leaf

heaping 1 cup red lentils

1¼ quarts vegetable or chicken stock, hot

2 tbsp chopped fresh cilantro

4 tbsp low-fat plain yogurt

salt and pepper

fresh cilantro sprigs, to garnish

1 Place the butter, onion, and celery in a large bowl. Cover and cook on HIGH power for 3 minutes.

2 Add the carrot, bay leaf, and lentils. Pour the stock over. Cover and cook on HIGH power for 15 minutes, stirring halfway through.

3 Remove from the microwave oven and stand, covered, for 5 minutes.

4 Remove the bay leaf, then blend in batches in a food processor until smooth. Alternatively, press the soup through a strainer.

5 Pour into a clean bowl. Season with salt and pepper to taste and stir in the cilantro. Cover and cook on HIGH power for 4–5 minutes until piping hot.

6 Serve in warmed bowls. Stir 1 tablespoon yogurt into each serving and garnish with sprigs of fresh cilantro.

COOK'S TIP

For an extra creamy soup try adding low-fat crème fraîche or sour cream instead of yogurt.

Minted Pea & Yogurt Soup

A deliciously refreshing soup that is full of goodness. It also tastes great served chilled in the summer.

NUTRITIONAL INFORMATION

Calories 208	Sugars 9g	
Protein 10g	Fat 7g	
Carbohydrate ...26g	Saturates 2g	

10 MINS   25 MINS

SERVES 4

INGREDIENTS

2 tbsp vegetable ghee or oil

2 onions, coarsely chopped

1½ cups peeled and coarsely chopped potatoes

2 garlic cloves, peeled

1-inch piece gingerroot, peeled and chopped

1 tsp ground coriander

1 tsp ground cumin

1 tbsp all-purpose flour

3½ cups vegetable stock

3½ cups frozen peas

2-3 tbsp chopped fresh mint, to taste

salt and freshly ground black pepper

⅔ cup low-fat plain yogurt

½ tsp cornstarch

1¼ cups skim milk

a little extra yogurt, for serving (optional)

mint sprigs, to garnish

1 Heat the ghee or oil in a saucepan. Add the onions and potato and cook gently for 3 minutes. Stir in the garlic, ginger, coriander, cumin, and flour and cook for 1 minute, stirring. Add the stock, peas, and half the mint and bring to a boil, stirring. Reduce the heat, cover, and simmer gently for 15 minutes.

2 Purée the soup in a blender or food processor. Return the soup to the pan and season with salt and pepper to taste. Blend the yogurt with the cornstarch and stir into the soup.

3 Add the milk and bring almost to a boil, stirring all the time. Cook very gently for 2 minutes. Serve hot, sprinkled with the remaining mint and a swirl of extra yogurt, if wished.

COOK'S TIP

The yogurt is mixed with a little cornstarch before being added to the hot soup – this helps to stabilize the yogurt and prevents it from separating when heated.

Avocado & Mint Soup

A rich and creamy pale green soup made with avocados and enhanced by a touch of chopped mint. Serve chilled in summer or hot in winter.

NUTRITIONAL INFORMATION

Calories ....199 Sugars 3g
Protein ....3g Fat 18g
Carbohydrate ....7g Saturates 6g

15 MINS   35 MINS

SERVES 6

INGREDIENTS

3 tbsp butter or margarine

6 scallions, sliced

1 garlic clove, crushed

2 tbsp all-purpose flour

2½ cups vegetable stock

2 ripe avocados

2–3 tsp lemon juice

pinch of grated lemon peel

⅔ cup milk

⅔ cup light cream

1–1½ tbsp chopped mint

salt and pepper

mint sprigs, to garnish

MINTED GARLIC BREAD

½ cup butter

1–2 tbsp chopped mint

1–2 garlic cloves, crushed

1 whole wheat or white French
  bread stick

1 Melt the butter or margarine in a large, heavy-based saucepan. Add the scallions and garlic clove and fry over a low heat, stirring occasionally, for about 3 minutes, until soft and translucent.

2 Stir in the flour and cook, stirring, for 1–2 minutes. Gradually stir in the stock, then bring to a boil. Simmer gently while preparing the avocados.

3 Peel the avocados, discard the pits and chop coarsely. Add to the soup with the lemon juice and peel and seasoning. Cover and simmer for about 10 minutes until tender.

4 Cool the soup slightly, then press through a strainer with the back of a spoon or process in a food processor or blender until a smooth purée forms; pour into a bowl.

5 Stir in the milk and cream, adjust the seasoning, and stir in the mint. Cover and chill thoroughly.

6 To make the minted garlic bread, soften the butter and beat in the mint and garlic. Slice the loaf diagonally but leave a hinge on the bottom crust. Spread each slice with the butter and reassemble the loaf. Wrap in foil and place in a preheated oven at 350°F for about 15 minutes.

7 Serve the soup garnished with a sprig of mint and accompanied by the minted garlic bread.

Thick Onion Soup

A delicious creamy soup with grated carrot and parsley for texture and color. Serve with crusty cheese biscuits for a hearty lunch.

NUTRITIONAL INFORMATION

Calories	277	Sugars	12g
Protein	6g	Fat	20g
Carbohydrate	19g	Saturates	8g

20 MINS   1HR 10 MINS

SERVES 6

I N G R E D I E N T S

5 tbsp butter

4 cups finely chopped onions

1 garlic clove, crushed

6 tbsp all-purpose flour

2½ cups vegetable stock

2½ cups milk

2–3 tsp lemon or lime juice

good pinch of ground allspice

1 bay leaf

1 carrot, coarsely grated

4–6 tbsp heavy cream

2 tbsp chopped fresh parsley

salt and pepper

C H E E S E   B I S C U I T S

2 cups malted wheat or wholewheat flour

2 tsp baking powder

4 tbsp butter

4 tbsp grated Parmesan cheese

1 egg, beaten

about ⅓ cup milk

1 Melt the butter in a saucepan and fry the onions and garlic over a low heat, stirring frequently, for 10–15 minutes until soft, but not colored. Stir in the flour and cook, stirring, for 1 minute, then gradually stir in the stock and bring to a boil, stirring frequently. Add the milk, then bring back to a boil.

2 Season to taste with salt and pepper and add 2 teaspoons of the lemon or lime juice, the allspice, and bay leaf. Cover and simmer for about 25 minutes until the vegetables are tender; discard the bay leaf.

3 Meanwhile, make the biscuits. Combine the flour, baking powder, and seasoning and cut in the butter until the

mixture resembles fine bread crumbs. Stir in 3 tablespoons of the cheese, the egg, and enough milk to mix to a soft dough.

4 Shape into a bar about ¾ inch thick. Place on a floured cookie sheet and mark into slices. Sprinkle with the remaining cheese and bake in a preheated oven at 425°F for about 20 minutes until risen and golden brown.

5 Stir the carrot into the soup and simmer for 2–3 minutes. Add more lemon or lime juice, if necessary. Stir in the cream and reheat. Garnish and serve with the warm biscuits.

Gardener's Broth

This hearty soup uses a variety of green vegetables with a flavoring of ground coriander. A finishing touch of thinly sliced leeks adds texture.

NUTRITIONAL INFORMATION

Calories	169	Sugars	........5g
Protein	.........4g	Fat	..........13g
Carbohydrate	....8g	Saturates	.......5g

 10 MINS   🕐 45 MINS

SERVES 6

INGREDIENTS

3 tbsp butter

1 onion, chopped

1–2 garlic cloves, crushed

1 large leek

8 oz Brussels sprouts

4 oz green or string beans

1¼ quarts vegetable stock

1 cup frozen peas

1 tbsp lemon juice

½ tsp ground coriander

4 tbsp heavy cream

salt and pepper

MELBA TOAST

4–6 slices white bread

1 Melt the butter in a saucepan. Add the onion and garlic and fry over a low heat, stirring occasionally, until they begin to soften, but not color.

2 Slice the white part of the leek very thinly and reserve; slice the remaining leek. Slice the Brussels sprouts and thinly slice the beans.

3 Add the green part of the leeks, the Brussels sprouts, and beans to the saucepan. Add the stock, bring to a boil, and simmer for 10 minutes.

4 Add the frozen peas, seasoning, lemon juice, and coriander and continue to simmer for 10–15 minutes until the vegetables are tender.

5 Cool the soup a little, then press through a strainer or process in a food processor or blender until smooth. Pour into a clean pan.

6 Add the reserved slices of leek to the soup, bring back to a boil, and simmer for about 5 minutes until the leek is tender. Adjust the seasoning, stir in the cream, and reheat gently.

7 To make the melba toast, toast the bread on both sides under a preheated broiler. Cut horizontally through the slices, then toast the uncooked sides until they curl up. Serve immediately with the soup.

Beet Soup

Quick and easy to prepare in a microwave oven, this deep-red soup of puréed beets and potatoes makes a stunning first course.

NUTRITIONAL INFORMATION

Calories ....120 Sugars 11g

Protein ....4g Fat 2g

Carbohydrate ...22g Saturates 1g

 20 MINS 🕐 30 MINS

SERVES 6

INGREDIENTS

1 onion, chopped

2½ cups diced potatoes

1 small cooking apple, peeled, cored, and grated

3 tbsp water

1 tsp cumin seeds

4 cups peeled and diced cooked beets

1 bay leaf

pinch of dried thyme

1 tsp lemon juice

2½ cups vegetable stock, hot

4 tbsp sour cream

salt and pepper

few dill sprigs, to garnish

1 Place the onion, potatoes, apple, and water in a large bowl. Cover and cook on HIGH power for 10 minutes.

2 Stir in the cumin seeds and cook on HIGH power for 1 minute.

3 Stir in the beets, bay leaf, thyme, lemon juice, and hot vegetable stock. Cover and cook on HIGH power for 12 minutes, stirring halfway through the cooking time.

4 Leave to stand, uncovered, for 5 minutes; remove and discard the bay leaf. Strain the vegetables and reserve the liquid. Process the vegetables with a little of the reserved liquid in a food processor or blender until they are smooth and creamy. Alternatively, either mash the vegetables with a potato masher or press them through a strainer with the back of a wooden spoon.

5 Pour the vegetable purée into a clean bowl with the reserved liquid and mix well. Season to taste. Cover and cook on HIGH power for 4–5 minutes until the soup is piping hot.

6 Serve the soup in warmed bowls. Swirl 1 tablespoon of sour cream into each serving and garnish with a few sprigs of fresh dill.

Appetizers

&Snacks

All of these recipes are easy to prepare and appetizing. They are colorful and flavorsome, providing an excellent beginning to any dinner party or just for an everyday snack. Depending on the main course, whet your guests'

appetite with a tasty Dipping Platter, Chinese Omelet or a pâté or delicious vegetable nibbles. Other quick-and-tasty snacks provide interesting colors and textures and can all be rustled up

at speed. In addition, all these quick recipes will satisfy your hunger pangs and taste buds. All of these dishes are sure to get your meal off to the right start.

Heavenly Garlic Dip

Anyone who loves garlic will adore this dip — it is very potent! Serve it at a barbecue and dip raw vegetables or chunks of French bread into it.

NUTRITIONAL INFORMATION

Calories . . . . . . .344 Sugars 2g
Protein . . . . .6g Fat 34g
Carbohydrate . . . .3g Saturates 5g

 15 MINS   20 MINS

SERVES 4

INGREDIENTS

2 bulbs garlic

6 tbsp olive oil

1 small onion, finely chopped

2 tbsp lemon juice

3 tbsp tahini paste

2 tbsp chopped fresh parsley

salt and pepper

TO SERVE

fresh vegetable crudités

French bread or warmed pita breads

1 Separate the bulbs of garlic into individual cloves. Place them on a cookie sheet and roast in a preheated oven at 400°F for 8–10 minutes; set aside to cool for a few minutes.

2 When they are cool enough to handle, peel the garlic cloves, and then chop them finely.

3 Heat the olive oil in a saucepan or skillet. Add the garlic and onion and fry over a low heat, stirring occasionally, for 8–10 minutes until softened; remove the pan from the heat.

4 Mix in the lemon juice, tahini paste, and parsley. Season to taste with salt and pepper. Transfer to a small heatproof bowl and keep warm at one side of the barbecue.

5 Serve with fresh vegetable crudités or chunks of French bread or warm pita breads.

VARIATION

If you come across smoked garlic, use it in this recipe — it tastes wonderful. There is no need to roast the smoked garlic, so omit the first step. This dip can also be used to baste kabobs and vegetarian burgers.

Mint & Cannellini Bean Dip

This dip is ideal for predinner drinks or for handing around at a party.
Don't forget the cannellini beans require soaking overnight.

NUTRITIONAL INFORMATION

Calories 208	Sugars 1g	
Protein 10g	Fat 12g	
Carbohydrate ...16g	Saturates 2g	

 40 MINS   30 MINS

SERVES 6

INGREDIENTS

1 cup dried cannellini beans

1 small garlic clove, crushed

1 bunch scallions, roughly chopped

handful of mint leaves

2 tbsp tahini paste

2 tbsp olive oil

1 tsp ground cumin

1 tsp ground coriander

lemon juice

salt and pepper

sprigs of mint, to garnish

TO SERVE

fresh vegetable crudités, such as
cauliflower flowerets, carrots, cucumber,
radishes, and bell peppers

1 Soak the cannellini beans overnight in plenty of cold water.

2 Rinse and drain the beans, put them into a large saucepan and cover them with cold water. Bring to a boil and boil rapidly for 10 minutes. Reduce the heat, cover, and simmer until tender.

3 Drain the beans and transfer them to a bowl or food processor. Add the garlic, scallions, mint, tahini paste, and olive oil.

4 Process the mixture for about 15 seconds, or mash well by hand until smooth.

5 Transfer the mixture to a bowl, stir in the cumin, coriander, and lemon juice, and season to taste with salt and pepper. Mix thoroughly, cover, and leave in a cool place for 30 minutes to allow the flavors to develop fully.

6 Spoon the dip into serving bowls, garnish with sprigs of fresh mint and surround with vegetable crudités. Serve at room temperature.

Buttered Nut & Lentil Dip

This tasty dip is very easy to make. It is perfect to have at barbecues, as it gives your guests something to nibble while they are waiting.

NUTRITIONAL INFORMATION

Calories 395	Sugars 4g
Protein 12g	Fat 31g
Carbohydrate ...18g	Saturates 10g

 5–10 MINS 40 MINS

SERVES 4

INGREDIENTS

4 tbsp butter

1 small onion, chopped

⅓ cup red lentils

1¼ cups vegetable stock

½ cup blanched almonds

½ cup pine nuts

½ tsp ground coriander

½ tsp ground cumin

½ tsp grated ginger root

1 tsp chopped fresh cilantro

salt and pepper

sprigs of fresh cilantro to garnish

TO SERVE

fresh vegetable crudités

bread sticks

VARIATION

Green or brown lentils can be used, but they will take longer to cook than red lentils. If you wish, substitute peanuts for the almonds. Ground ginger can be used instead of fresh – substitute ½ teaspoon and add it with the other spices.

1 Melt half the butter in a saucepan and fry the onion over a medium heat, stirring frequently, until golden brown.

2 Add the lentils and vegetable stock. Bring to a boil, then reduce the heat and simmer gently, uncovered, for about 25–30 minutes until the lentils are tender; drain well.

3 Melt the remaining butter in a small skillet. Add the almonds and pine nuts and fry them over a low heat, stirring frequently, until golden brown; remove from the heat.

4 Put the lentils, almonds, and pine nuts, with any remaining butter, into a food processor blender. Add the ground coriander, cumin, ginger, and fresh cilantro. Process for about 15–20 seconds until the mixture is smooth. Alternatively, press the lentils through a strainer to purée them and then mix with the finely chopped nuts, spices, and herbs.

5 Season the dip with salt and pepper and garnish with sprigs of fresh cilantro. Serve with fresh vegetable crudités and bread sticks.

Cheese, Garlic & Herb Pâté

This wonderful soft cheese pâté is fragrant with the aroma of fresh herbs and garlic. Serve with Melba toast for a perfect first course.

NUTRITIONAL INFORMATION

Calories 392	Sugars 1g	
Protein 17g	Fat 28g	
Carbohydrate ...18g	Saturates 18g	

20 MINS   10 MINS

SERVES 4

I N G R E D I E N T S

1 tbsp butter

1 garlic clove, crushed

3 scallions, finely chopped

½ cup full-fat soft cheese

2 tbsp chopped mixed herbs,
    such as parsley, chives, marjoram,
    oregano, and basil

1½ cups finely grated sharp cheddar cheese

pepper

4–6 slices of white bread from a
    medium-cut sliced loaf

mixed salad greens and cherry tomatoes,
to serve

TO GARNISH

ground paprika

herb sprigs

1 Melt the butter in a small skillet and gently fry the garlic and scallions together for 3–4 minutes until softened; allow to cool.

2 Beat the soft cheese in a large mixing bowl until smooth, then add the garlic and scallions. Stir in the herbs, mixing well.

3 Add the cheddar and work the mixture together to form a stiff paste. Cover and chill until ready to serve.

4 To make the Melba toast, toast the slices of bread on both sides, and then cut off the crusts. Using a sharp bread knife, cut through the slices horizontally to make very thin slices. Cut into triangles and then lightly broil the untoasted sides until golden.

5 Arrange the mixed salad greens on 4 serving plates with the cherry tomatoes. Pile the cheese pâté on top and sprinkle with a little paprika. Garnish with sprigs of fresh herbs and serve with the Melba toast.

Walnut, Egg & Cheese Pâté

This unusual pâté, flavored with parsley and dill, can be served with crackers, crusty bread, or toast. The pâté requires chilling until set.

NUTRITIONAL INFORMATION

Calories	438	Sugars	.........2g
Protein	........21g	Fat	..........38g
Carbohydrate	....2g	Saturates	......18g

 20 MINS   2 MINS

SERVES 2

INGREDIENTS

1 celery stalk

1–2 scallions, trimmed

¼ cup shelled walnuts

1 tbsp chopped fresh parsley

1 tsp chopped fresh dill, or ½ tsp dried dill

1 garlic clove, crushed

dash of Worcestershire sauce

½ cup cottage cheese

½ cup blue cheese, such as
    Stilton or Danish blue

1 hard-cooked egg

2 tbsp butter

salt and pepper

herbs, to garnish

crackers, toast, or crusty bread and
    crudités, to serve

COOK'S TIP

You can also use this as a stuffing for vegetables. Cut the tops off extra-large tomatoes, scoop out the seeds, and fill with the pâté, piling it well up, or spoon into the hollows of celery stalks cut into 2-inch pieces.

1 Finely chop the celery, slice the scallions very finely, and chop the walnuts evenly; place in a bowl.

2 Add the chopped herbs, garlic, and Worcestershire sauce to taste and mix well, then stir the cottage cheese evenly through the mixture.

3 Grate the blue cheese and hard-cooked egg finely into the pâté mixture, and season with salt and pepper.

4 Melt the butter and stir through the pâté, then spoon into one serving dish or individual dishes, but do not press down firmly; chill until set.

5 Garnish with fresh herbs and serve with crackers, toast, or fresh, crusty bread and a few crudités, if liked.

Smoked Fish & Potato Pâté

This smoked fish pâté is given a tart fruity flavor by the gooseberries, which complement the fish perfectly.

NUTRITIONAL INFORMATION

Calories 418	Sugars 4g
Protein 18g	Fat 25g
Carbohydrate . . .32g	Saturates 6g

20 MINS   10 MINS

SERVES 4

I N G R E D I E N T S

5 cups diced potatoes

10 oz smoked mackerel, skinned and flaked

½ cup cooked gooseberries

2 tsp lemon juice

2 tbsp low-fat crème fraîche or sour cream

1 tbsp capers

1 gherkin, chopped

1 tbsp chopped dill pickle

1 tbsp chopped fresh dill

salt and pepper

lemon wedges, to garnish

toast or warm crusty bread, to serve

1 Cook the diced potatoes in a saucepan of boiling water for 10 minutes until tender, then drain well.

2 Place the cooked potatoes in a food processor or blender.

3 Add the skinned and flaked smoked mackerel and process for 30 seconds until fairly smooth. Alternatively, place the ingredients in a bowl and mash with a fork.

4 Add the cooked gooseberries, lemon juice, and crème fraîche to the fish and potato mixture. Blend for a further 10 seconds or mash well.

5 Stir in the capers, chopped gherkin and dill pickle, and chopped fresh dill. Season well with salt and pepper.

6 Turn the fish pâté into a serving dish, garnish with lemon wedges, and serve with slices of toast or warm crusty bread cut into chunks or slices.

COOK'S TIP

Use stewed, canned, or bottled cooked gooseberries for convenience and to save time, or when fresh gooseberries are out of season.

Lentil Pâté

Red lentils are used in this spicy recipe for speed because they do not require presoaking. You can substitute other types of lentils, if preferred.

NUTRITIONAL INFORMATION

Calories	267	Sugars	........12g
Protein	........14g	Fat	...........8g
Carbohydrate	...37g	Saturates	.......1g

 30 MINS   1¼ HOURS

SERVES 4

I N G R E D I E N T S

1 tbsp vegetable oil, plus extra for greasing

1 onion, chopped

2 garlic cloves, crushed

1 tsp garam masala

½ tsp ground coriander

3¾ cups vegetable stock

¾ cup red lentils

1 small egg

2 tbsp milk

2 tbsp mango chutney

2 tbsp chopped fresh parsley

fresh parsley sprigs, to garnish

salad greens and toast, to serve

1 Heat the oil in a large saucepan and sauté the onion and garlic, stirring constantly, for 2–3 minutes. Add the spices and cook for a further 30 seconds.

2 Stir in the stock and lentils and bring the mixture to a boil. Reduce the heat and simmer for 20 minutes until the lentils are cooked and softened. Remove the pan from the heat and drain off any excess moisture.

3 Put the mixture in a food processor and add the egg, milk, mango chutney, and parsley; process until smooth.

4 Grease and line the base of an 8- x 4-inch bread pan and spoon in the mixture, leveling the surface. Cover and cook in a preheated oven at 400°F for 40–45 minutes, or until the pâté is firm to the touch.

5 Cool in the pan for 20 minutes, then transfer to the refrigerator.

6 Turn out the pâté on to a serving plate, slice and garnish with fresh parsley. Serve with salad greens and toast.

COOK'S TIP

It is always better to make your own stock, if you have time, rather than use bouillon cubes, as the flavor of homemade stock is far superior.

Mixed Bean Pâté

This is a really quick appetizer to prepare if canned beans are used. Choose a wide variety of beans for color and flavor.

NUTRITIONAL INFORMATION

Calories 126	Sugars 3g
Protein 5g	Fat 6g
Carbohydrate ...13g	Saturates 1g

 45 MINS   0 MINS

SERVES 4

INGREDIENTS

14-oz can mixed beans, drained

2 tbsp olive oil

juice of 1 lemon

2 garlic cloves, crushed

1 tbsp chopped cilantro

2 scallions, chopped

salt and pepper

shredded scallions to garnish

1 Rinse the beans thoroughly under cold running water and drain well.

2 Transfer the beans to a food processor or blender and process until smooth. Alternatively, place the beans in a bowl and mash thoroughly with a fork or potato masher.

3 Add the olive oil, lemon juice, garlic, cilantro, and scallions and blend until fairly smooth. Season with salt and pepper to taste.

4 Transfer the pâté to a serving bowl and chill in the refrigerator for at least 30 minutes.

5 Garnish with shredded scallions and serve.

Toasted Nibbles

These tiny cheese balls are rolled in fresh herbs, toasted nuts, or paprika to make nibbles for parties, buffets, or predinner drinks.

NUTRITIONAL INFORMATION

Calories 310	Sugars 1g
Protein 15g	Fat 27g
Carbohydrate 1g	Saturates 12g

🍐 40 MINS   🕐 5 MINS

SERVES 4

INGREDIENTS

½ cup ricotta cheese

1 cup finely grated brick cheese

2 tsp chopped parsley

½ cup chopped mixed nuts

3 tbsp chopped herbs, such as parsley,
    chives, marjoram, lovage, and chervil

2 tbsp mild paprika

pepper

herb sprigs, to garnish

1 Mix together the ricotta and brick cheeses. Add the parsley and pepper and work together until thoroughly combined.

2 Form the mixture into small balls and place on a plate. Cover and chill in the refrigerator for about 20 minutes until they are firm.

3 Scatter the chopped nuts onto a cookie sheet and place them under a preheated broiler until lightly browned; take care because they can easily burn. Set aside to cool.

4 Sprinkle the nuts, herbs, and paprika into 3 separate small bowls. Remove the cheese balls from the refrigerator and

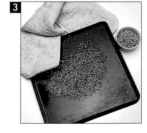

divide into 3 equal piles. Roll one quantity of the cheese balls in the nuts, one quantity in the herbs, and one quantity in the paprika until they are all well coated.

5 Arrange the coated cheese balls alternately on a large serving platter. Chill in the refrigerator until ready to serve and then garnish with sprigs of fresh herbs.

Tzatziki & Black Olive Dip

Tzatziki is a Greek dish, made with yogurt, mint, and cucumber.
It tastes superb served with warm pita bread.

NUTRITIONAL INFORMATION

Calories 381	Sugars 8g
Protein 11g	Fat 15g
Carbohydrate . . .52g	Saturates 2g

 1 HOUR   3 MINS

SERVES 4

I N G R E D I E N T S

½ cucumber

1 cup thick plain yogurt

1 tbsp chopped mint

salt and pepper

4 pita breads

D I P

2 garlic cloves, crushed

1 cup pitted black olives

4 tbsp olive oil

2 tbsp lemon juice

1 tbsp chopped parsley

T O   G A R N I S H

mint sprigs

parsley sprigs

COOK'S TIP

Sprinkling the cucumber
with salt draws out some of its
moisture, making it crisper. If
you are in a hurry, you can omit
this procedure. Use green olives
instead of black ones, if you prefer.

1 To make the tzatziki, peel the cucumber and chop roughly. Sprinkle it with salt and leave to stand for 15–20 minutes. Rinse with cold water and drain well.

2 Mix the cucumber, yogurt, and mint together. Season to taste with salt and pepper and transfer to a serving bowl. Cover and chill for 20–30 minutes.

3 To make the black olive dip, put the crushed garlic and olives into a blender or food processor and process for 15–20 seconds. Alternatively, chop them very finely.

4 Add the olive oil, lemon juice, and parsley to the blender or food processor and process for a few more seconds. Alternatively, mix with the chopped garlic and olives and mash together; season with salt and pepper.

5 Wrap the pita breads in foil and place over a barbecue for 2–3 minutes, turning once to warm through. Alternatively, heat in the oven or under the broiler. Cut into pieces and serve with the tzatziki and black olive dip, garnished with sprigs of fresh mint and parsley.

Hummus & Garlic Toasts

Hummus, made from garbanzo beans, is a real favorite spread on these flavorsome garlic toasts for a delicious appetizer or snack.

NUTRITIONAL INFORMATION

Calories	731	Sugars	.........2g
Protein	........22g	Fat	..........55g
Carbohydrate	...39g	Saturates	.......8g

 20 MINS   3 MINS

SERVES 4

INGREDIENTS

HUMMUS

14-oz can garbanzo beans

juice of 1 large lemon

6 tbsp tahini paste

2 tbsp olive oil

2 garlic cloves, crushed

salt and pepper

chopped cilantro and black olives,
   to garnish

TOASTS

1 loaf ciabatta, sliced

2 garlic cloves, crushed

1 tbsp chopped cilantro

4 tbsp olive oil

COOK'S TIP

Make the hummus one day in advance, and chill, covered, in the refrigerator until required. Garnish and serve.

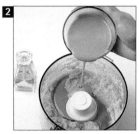

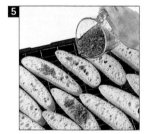

1 To make the hummus, drain the garbanzo beans, reserving a little of the liquid. Put the garbanzo beans and liquid in a food processor and process, gradually adding the reserved liquid and lemon juice. Blend well after each addition until smooth.

2 Stir in the tahini paste and all but 1 teaspoon of the olive oil. Add the garlic, season to taste, and blend again until smooth.

3 Spoon the hummus into a serving dish and smooth the top. Drizzle the remaining olive oil over the top, then garnish with chopped cilantro and olives. Set the hummus aside in the refrigerator to chill while you are preparing the garlic toasts.

4 Place the slices of ciabatta on a broiler rack in a single layer.

5 Mix the garlic, cilantro and olive oil together and drizzle over the bread slices. Cook under a hot broiler, turning once, for about 2–3 minutes until golden brown. Serve the toasts immediately with the hummus.

Onions à la Grecque

This is a traditional method of cooking vegetables in Greece, and this dish is perfect made with shallots or onions, served with a crisp salad.

NUTRITIONAL INFORMATION

Calories	200	Sugars	........26g
Protein	.........2g	Fat	...........9g
Carbohydrate	...28g	Saturates	.......1g

 10 MINS   15 MINS

SERVES 4

I N G R E D I E N T S

1 lb shallots

3 tbsp olive oil

3 tbsp honey

2 tbsp garlic wine vinegar

3 tbsp dry white wine

1 tbsp tomato paste

2 celery stalks, sliced

2 tomatoes, seeded and chopped

salt and pepper

chopped celery leaves, to garnish

1 Peel the shallots. Heat the oil in a large saucepan, add the shallots, and cook, stirring, for 3–5 minutes, or until they begin to brown.

2 Add the honey and cook over a high heat for a further 30 seconds, then add the garlic wine vinegar and dry white wine, stirring well.

3 Stir in the tomato paste, celery, and tomatoes and bring the mixture to a boil. Cook over a high heat for 5–6 minutes. Season to taste and leave to cool slightly.

4 Garnish with chopped celery leaves and serve warm. Alternatively, chill in the refrigerator before serving.

Bell Pepper Salad

Colorful marinated Mediterranean vegetables make a flavor-packed first course. Serve with Tomato Toasts or fresh bread.

NUTRITIONAL INFORMATION

Calories 234	Sugars 4g
Protein 6g	Fat 17g
Carbohydrate ...15g	Saturates 2g

 5–10 MINS   35 MINS

SERVES 4

INGREDIENTS

1 onion

2 red bell peppers

2 yellow bell peppers

3 tbsp olive oil

2 large zucchini, sliced

2 garlic cloves, sliced

1 tbsp balsamic vinegar

1¾-oz can anchovy fillets, chopped

¼ cup halved and pitted black olives

1 tbsp chopped fresh basil

salt and pepper

TOMATO TOASTS

small stick of French bread

1 garlic clove, crushed

1 tomato, peeled and chopped

2 tbsp olive oil

1 Cut the onion into wedges. Core and seed the bell peppers and cut into thick slices.

2 Heat the oil in a large heavy-based skillet. Add the onion, bell peppers, zucchini, and garlic and fry gently for 20 minutes, stirring occasionally.

3 Add the vinegar, anchovies, olives, and seasoning to taste, mix thoroughly and leave to cool.

4 Spoon onto individual plates and sprinkle with the basil.

5 To make the tomato toasts, cut the French bread diagonally into ½-inch slices.

6 Mix the garlic, tomato, oil, and seasoning together, and spread thinly over each slice of bread.

7 Place the bread on a cookie sheet, drizzle with the olive oil, and bake in a preheated oven at 425°F for 5–10 minutes until crisp. Serve the Tomato Toasts with the Bell Pepper Salad.

Bruschetta with Tomatoes

Using ripe tomatoes and the best olive oil will make this classic Tuscan dish absolutely delicious.

NUTRITIONAL INFORMATION

Calories	 330	Sugars	.... 4g
Protein	.... 8g	Fat	.... 14g
Carbohydrate	... 45g	Saturates	.... 2g

15 MINS 5 MINS

SERVES 4

INGREDIENTS

10 oz cherry tomatoes

4 sun-dried tomatoes

4 tbsp extra-virgin olive oil

16 fresh basil leaves, shredded

2 garlic cloves, peeled

8 slices ciabatta

salt and pepper

1 Using a sharp knife, cut the cherry tomatoes in half.

2 Using a sharp knife, slice the sun-dried tomatoes into strips.

3 Place the cherry tomatoes and sun-dried tomatoes in a bowl. Add the olive oil and the shredded basil leaves and toss to mix well. Season to taste with a little salt and pepper.

4 Using a sharp knife, cut the garlic cloves in half. Lightly toast the ciabatta bread.

5 Rub the garlic, cut-side down, over both sides of the lightly toasted ciabatta bread.

6 Top the ciabatta bread with the tomato mixture and serve.

Cured Meats, Olives & Tomatoes

This is a typical *antipasto* dish with the cold cured meats, stuffed olives, fresh tomatoes, basil, and balsamic vinegar.

NUTRITIONAL INFORMATION

Calories 312	Sugars 1g
Protein 12g	Fat 28g
Carbohydrate 2g	Saturates 1g

 10 MINS   5 MINS

SERVES 4

INGREDIENTS

4 plum tomatoes

1 tbsp balsamic vinegar

6 canned anchovy fillets, drained and rinsed

2 tbsp capers, drained and rinsed

1 cup green olives, pitted

6 oz mixed cured meats, sliced

8 fresh basil leaves

1 tbsp extra-virgin olive oil

salt and pepper

crusty bread, to serve

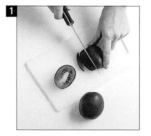

1 Using a sharp knife, cut the tomatoes into evenly-sized slices. Sprinkle the tomato slices with the balsamic vinegar and a little salt and pepper to taste; set aside.

2 Chop the anchovy fillets into pieces measuring about the same length as the olives.

3 Push a piece of anchovy and a caper into each olive.

4 Arrange the sliced meat on 4 individual serving plates together with the tomatoes, filled olives, and basil leaves.

5 Lightly drizzle the olive oil over the sliced meat, tomatoes, and olives.

6 Serve the cured meats, olives, and tomatoes with plenty of fresh crusty bread.

COOK'S TIP

The cured meats for this recipe are up to your individual taste. They can include a selection of prosciutto, pancetta, dried salt beef, and *salame di Milano* (pork and beef sausage).

Baked Fennel

Fennel is used extensively in northern Italy. It is a very versatile vegetable, good both cooked or used raw in salads.

NUTRITIONAL INFORMATION

Calories	111	Sugars	.........6g
Protein	.........7g	Fat	...........7g
Carbohydrate	....7g	Saturates	.......3g

10 MINS   35 MINS

SERVES 4

INGREDIENTS

2 fennel bulbs

2 celery stalks, cut into 3-inch sticks

6 sun-dried tomatoes, halved

1 cup puréed strained tomatoes

2 tsp dried oregano

3 tbsp grated Parmesan cheese

1 Using a sharp knife, trim the fennel, discarding any tough outer leaves, and cut the bulb into quarters.

2 Bring a large pan of water to a boil, add the fennel and celery, and cook for 8–10 minutes, or until just tender. Remove with a draining spoon and drain.

3 Place the fennel pieces, celery, and sun-dried tomatoes in a large baking dish.

4 Mix the tomatoes and oregano and pour over the fennel mixture.

5 Sprinkle with the Parmesan cheese and bake in a preheated oven at 375°F for 20 minutes or until hot. Serve as an appetizer with bread or as a vegetable side dish.

Figs & Prosciutto

This colorful fresh salad is delicious at any time of the year. Prosciutto di Parma is considered by many to be the best ham in the world.

NUTRITIONAL INFORMATION

Calories	121	Sugars	6g
Protein	1g	Fat	11g
Carbohydrate	6g	Saturates	2g

 15 MINS   5 MINS

SERVES 4

INGREDIENTS

1½ oz arugula

4 fresh figs

4 slices prosciutto

4 tbsp olive oil

1 tbsp fresh orange juice

1 tbsp honey

1 small red chili

1 Tear the arugula into more manageable pieces and arrange on 4 serving plates.

2 Using a sharp knife, cut each of the figs into quarters and place them on top of the arugula leaves.

3 Using a sharp knife, cut the prosciutto into strips and scatter over the arugula and figs.

4 Place the oil, orange juice, and honey in a screw-top jar. Shake the jar until the mixture emulsifies and forms a thick dressing; transfer to a bowl.

5 Using a sharp knife, dice the chili, remembering not to touch your face before you have washed your hands (see Cook's Tip, below). Add the chopped chili to the dressing and mix well.

6 Drizzle the dressing over the prosciutto, arugula, and figs, tossing to mix well. Serve at once.

COOK'S TIP

Chilies can burn the skin for several hours after chopping, so it is advisable to wear rubber gloves when you are handling the very hot varieties.

Deep-Fried Seafood

Deep-fried seafood is popular all around the Mediterranean, where fish of all kinds is fresh and abundant.

NUTRITIONAL INFORMATION

Calories	393	Sugars	.......0.2g
Protein	........27g	Fat	..........26g
Carbohydrate	...12g	Saturates	.......3g

5 MINS 　 15 MINS

SERVES 4

I N G R E D I E N T S

7 oz prepared squid

7 oz raw tiger prawns or jumbo
　　shrimp, peeled

5 oz whitebait

vegetable oil for deep-frying

4 tbsp all-purpose flour

1 tsp dried basil

salt and pepper

TO SERVE

garlic-flavored mayonnaise

lemon wedges

1 Carefully rinse the squid, prawns or shrimp, and whitebait under cold running water, completely removing any dirt or grit.

2 Using a sharp knife, slice the squid into rings, leaving the tentacles whole.

3 Heat the oil in a large saucepan to 350° to 375°F, or until a cube of bread browns in 30 seconds.

4 Place the flour in a bowl, add the basil, and season with salt and pepper to taste; mix together well.

5 Roll the squid, prawns or shrimp, and whitebait in the seasoned flour until coated all over. Carefully shake off any excess flour.

6 Cook the seafood in the heated oil, in batches, for 2–3 minutes, or until crispy and golden all over. Remove all of the seafood with a draining spoon and leave to drain thoroughly on paper towels.

7 Transfer the deep-fried seafood to serving plates and serve with garlic-flavored mayonnaise and a few lemon wedges.

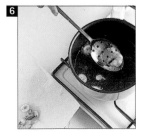

Mussels in White Wine

This soup of mussels, cooked in white wine with onions and cream, can be served as an appetizer or a main dish with plenty of crusty bread.

NUTRITIONAL INFORMATION

Calories 396   Sugars 2g
Protein . . . . .23g   Fat 24g
Carbohydrate . . . .8g   Saturates 15g

  5-10 MINS   25 MINS

SERVES 4

INGREDIENTS

about 3 quarts fresh mussels

4 tbsp butter

1 large onion, very finely chopped

2–3 garlic cloves, crushed

1½ cups dry white wine

⅔ cup water

2 tbsp lemon juice

good pinch of finely grated lemon peel

1 bouquet garni

1 tbsp all-purpose flour

4 tbsp light or heavy cream

2–3 tbsp chopped fresh parsley

salt and pepper

warm crusty bread, to serve

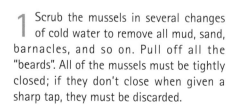  

1 Scrub the mussels in several changes of cold water to remove all mud, sand, barnacles, and so on. Pull off all the "beards". All of the mussels must be tightly closed; if they don't close when given a sharp tap, they must be discarded.

2 Melt half the butter in a large saucepan. Add the onion and garlic, and fry gently until soft but not colored.

3 Add the wine, water, lemon juice and peel, bouquet garni, and plenty of seasoning. Bring to a boil, then cover and simmer for 4–5 minutes.

4 Add the mussels to the pan, cover tightly, and simmer for 5 minutes, shaking the pan frequently, until all the mussels have opened; discard any mussels which have not opened. Remove the bouquet garni.

5 Remove the empty half shell from each mussel. Blend the remaining butter with the flour and whisk into the soup, a little at a time. Simmer gently for 2–3 minutes until slightly thickened.

6 Add the cream and half the parsley to the soup and reheat gently. Adjust the seasoning. Ladle the mussels and soup into warmed large soup bowls, sprinkle with the remaining parsley, and serve with plenty of warm crusty bread.

Tagliarini with Gorgonzola

This simple, creamy pasta sauce is a classic Italian recipe. You could use Danish blue cheese instead of the gorgonzola, if you prefer.

NUTRITIONAL INFORMATION

Calories	904	Sugars	.........4g
Protein	........27g	Fat	..........53g
Carbohydrate	...83g	Saturates	......36g

5 MINS   20 MINS

SERVES 4

INGREDIENTS

2 tbsp butter

1½ cups roughly crumbled
    gorgonzola cheese

⅔ cup heavy cream

2 tbsp dry white wine

1 tsp cornstarch

4 fresh sage sprigs, finely chopped

14 oz dried tagliarini

2 tbsp olive oil

salt and white pepper

1 Melt the butter in a heavy-based pan. Stir in 1 cup of the cheese and melt, over a low heat, for about 2 minutes.

2 Add the cream, wine, and cornstarch and beat with a whisk until fully incorporated.

COOK'S TIP

Gorgonzola is one of the world's oldest veined cheeses and, arguably, its finest. When buying, always check that it is creamy yellow with delicate green veining; avoid hard or discolored cheese. It should have a rich, piquant aroma, not a bitter smell.

3 Stir in the sage and season to taste with salt and white pepper. Bring to a boil over a low heat, whisking constantly, until the sauce thickens. Remove from the heat and set aside while you cook the pasta.

4 Bring a large saucepan of lightly salted water to the boil. Add the tagliarini and 1 tbsp of the olive oil. Cook the pasta for 8–10 minutes, or until just

tender, then drain thoroughly and toss in the remaining olive oil. Transfer the pasta to a serving dish and keep warm.

5 Reheat the sauce over a low heat, whisking constantly. Spoon the gorgonzola sauce over the tagliarini, generously sprinkle the remaining cheese over, and serve immediately.

Ciabatta Rolls

Sandwiches are always a welcome snack, but can be mundane. These crisp rolls filled with roasted bell peppers and cheese are irresistible.

NUTRITIONAL INFORMATION

Calories	328	Sugars	.........6g
Protein	.........8g	Fat	..........19g
Carbohydrate	...34g	Saturates	.......9g

  15 MINS   🕙 10 MINS

SERVES 4

INGREDIENTS

4 ciabatta rolls

2 tbsp olive oil

1 garlic clove, crushed

FILLING

1 red bell pepper

1 green bell pepper

1 yellow bell pepper

4 radishes, sliced

1 bunch watercress

½ cup cream cheese

1 Slice the ciabatta rolls in half. Heat the olive oil and crushed garlic in a saucepan. Pour the garlic and oil mixture over the cut surfaces of the rolls and leave to stand.

2 Halve the bell peppers and place, skin side uppermost, on a broiler rack. Cook under a hot broiler for 8–10 minutes until just beginning to char. Remove the peppers from the broiler, peel, and slice thinly.

3 Arrange the radish slices on one half of each roll with a few watercress leaves. Spoon the cream cheese on top. Pile the bell peppers on top of the cream cheese and top with the other half of the roll. Serve immediately.

Eggplant Dipping Platter

Dipping platters are a very sociable dish, bringing together all the diners at the table.

NUTRITIONAL INFORMATION

Calories 81   Sugars 4g
Protein . . . . .4g   Fat 5g
Carbohydrate . . . .5g   Saturates 1g

🍴 15 MINS   🕐 10 MINS

SERVES 4

I N G R E D I E N T S

1 eggplant, peeled and cut into 1-inch cubes

3 tbsp sesame seeds, toasted in a dry pan over a low heat

1 tsp sesame oil

grated peel and juice of ½ lime

1 small shallot, diced

1 tsp sugar

1 red chili, seeded and sliced

1¼ cups broccoli flowerets

2 carrots, cut into matchsticks

8 baby corn cobs, cut in half lengthways

2 celery stalks, cut into matchsticks

1 baby red cabbage, cut into 8 wedges, the leaves of each wedge held together by the core

salt and pepper

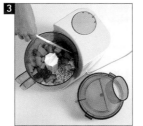

1 Cook the diced eggplant in a saucepan of boiling water for 7–8 minutes.

2 Meanwhile, grind the sesame seeds with the oil in a food processor or mortar and pestle.

3 Add the eggplant, lime peel and juice, shallot, ½ teaspoon salt, pepper, sugar, and chili in that order to the sesame seeds. Process, or chop and mash by hand, until smooth.

4 Adjust the seasoning to taste then spoon the dip into a bowl.

5 Serve the eggplant dipping platter surrounded by the broccoli, carrots, baby corn cobs, celery, and red cabbage.

VARIATION

You can vary the selection of vegetables depending on your preference or whatever you have at hand. Other vegetables you can use are cauliflower flowerets and cucumber sticks.

Son-in-Law Eggs

This recipe is supposedly so called because it is an easy enough dish for a son-in-law to cook to impress his new mother-in-law!

NUTRITIONAL INFORMATION

Calories 229   Sugars 8g
Protein . . . . .9g   Fat 18g
Carbohydrate . . . .8g   Saturates 3g

15 MINS   15 MINS

SERVES 4

I N G R E D I E N T S

6 eggs, hard-cooked and shelled

4 tbsp sunflower oil

1 onion, thinly sliced

2 fresh red chilies, sliced

2 tbsp sugar

1 tbsp water

2 tsp tamarind pulp

1 tbsp liquid seasoning, such as Maggi

rice, to serve

1 Prick the hard-cooked eggs 2 or 3 times with a toothpick.

2 Heat the sunflower oil in a wok and fry the eggs until crispy and golden. Drain on absorbent paper towels.

3 Halve the eggs lengthways and put on a serving dish.

4 Pour off all but one tablespoon of the oil. Heat the oil and cook the onion and chilies over a high heat until golden and slightly crisp. Drain on paper towels.

5 Heat the sugar, water, tamarind pulp, and liquid seasoning in the wok and simmer for 5 minutes until thickened.

6 Pour the sauce over the eggs and spoon over the onion and chilies. Serve immediately with rice.

COOK'S TIP

Tamarind pulp is sold in oriental stores, and is very sour. If it is not available, use twice the amount of lemon juice in its place.

Crispy Seaweed

This tasty Chinese appetizer is not all that it seems — the "seaweed" is, in fact, fried and salted pak choi tossed with pine nuts.

NUTRITIONAL INFORMATION

Calories . . . . .214 Sugars 14g
Protein . . . . .6g Fat 15g
Carbohydrate . . .15g Saturates 2g

10 MINS   5 MINS

SERVES 4

INGREDIENTS

2 lb 4 oz pak choi

peanut oil for deep-frying (about 3¾ cups)

1 tsp salt

1 tbsp sugar

2½ tbsp toasted pine nuts

1 Rinse the pak choi leaves under cold running water and then pat dry thoroughly with paper towels.

2 Discarding any tough outer leaves, roll each pak choi leaf up, then slice them thinly so the leaves are finely

shredded. Alternatively, use a food processor to shred the pak choi.

3 Heat the peanut oil in a large wok or heavy-based skillet.

4 Carefully add the shredded pak choi leaves to the wok or skillet and fry for about 30 seconds, or until they shrivel up and become crispy: you will probably need to do this in

several batches, depending on the size of the wok.

5 Remove the crispy seaweed from the wok with a draining spoon and drain on paper towels.

6 Transfer the crispy seaweed to a large bowl and toss with the salt, sugar, and pine nuts. Serve immediately.

COOK'S TIP

The tough, outer leaves of pak choi are discarded because they will spoil the overall taste and texture of the dish.

Use savoy cabbage instead of the pak choi if it is unavailable, drying the leaves thoroughly before frying.

Spicy Corn Fritters

Cornmeal acts as a binding agent in this recipe, which makes a simple first course.

NUTRITIONAL INFORMATION

Calories	....	.213
Protein	....	.5g
Carbohydrate	...	30g

Sugars	....	.6g
Fat	....	.8g
Saturates	....	.1g

 5 MINS   15 MINS

SERVES 4

I N G R E D I E N T S

¾ cup canned or frozen corn kernels

2 red chilies, seeded and very finely chopped

2 garlic cloves, crushed

10 kaffir lime leaves, very finely chopped

2 tbsp fresh cilantro, chopped

1 large egg

½ cup cornmeal

½ cup fine green beans, very finely chopped

peanut oil for frying

1 Place the corn, chilies, garlic, lime leaves, cilantro, egg, and cornmeal in a large mixing bowl and stir to combine.

2 Add the green beans to the ingredients in the bowl and stir, using a wooden spoon.

3 Divide the mixture into small, evenly sized balls. Flatten the balls of mixture between the palms of your hands to form patties.

4 Heat a little peanut oil in a preheated wok or large skillet until really hot. Cook the fritters, in batches, until brown and crispy on the outside, turning occasionally: leave the fritters to drain on paper towels while frying the remaining fritters.

5 Transfer the fritters to warm serving plates and serve immediately.

COOK'S TIP

Kaffir lime leaves are dark green, glossy leaves that have a lemon-lime flavor. They are sold at specialist Asian stores, either fresh or dried. Fresh leaves impart the most delicious flavor.

Chinese Omelet

This is a fairly filling omelet, because it contains chicken and shrimp.
It is cooked as a whole omelet and then sliced for serving.

NUTRITIONAL INFORMATION

Calories 309	Sugars 0g	
Protein 34g	Fat 19g	
Carbohydrate ...0.2g	Saturates 5g	

5 MINS   5 MINS

SERVES 4

I N G R E D I E N T S

8 eggs

2 cups shredded cooked chicken

12 tiger prawns or jumbo shrimp,
   peeled and deveined

2 tbsp snipped chives

2 tsp light soy sauce

dash of chili sauce

2 tbsp vegetable oil

1 Lightly beat the eggs in a large mixing bowl.

2 Add the shredded chicken and tiger prawns or jumbo shrimp to the eggs, mixing well.

3 Stir in the snipped chives, light soy sauce, and chili sauce, stirring well to combine all the ingredients.

4 Heat the vegetable oil in a large preheated skillet over a medium heat.

5 Add the egg mixture to the skillet, tilting the pan to coat the base completely.

6 Cook over a medium heat, gently stirring the omelet with a fork until the surface is just set and the underside is a golden brown color.

7 When the omelet is set, slide it carefully out of the pan, with the aid of a spatula.

8 Cut the Chinese omelet into squares or slices and serve immediately. Alternatively, serve the omelet as a main course for two people.

VARIATION

You can add extra flavour to the omelet by stirring in 3 tablespoons of finely chopped fresh cilantro or 1 teaspoon of sesame seeds with the chives in step 3.

Pork-Sesame Toasts

This classic Chinese appetizer is also a great nibble for serving at parties – but be sure to make plenty!

NUTRITIONAL INFORMATION

Calories	674	Sugars	........2g
Protein	........33g	Fat	..........46g
Carbohydrate	...33g	Saturates	.......7g

5 MINS   35 MINS

SERVES 4

INGREDIENTS

9 oz lean, boneless pork

9 oz uncooked peeled shrimp, deveined

4 scallions, trimmed

1 garlic clove, crushed

1 tbsp chopped fresh cilantro leaves
   and stems

1 tbsp fish sauce

1 egg

8–10 slices of thick-cut white bread

3 tbsp sesame seeds

⅔ cup vegetable oil

salt and pepper

TO GARNISH

sprigs of fresh cilantro

red bell pepper, finely sliced

1 Put the pork, shrimp, scallions, garlic, cilantro, fish sauce, egg, and seasoning into a food processor or blender. Process for a few seconds until the ingredients are finely chopped; transfer the mixture to a bowl. Alternatively, chop the pork, shrimp and scallions very finely, and mix with the garlic, cilantro, fish sauce, beaten egg, and seasoning until all the ingredients are well combined.

2 Spread the pork and shrimp mixture thickly over the bread so it reaches right up to the edges. Cut off the crusts and slice each piece of bread into 4 squares or triangles.

3 Sprinkle the topping liberally with sesame seeds.

4 Heat the oil in a wok or skillet. Fry a few pieces of the bread, topping side down first so it sets the egg, for about 2 minutes, or until golden brown. Turn the pieces over to cook on the other side, for about 1 minute.

5 Drain the pork and shrimp toasts and place them on paper towels; fry the remaining pieces. Serve garnished with sprigs of fresh cilantro and strips of red bell pepper.

Sesame-Ginger Chicken

Chunks of chicken breast are marinated in a mixture of lime juice, garlic, sesame oil, and fresh gingerroot to give them a great flavor.

NUTRITIONAL INFORMATION

Calories	204	Sugars	.........0g
Protein	........28g	Fat	..........10g
Carbohydrate	....1g	Saturates	.......2g

  2¼ HOURS   10 MINS

SERVES 4

I N G R E D I E N T S

4 wooden satay sticks, soaked in
  warm water

1 lb 2 oz boneless chicken
  breasts

sprigs of fresh mint, to garnish

MARINADE

1 garlic clove, crushed

1 shallot, very finely chopped

2 tbsp sesame oil

1 tbsp fish sauce or light soy sauce

finely grated peel of 1 lime or
  ½ lemon

2 tbsp lime juice or lemon juice

1 tsp sesame seeds

2 tsp finely grated fresh gingerroot

2 tsp chopped fresh mint

salt and pepper

COOK'S TIP

The kabobs taste delicious if dipped into an accompanying bowl of hot chili sauce.

1 To make the marinade, put the crushed garlic, chopped shallot, sesame oil, fish sauce or soy sauce, lime or lemon peel and juice, sesame seeds, grated gingerroot, and chopped mint into a large, nonmetallic bowl. Season with a little salt and pepper and mix together until all the ingredients are thoroughly combined.

2 Remove the skin from the chicken breasts and cut the flesh into chunks.

3 Add the chicken to the marinade, stirring to coat the chicken completely in the mixture. Cover with plastic wrap and chill in the refrigerator for at least 2 hours so the flavours are absorbed.

4 Thread the chicken onto wooden satay sticks. Place them on the rack of a broiler pan and baste with the marinade.

5 Place the kabobs under a preheated broiler for 8–10 minutes. Turn them frequently, basting them with the remaining marinade.

6 Serve the chicken skewers at once, garnished with sprigs of fresh mint.

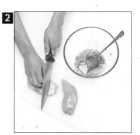

Spicy Salt & Pepper Shrimp

For best results, use raw jumbo shrimp in their shells. They are 3-4 inches long, and you should get 18 to 20 per 18 ounces.

NUTRITIONAL INFORMATION

Calories	160	Sugars	.......0.2g
Protein	........17g	Fat	..........10g
Carbohydrate	...0.5g	Saturates	.......1g

  35 MINS   20 MINS

SERVES 4

I N G R E D I E N T S

9-10 oz raw shrimp in their shells, defrosted if frozen

1 tbsp light soy sauce

1 tsp Chinese rice wine or dry sherry

2 tsp cornstarch

vegetable oil for deep-frying

2-3 scallions, to garnish

SPICY SALT AND PEPPER

1 tbsp salt

1 tsp ground Szechuan peppercorns

1 tsp five-spice powder

1 Pull the soft legs off the shrimp, but keep the body shells on; dry well on paper towels.

2 Place the shrimp in a bowl with the soy sauce, rice wine or sherry, and cornstarch. Turn the shrimp to coat thoroughly in the mixture and leave to marinate for about 25-30 minutes.

3 To make the Spicy Salt and Pepper, mix the salt, ground Szechuan peppercorns, and five-spice powder together. Place in a dry skillet and stir-fry for about 3-4 minutes over a low heat, stirring constantly to prevent the spices burning on the bottom of the pan; remove from the heat and allow to cool.

4 Heat the vegetable oil in a preheated wok or large skillet until smoking. Deep-fry the shrimp in batches until golden brown. Remove the shrimp from the wok with a draining spoon and drain on paper towels.

5 Place the scallions in a bowl, pour in 1 tablespoon of the hot oil, and leave for 30 seconds. Serve the shrimp garnished with the scallions, and with the Spicy Salt and Pepper as a dip.

COOK'S TIP

The roasted spice mixture made with Szechuan peppercorns is used throughout China as a dip for deep-fried food. The peppercorns are sometimes roasted first and then ground. Dry-frying is a way of releasing the flavors of the spices.

Crostini alla Fiorentina

Serve as an appetizer, or simply spread on small pieces of crusty fried bread (crostini) to enjoy with drinks.

NUTRITIONAL INFORMATION

Calories 393	Sugars 2g
Protein 17g	Fat 25g
Carbohydrate ...19g	Saturates 9g

10 MINS   40–45 MINS

SERVES 4

INGREDIENTS

3 tbsp olive oil

1 onion, chopped

1 celery stalk, chopped

1 carrot, chopped

1–2 garlic cloves, crushed

4 oz chicken livers

4 oz calf, lamb, or pig liver

⅔ cup red wine

1 tbsp tomato paste

2 tbsp chopped fresh parsley

3 or 4 canned anchovy fillets, finely chopped

2 tbsp stock or water

2–3 tbsp butter

1 tbsp capers

salt and pepper

small pieces of fried crusty bread, to serve

chopped parsley, to garnish

1 Heat the oil in a pan. Add the onion, celery, carrot, and garlic and cook gently for 4–5 minutes, or until the onion is soft, but not colored.

2 Meanwhile, rinse and dry the chicken livers. Dry the calf or other liver, and slice into strips. Add the liver to the pan and fry gently for a few minutes until the strips are well sealed on all sides.

3 Add half of the wine and cook until it has mostly evaporated. Then add the rest of the wine, tomato paste, half of the parsley, the anchovy fillets, stock or water, a little salt and plenty of black pepper.

4 Cover the pan and leave to simmer, stirring occasionally, for 15–20 minutes, or until tender and most of the liquid has been absorbed.

5 Leave the mixture to cool a little, then either coarsely chop or put into a food processor and process to a chunky purée.

6 Return to the pan and add the butter, capers, and remaining parsley. Heat through gently until the butter melts. Adjust the seasoning and spoon into a bowl. Serve warm or cold spread on the slices of crusty bread and sprinkled with chopped parsley.

Chicken or Beef Satay

In this dish, strips of chicken or beef are threaded onto skewers, broiled, and served with a spicy peanut sauce.

NUTRITIONAL INFORMATION

Calories 314	Sugars 8g	
Protein 32g	Fat 16g	
Carbohydrate . . .10g	Saturates 4g	

  2¼ HOURS 15 MINS

SERVES 6

INGREDIENTS

4 boneless, skinned chicken breasts, or
1 lb 10 oz sirloin steak, trimmed

MARINADE

1 small onion, finely chopped

1 garlic clove, crushed

1-inch piece gingerroot, peeled
and grated

2 tbsp dark soy sauce

2 tsp ground red chili

1 tsp ground coriander

2 tsp dark brown sugar

1 tbsp lemon or lime juice

1 tbsp vegetable oil

SAUCE

1¼ cups coconut milk

4 tbsp crunchy peanut butter

1 tbsp fish sauce

1 tsp lemon or lime juice

salt and pepper

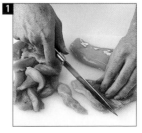  

1 Using a sharp knife, trim any fat from the chicken or beef then cut into thin strips, about 3 inches long.

2 To make the marinade, place all the ingredients in a shallow dish and mix well. Add the chicken or beef strips and turn in the marinade until well coated.

Cover with plastic wrap and leave to marinate for 2 hours, or overnight in the refrigerator.

3 Remove the meat from the marinade and thread the pieces, concertina style, on presoaked bamboo or thin wooden skewers.

4 Broil the chicken and beef satays for 8-10 minutes, turning and brushing

occasionally with the marinade, until cooked through.

5 Meanwhile, to make the sauce, mix the coconut milk with the peanut butter, fish sauce, and lemon or lime juice in a saucepan. Bring to a boil and cook for 3 minutes; season to taste.

6 Transfer the sauce to a serving bowl and serve with the cooked satays.

Pasta & Anchovy Sauce

This is an ideal dish for cooks in a hurry, as it is prepared in minutes from pantry ingredients.

NUTRITIONAL INFORMATION

Calories 712	Sugars 4g
Protein 25g	Fat 34g
Carbohydrate . . .81g	Saturates 8g

 10 MINS 25 MINS

SERVES 4

I N G R E D I E N T S

6 tbsp olive oil

2 garlic cloves, crushed

2-oz can anchovy fillets, drained

1 lb dried spaghetti

¼ cup Pesto Dressing (see page 223)

2 tbsp finely chopped fresh oregano

1 cup grated Parmesan cheese,
    plus extra for serving (optional)

salt and pepper

2 fresh oregano sprigs, to garnish

1 Reserve 1 tbsp of the oil and heat the remainder in a small saucepan. Add the garlic and fry for 3 minutes.

2 Lower the heat, stir in the anchovies and cook, stirring occasionally, until the anchovies have disintegrated.

3 Bring a large saucepan of lightly salted water to a boil. Add the spaghetti and the remaining olive oil and cook for 8–10 minutes, or until just tender, but still firm to the bite.

4 Add the Pesto Dressing and chopped fresh oregano to the anchovy mixture and then season with pepper to taste.

5 Drain the spaghetti, using a draining spoon, and transfer to a warm serving dish. Pour the Pesto Dressing over the spaghetti and then sprinkle over the grated Parmesan cheese.

6 Garnish with oregano sprigs and serve with extra cheese, if using.

COOK'S TIP

If you find canned anchovies too salty, soak them in a saucer of cold milk for 5 minutes, drain and pat dry with paper towels before using; the milk absorbs the salt.

Fish & Seafood

The wealth of species and flavors of fish and seafood that the world's oceans and rivers provide is immense. Each country combines its local catch with the region's favorite herbs and spices to create a variety of dishes. All of the recipes featured

in this chapter are easy to prepare and delicious to eat. Moreover, not only are fish and seafood quick to cook, but they are packed full with nutritional goodness. Naturally low in fat, yet rich in minerals and protein, fish and seafood are important to help balance any diet. The variety of fish and fish prices helps us to choose dishes to suit both mood and pocket.

Seafood Salad

Seafood is plentiful in Italy and each region has its own version of seafood salad. The dressing needs to be chilled for several hours in advance.

NUTRITIONAL INFORMATION

Calories 471	Sugars 2g
Protein 34g	Fat 33g
Carbohydrate 4g	Saturates 5g

🕒 45-55 MINS ⏱ 40 MINS

SERVES 4

I N G R E D I E N T S

6 oz squid rings, defrosted if frozen

2½ cups water

⅔ cup dry white wine

8 oz hake or monkfish, cut into cubes

16–20 mussels, scrubbed and bearded

20 clams in shells, scrubbed, if available
   (otherwise use extra mussels)

4–6 oz peeled shrimp

3–4 scallions, trimmed and
   sliced (optional)

radicchio and chicory leaves, to serve

lemon wedges, to garnish

D R E S S I N G

6 tbsp olive oil

1 tbsp wine vinegar

2 tbsp chopped fresh parsley

1–2 garlic cloves, crushed

salt and pepper

G A R L I C   M A Y O N N A I S E

5 tbsp thick mayonnaise

2–3 tbsp fromage blanc or plain yogurt

2 garlic cloves, crushed

1 tbsp capers

2 tbsp chopped fresh parsley or mixed herbs

1 Poach the squid in the water and wine for 20 minutes, or until almost tender. Add the fish and continue to cook gently for 7–8 minutes, or until tender; strain, reserving the fish. Pour the stock into a clean pan.

2 Bring the fish stock to a boil and add the mussels and clams. Cover the pan and simmer gently for about 5 minutes, or until the shells open; discard any that remain closed.

3 Drain the shellfish and remove from their shells. Put into a bowl with the cooked fish and add the shrimp and scallions, if using.

4 For the dressing, whisk together the oil, vinegar, parsley, garlic, and salt and pepper to taste. Pour over the fish, mixing well. Cover and chill for several hours.

5 Arrange small leaves of radicchio and chicory on 4 plates and spoon the fish salad into the center. Garnish with lemon wedges. Combine all the ingredients for the garlic mayonnaise and serve with the salad.

Mussel Salad

A colorful combination of cooked mussels tossed together with chargrilled red bell peppers and salad leaves in a lemon dressing.

NUTRITIONAL INFORMATION

Calories	124	Sugars	.........5g
Protein	........16g	Fat	...........5g
Carbohydrate	....5g	Saturates	......1g

40 MINS   10 MINS

SERVES 4

INGREDIENTS

2 large red bell peppers

12 oz cooked shelled mussels, thawed if frozen

1 head of radicchio

1 oz arugula leaves

8 cooked New Zealand mussels in their shells

TO SERVE

lemon wedges

crusty bread

DRESSING

1 tbsp olive oil

1 tbsp lemon juice

1 tsp finely grated lemon peel

2 tsp honey

1 tsp Dijon mustard

1 tbsp snipped fresh chives

salt and pepper

1 Preheat the broiler to hot. Halve and seed the bell peppers and place them skin-side up on the rack.

2 Cook for 8–10 minutes until the skin is charred and blistered and the flesh is soft. Leave to cool for 10 minutes, then peel off the skins.

3 Slice the bell pepper flesh into thin strips and place in a bowl. Gently mix in the shelled mussels and set aside until required.

4 To make the dressing, mix all of the ingredients until well blended.

5 Stir into the bell pepper and mussel mixture until coated.

6 Remove the central core of the radicchio and shred the leaves. Place in a serving bowl with the arugula leaves and toss together.

7 Pile the mussel mixture into the center of the leaves and arrange the large mussels in their shells around the edge of the dish. Serve with lemon wedges and crusty bread.

Sweet & Sour Tuna Salad

Small navy beans, zucchini, and tomatoes are quickly cooked in a sweet-and-sour sauce, before being combined with tuna.

NUTRITIONAL INFORMATION

Calories	245	Sugars	.........5g
Protein	.......22g	Fat	...........8g
Carbohydrate	...24g	Saturates	......1g

  15 MINS   10 MINS

SERVES 4

I N G R E D I E N T S

2 tbsp olive oil

1 onion, chopped

2 garlic cloves, chopped

2 zucchini, sliced

4 tomatoes, skinned

14-oz can small navy beans, drained and rinsed

10 black olives, halved and pitted

1 tbsp capers

1 tsp sugar

1 tbsp wholegrain mustard

1 tbsp white-wine vinegar

7-oz can tuna, drained

2 tbsp chopped fresh parsley

chopped fresh parsley, to garnish

crusty bread, to serve

1   Heat the oil in a skillet and fry the onion and garlic for 5 minutes until soft.

2   Add the zucchini and cook for 3 minutes, stirring occasionally.

3   Cut the tomatoes in half, then into thin wedges.

4   Add the tomatoes to the pan with the beans, olives, capers, sugar, mustard, and vinegar.

5   Simmer for 2 minutes, stirring gently, then allow to cool slightly.

6   Flake the tuna and stir into the bean mixture with the parsley.

7   Garnish with parsley and serve lukewarm with crusty bread.

COOK'S TIP

Capers are the flower buds of the caper bush, which is native to the Mediterranean region. Capers are preserved in vinegar and salt and give a distinctive flavor to this salad. They are often featured in Italian and Provençale cooking.

Smoked Trout & Apple Salad

Smoked trout and horseradish are natural partners, and when combined with apple and watercress make a wonderful first course.

NUTRITIONAL INFORMATION

Calories	133	Sugars	........11g
Protein	........12g	Fat	...........5g
Carbohydrate	....11g	Saturates	......1g

 10 MINS   0 MINS

SERVES 4

I N G R E D I E N T S

2 orange-red eating apples

2 tbsp vinaigrette dressing

½ bunch watercress

1 smoked trout, about 6 oz

HORSERADISH DRESSING

½ cup low-fat plain yogurt

½–1 tsp lemon juice

1 tbsp horseradish sauce

milk (optional)

salt and pepper

TO GARNISH

1 tbsp chopped chives

chive flowers (optional)

1 Leaving the skin on, cut the apples into quarters and remove the cores. Slice the apples into a bowl and toss in the vinaigrette to prevent them from browning.

2 Break the watercress into sprigs and arrange on 4 serving plates.

3 Skin the trout and take out the bone; carefully remove any fine bones that remain. Flake the trout into fairly large pieces and arrange between the watercress with the apple.

4 To make the horseradish dressing, whisk all the ingredients together, adding a little milk if too thick, then drizzle over the trout. Sprinkle the chopped chives and flowers (if using) over the trout, then serve.

COOK'S TIP

To make Melba toast, toast thinly sliced bread, then cut off the crusts and carefully slice in half horizontally using a sharp knife. Cut in half diagonally and place toasted side down in a warm oven for 15–20 minutes until the edges start to curl and the toast is crisp.

Tuna, Bean & Anchovy Salad

Serve as part of a selection of *antipasti*, or for a summer lunch with hot garlic bread.

NUTRITIONAL INFORMATION

Calories 397	Sugars 8g
Protein 23g	Fat 30g
Carbohydrate . . .10g	Saturates 4g

 35 MINS　　 0 MINS

SERVES 4

I N G R E D I E N T S

1 lb 2 oz tomatoes

7-oz can tuna, drained

2 tbsp chopped fresh parsley

½ cucumber

1 small red onion, sliced

8 oz green beans, cooked

1 small red bell pepper, cored and
　　seeded

1 small crisp lettuce

6 tbsp Italian-style dressing

3 hard-cooked eggs

2-oz can anchovies, drained

12 black olives, pitted

1　Cut the tomatoes into wedges and flake the tuna. Put both into the bowl with the parsley.

2　Cut the cucumber in half lengthways, then cut into slices. Slice the onion. Add the cucumber and onion to the bowl.

3　Cut the beans in half, chop the bell pepper, and add both to the bowl with the lettuce leaves. Pour the dressing over and toss to mix, then spoon into a salad bowl. Cut the eggs into quarters, arrange over the top with the anchovies, and scatter with the olives.

Neapolitan Seafood Salad

This delicious mix of seafood, salad greens, and ripe tomatoes conjures up all the warmth and sunshine of Naples.

NUTRITIONAL INFORMATION

Calories	1152	Sugars	.........3g
Protein	........67g	Fat	..........81g
Carbohydrate	...35g	Saturates	......12g

6½ HOURS   25 MINS

SERVES 4

I N G R E D I E N T S

1 lb prepared squid, cut into strips

1 lb 10 oz cooked mussels

1 lb cooked cockles in brine

⅔ cup white wine

1¼ cups olive oil

8 oz dried campanelle, or other
   small pasta shapes

juice of 1 lemon

1 bunch chives, snipped

1 bunch fresh parsley, finely chopped

4 large tomatoes

mixed salad greens

salt and pepper

sprig of fresh basil, to garnish

1 Put all of the seafood into a large bowl, pour the wine and half of the olive oil over, and set aside for 6 hours.

2 Put the seafood mixture into a saucepan and simmer over a low heat for 10 minutes; set aside to cool.

3 Bring a large saucepan of lightly salted water to a boil. Add the pasta and 1 tbsp of the remaining olive oil and cook for 8–10 minutes, or until tender, but still firm to the bite. Drain thoroughly and refresh in cold water.

4 Strain off about half of the cooking liquid from the seafood and discard the rest. Stir in the lemon juice, chives, parsley, and the remaining olive oil. Season to taste with salt and pepper. Drain the pasta and add to the seafood.

5 Cut the tomatoes into quarters. Shred the salad greens and arrange them at the base of a salad bowl. Spoon in the seafood salad and garnish with the tomatoes and a sprig of basil. Serve at once.

VARIATION

You can substitute cooked scallops for the mussels and clams in brine for the cockles, if you prefer. The seafood needs to be marinated for 6 hours, so prepare it well in advance.

Seafood Stir-Fry

This combination of assorted seafood and tender vegetables flavored with ginger makes an ideal light meal served with thread noodles.

NUTRITIONAL INFORMATION

Calories 226   Sugars 5g
Protein ....35g   Fat 7g
Carbohydrate ....6g   Saturates 1g

5 MINS   15 MINS

SERVES 4

I N G R E D I E N T S

3½ oz small, thin asparagus spears, trimmed

1 tbsp sunflower oil

1-inch piece gingerroot, cut into thin strips

1 leek, shredded

2 carrots, julienned

3½ oz baby corn cobs, quartered lengthwise

2 tbsp light soy sauce

1 tbsp oyster sauce

1 tsp honey

1 lb cooked, assorted shellfish, thawed if frozen

freshly cooked egg noodles, to serve

T O   G A R N I S H

4 large cooked shrimp

small bunch fresh chives, freshly snipped

1 Bring a small saucepan of water to a boil and blanch the asparagus for 1–2 minutes.

2 Drain the asparagus; set aside and keep warm.

3 Heat the oil in a wok or large skillet and stir-fry the ginger, leek, carrot, and corn for about 3 minutes; do not allow the vegetables to brown.

4 Add the soy sauce, oyster sauce and honey to the wok or skillet.

5 Stir in the cooked shellfish and continue to stir-fry for 2–3 minutes until the vegetables are just tender and the shellfish are thoroughly heated through. Add the blanched asparagus and stir-fry for about 2 minutes.

6 To serve, pile the cooked noodles onto 4 warm serving plates and spoon the seafood and vegetable stir fry over them.

7 Garnish with the cooked shrimp and freshly snipped chives and serve immediately.

Fillets of Red Mullet & Pasta

This simple recipe perfectly complements the sweet flavor and delicate texture of the fish.

NUTRITIONAL INFORMATION

Calories	457	Sugars	.........3g
Protein	........39g	Fat	..........12g
Carbohydrate	...44g	Saturates	.......5g

15 MINS   1 HOUR

SERVES 4

I N G R E D I E N T S

2 lb 4 oz red mullet or goatfish fillets

1¼ cups dry white wine

4 shallots, finely chopped

1 garlic clove, crushed

3 tbsp finely chopped mixed fresh herbs

finely grated peel and juice of 1 lemon

pinch of freshly grated nutmeg

3 anchovy fillets, roughly chopped

2 tbsp heavy cream

1 tsp cornstarch

1 lb dried vermicelli

1 tbsp olive oil

salt and pepper

TO GARNISH

1 fresh mint sprig

lemon slices

lemon peel

1 Put the fish fillets in a large Dutch oven. Pour the wine over and add the shallots, garlic, herbs, lemon peel and juice, nutmeg, and anchovies. Season. Cover and bake in a preheated oven at 350°F for 35 minutes.

2 Transfer the fish to a warm dish; set aside and keep warm.

3 Pour the cooking liquid into a pan and bring to a boil. Simmer for 25 minutes until reduced by half. Mix the cream and cornstarch and stir into the sauce to thicken.

4 Meanwhile, bring a pan of lightly salted water to a boil. Add the vermicelli and oil and cook for 8–10 minutes until tender, but still firm to the bite. Drain the pasta and transfer to a warm serving dish.

5 Arrange the fish fillets on top of the vermicelli and pour the sauce over. Garnish with a fresh mint sprig, slices of lemon, and strips of lemon peel. Serve immediately.

Trout with Smoked Bacon

Most trout available nowadays is farmed rainbow trout, however, if you can, buy wild brown trout for this recipe.

NUTRITIONAL INFORMATION

Calories 802	Sugars 8g	
Protein 68g	Fat 36g	
Carbohydrate ...54g	Saturates 10g	

35 MINS   25 MINS

SERVES 4

INGREDIENTS

butter for greasing

4 x 9-oz trout, drawn and cleaned

12 anchovies in oil, drained and chopped

2 apples, peeled, cored, and sliced

4 fresh mint sprigs

juice of 1 lemon

12 slices smoked fatty bacon

1 lb dried tagliatelle

1 tbsp olive oil

salt and pepper

TO GARNISH

2 apples, cored and sliced

4 fresh mint sprigs

1 Grease a deep baking pan with butter.

2 Open up the cavities of each trout and rinse with warm saltwater.

3 Season each cavity with salt and pepper. Divide the anchovies, sliced apples and mint sprigs between each of the cavities. Sprinkle the lemon juice into each cavity.

4 Carefully cover the whole of each trout, except the head and tail, with 3 slices of smoked bacon in a spiral.

5 Arrange the trout on the baking pan with the loose ends of bacon tucked underneath. Season with pepper and bake in a preheated oven at 400°F for 20 minutes, turning the trout over after 10 minutes.

6 Meanwhile, bring a large pan of lightly salted water to a boil. Add the tagliatelle and olive oil and cook for about 12 minutes until tender, but still firm to the bite. Drain the pasta and transfer to a large, warm serving dish.

7 Remove the trout from the oven and arrange on the tagliatelle. Garnish with sliced apples and fresh mint sprigs and serve immediately.

Poached Salmon with Penne

Fresh salmon and pasta in a mouthwatering lemon and watercress sauce — a wonderful summer evening treat.

NUTRITIONAL INFORMATION

Calories 968   Sugars 3g
Protein . . . . .59g   Fat 58g
Carbohydrate . . .49g   Saturates 19g

   10 MINS   30 MINS

SERVES 4

INGREDIENTS

4 x 9-oz fresh salmon steaks

4 tbsp butter

¾ cup dry white wine

sea salt

8 peppercorns

fresh dill sprig

fresh tarragon sprig

1 lemon, sliced

1 lb dried penne

2 tbsp olive oil

lemon slices and fresh watercress,
    to garnish

LEMON & WATERCRESS SAUCE

2 tbsp butter

¼ cup all-purpose flour

⅔ cup milk, warm

juice and finely grated peel of 2 lemons

½ cup chopped watercress

salt and pepper

1 Put the salmon in a large, nonstick pan. Add the butter, wine, a pinch of sea salt, the peppercorns, dill, tarragon, and lemon. Cover, bring to a boil, and simmer for 10 minutes.

2 Using a pancake turner, carefully remove the salmon; strain and reserve the cooking liquid. Remove and discard the salmon skin and center bones. Place on a warm dish, cover, and keep warm.

3 Meanwhile, bring a saucepan of salted water to a boil. Add the penne and 1 tbsp of the oil and cook for 8–10 minutes until tender, but still firm to the bite. Drain and sprinkle the remaining olive oil over. Place on a warm serving dish, top with the salmon steaks, and keep warm.

4 To make the sauce, melt the butter and stir in the flour for 2 minutes. Stir in the milk and about 7 tbsp of the reserved cooking liquid. Add the lemon juice and peel and cook, stirring, for a further 10 minutes.

5 Add the watercress to the sauce, stir gently, and season to taste with salt and pepper.

6 Pour the sauce over the salmon and penne, garnish with slices of lemon, and fresh watercress and serve.

Shrimp & Pasta Bake

This dish is ideal for a substantial supper. You can use whatever pasta you like, but the tricolor varieties give the most colorful results.

NUTRITIONAL INFORMATION

Calories 723	Sugars 9g
Protein 56g	Fat 8g
Carbohydrate ...114g	Saturates 2g

 10 MINS   50 MINS

SERVES 4

I N G R E D I E N T S

8 oz tricolor pasta shapes

1 tbsp vegetable oil

2½ cups sliced button mushrooms

1 bunch scallions, trimmed and chopped

14-oz can tuna in brine, drained and flaked

6 oz peeled shrimp, thawed if frozen

2 tbsp cornstarch

1¾ cups skim milk

4 tomatoes, thinly sliced

¼ cup fresh breadcrumbs

¼ cup grated reduced-fat cheddar cheese

salt and pepper

TO SERVE

wholewheat bread

fresh salad

1 Preheat the oven to 375°F. Bring a large saucepan of water to a boil and cook the pasta according to the directions on the package. Drain well.

2 Meanwhile, heat the vegetable oil in a skillet and fry the mushrooms and all but a handful of the scallions for 4–5 minutes until softened.

3 Place the cooked pasta in a bowl and stir in the scallions, mushrooms, tuna, and shrimp.

4 Blend the cornstarch with a little milk to make a paste. Pour the remaining milk into a saucepan and stir in the paste. Heat, stirring, until the sauce begins to thicken; season well. Add the sauce to the pasta mixture and mix well. Transfer to a baking dish and place on a cookie sheet.

5 Arrange the tomato slices over the pasta and sprinkle with the bread crumbs and cheese. Bake for 25–30 minutes until golden. Serve sprinkled with the reserved scallions and accompanied with bread and salad.

Spaghetti al Tonno

The classic Italian combination of pasta and tuna is enhanced in this recipe with a delicious parsley sauce.

NUTRITIONAL INFORMATION

Calories 1065	Sugars 3g	
Protein 27g	Fat 85g	
Carbohydrate . . .52g	Saturates 18g	

10 MINS   15 MINS

SERVES 4

INGREDIENTS

7-oz can tuna, drained

2-oz can anchovies, drained

1 cup olive oil

1 cup roughly chopped flat-leaf parsley

⅔ cup crème fraîche or sour cream

1 lb dried spaghetti

2 tbsp butter

salt and pepper

black olives, to garnish

crusty bread, to serve

1 Remove any bones from the tuna. Put the tuna into a food processor or blender, together with the anchovies, 1 cup of the olive oil, and the flat-leaf parsley; process until the sauce is very smooth.

VARIATION

If liked, you can add 1–2 garlic cloves to the sauce, substitute ½ cup chopped fresh basil for half the parsley, and garnish with capers instead of black olives.

2 Spoon the crème fraîche or sour cream into the food processor or blender and process again for a few seconds to blend thoroughly. Season with salt and pepper to taste.

3 Bring a large pan of lightly salted water to a boil. Add the spaghetti and the remaining olive oil and cook for 8–10 minutes until tender, but still firm to the bite.

4 Drain the spaghetti, return to the pan and place over a medium heat. Add the butter and toss well to coat. Spoon in the sauce and quickly toss into the spaghetti, using 2 forks.

5 Remove the pan from the heat and divide the spaghetti between 4 warm individual serving plates. Garnish with the olives and serve immediately with warm, crusty bread.

Pasta Shells with Mussels

Serve this aromatic seafood dish to family and friends who admit to a love of garlic.

NUTRITIONAL INFORMATION

Calories 686	Sugars 2g
Protein 30g	Fat 45g
Carbohydrate ...36g	Saturates 27g

15 MINS   25 MINS

SERVES 6

INGREDIENTS

2 lb 12 oz mussels

1 cup dry white wine

2 large onions, chopped

½ cup unsalted butter

6 large garlic cloves, finely chopped

5 tbsp chopped fresh parsley

1¼ cups heavy cream

14 oz dried pasta shells

1 tbsp olive oil

salt and pepper

crusty bread, to serve

1 Scrub and debeard the mussels under cold running water; discard any mussels that do not close immediately when sharply tapped. Put the mussels into a large saucepan, together with the wine and half of the onions. Cover and cook over a medium heat, shaking the pan frequently, for 2–3 minutes, or until the shells open.

2 Remove the pan from the heat. Drain the mussels and reserve the cooking liquid; discard any mussels that have not opened. Strain the cooking liquid through a clean cloth into a glass pitcher or bowl and reserve.

3 Melt the butter in a pan over a medium heat. Add the remaining onion and fry until translucent. Stir in the garlic and cook for 1 minute. Gradually stir in the reserved cooking liquid. Stir in the parsley and cream and season to taste with salt and pepper. Bring to the simmering point over a low heat.

4 Meanwhile, bring a large pan of lightly salted water to the boil. Add the pasta and oil and cook for 8–10 minutes until just tender, but still firm to the bite. Drain the pasta, return to the pan, cover, and keep warm.

5 Reserve a few mussels for the garnish and remove the remainder from their shells. Stir the shelled mussels into the cream sauce and warm briefly.

6 Transfer the pasta to a serving dish. Pour the sauce over and toss to coat. Garnish with the reserved mussels.

Mussel & Scallop Spaghetti

Juicy mussels and scallops poached gently in white wine are the perfect accompaniment to pasta to make a sophisticated meal.

NUTRITIONAL INFORMATION

Calories 301	Sugars 1g
Protein 42g	Fat 5g
Carbohydrate . . .17g	Saturates 1g

55 MINS   30 MINS

SERVES 4

I N G R E D I E N T S

8 oz dried whole-wheat spaghetti

2 slices lean slab bacon, chopped

2 shallots, finely chopped

2 celery stalks, fincly chopped

⅔ cup dry white wine

⅔ cup fish stock

1 lb 2 oz fresh mussels, prepared

8 oz shelled queen or China bay scallops

1 tbsp chopped fresh parsley

salt and pepper

1 Cook the spaghetti in a saucepan of boiling water according to the package directions, or until the pasta is cooked but still "al dente" (firm to the bite) — this will take about 10 minutes.

2 Meanwhile, gently dry-fry the bacon in a large nonstick skillet for 2–3 minutes. Stir in the shallots, celery, and wine. Simmer gently, uncovered, for 5 minutes until softened.

3 Add the stock, mussels, and scallops, cover, and cook for a further 6–7 minutes; discard any mussels that remain unopened after cooking.

4 Drain the spaghetti and add to the skillet. Add the parsley, season to taste and toss together. Continue to cook for 1–2 minutes to heat through. Pile onto warmed serving plates, spooning over the cooking juices.

COOK'S TIP

Whole-wheat pasta doesn't have any egg added to the dough, so it is low in fat, and has higher fiber than other pastas.

Seafood Medley

You can use almost any kind of sea fish in this recipe. Red sea bream is an especially good choice.

NUTRITIONAL INFORMATION

Calories . . . . . . .699 Sugars 4g
Protein . . . . .56g Fat 35g
Carbohydrate . . .35g Saturates 20g

 20 MINS   30 MINS

SERVES 4

I N G R E D I E N T S

12 raw tiger prawns or jumbo shrimp

12 raw small shrimp

1 lb fillet of sea bream

4 tbsp butter

12 scallops, shelled

4 oz freshwater shrimp

juice and finely grated peel of 1 lemon

pinch of saffron powder or threads

1 quart vegetable stock

⅔ cup rose-petal vinegar

1 lb dried farfalle

1 tbsp olive oil

⅔ cup white wine

1 tbsp pink peppercorns

4 oz baby carrots

⅔ cup heavy cream or fromage blanc

salt and pepper

1 Peel and devein all the shrimp. Thinly slice the sea bream. Melt the butter in a skillet, add the sea bream, scallops, and both shrimp and cook for 1–2 minutes.

2 Season with pepper to taste. Add the lemon juice and grated peel. Very carefully add a pinch of saffron powder or a few strands of saffron to the cooking juices (not to the seafood).

3 Remove the seafood from the pan; set aside and keep warm.

4 Return the pan to the heat and add the stock. Bring to a boil and reduce by one third. Add the rose-petal vinegar and cook for 4 minutes until reduced.

5 Bring a pan of salted water to a boil. Add the farfalle and oil and cook for 8–10 minutes until tender, but still firm to the bite. Drain the pasta, transfer to a serving plate, and top with the seafood.

6 Add the wine, peppercorns, and carrots to the pan and reduce the sauce for 6 minutes. Add the cream or fromage blanc and simmer for 2 minutes.

7 Pour the sauce over the seafood and pasta and serve immediately.

Spaghetti & Seafood Sauce

Peeled shrimp from the freezer become the star ingredient in this colorful and tasty dish, ideal for midweek family meals.

NUTRITIONAL INFORMATION

Calories	498	Sugars	.........5g
Protein	........32g	Fat	..........23g
Carbohydrate	...43g	Saturates	......11g

 30 MINS   35 MINS

SERVES 4

INGREDIENTS

8 oz dried spaghetti, broken into
   6-inch pieces

2 tbsp olive oil

1¼ cups chicken stock

1 tsp lemon juice

1 small cauliflower, cut into flowerets

2 carrots, thinly sliced

4 oz snow peas

4 tbsp butter

1 onion, sliced

1½ cups sliced zucchini

1 garlic clove, chopped

12 oz frozen, cooked, peeled shrimp,
   defrosted

2 tbsp chopped fresh parsley

¼ cup freshly grated
   Parmesan cheese

½ tsp paprika

salt and pepper

4 unpeeled, cooked shrimp,
   to garnish

1 Bring a pan of lightly salted water to a boil. Add the spaghetti and 1 tbsp of the olive oil and cook for 8–10 minutes until tender, but still firm to the bite. Drain the spaghetti and return to the pan. Toss with the remaining olive oil, cover, and keep warm.

2 Bring the chicken stock and lemon juice to a boil. Add the cauliflower and carrots and cook for 3–4 minutes; remove from the pan and set aside. Add the snow peas to the pan and cook for 1–2 minutes; set aside with the other vegetables.

3 Melt half of the butter in a skillet over a medium heat. Add the onion and zucchini and fry for about 3 minutes. Add the garlic and shrimp and cook for a further 2–3 minutes, until thoroughly heated through.

4 Stir in the reserved vegetables and heat through. Season to taste and stir in the remaining butter.

5 Transfer the spaghetti to a warm serving dish. Pour the sauce over and add the chopped parsley; toss well with 2 forks until coated. Sprinkle the Parmesan cheese and paprika over, garnish with the unpeeled shrimp and serve immediately.

Seafood Chow Mein

Use whatever seafood is available for this delicious noodle dish — mussels and crab are also suitable.

NUTRITIONAL INFORMATION

Calories 281   Sugars 1g
Protein . . . . .15g   Fat 18g
Carbohydrate . . .16g   Saturates 2g

 15 MINS   15 MINS

SERVES 4

I N G R E D I E N T S

3 oz squid, dressed and cleaned

3-4 fresh scallops

3 oz raw shrimp, shelled

½ egg white, lightly beaten

1 tbsp cornstarch paste

9 oz egg noodles

5-6 tbsp vegetable oil

2 tbsp light soy sauce

2 oz snow peas

½ tsp salt

½ tsp sugar

1 tsp Chinese rice wine

2 scallions, finely shredded

a few drops of sesame oil

1 Open up the squid and score the inside in a crisscross pattern, then cut into pieces about the size of a postage stamp. Soak the squid in a bowl of boiling water until all the pieces curl up; rinse in cold water and drain.

2 Cut each scallop into 3-4 slices. Cut the shrimp in half lengthways, if large. Mix the scallops and shrimp with the egg white and cornstarch paste.

3 Cook the noodles in boiling water according to the package directions, then drain and rinse under cold water. Drain well, then toss with about 1 tablespoon of oil.

4 Heat 3 tablespoons of oil in a preheated wok. Add the noodles and 1 tablespoon of the soy sauce and stir-fry for 2-3 minutes; transfer to a large serving dish.

5 Heat the remaining oil in the wok and add the snow peas and seafood. Stir-fry for about 2 minutes, then add the salt, sugar, wine, remaining soy sauce, and about half the scallions. Blend well and add a little stock or water if necessary. Pour the seafood mixture on top of the noodles and sprinkle with sesame oil. Garnish with the remaining scallions and serve.

COOK'S TIP

Chinese rice wine, made from glutinous rice, is also known as "yellow wine" because of its golden amber color. If it is unavailable, a good dry or medium sherry is an acceptable substitute.

Cellophane Noodles & Shrimp

Tiger prawns or jumbo shrimp are cooked with orange juice, peppers, soy sauce, and vinegar and served on a bed of cellophane noodles.

NUTRITIONAL INFORMATION

Calories 118	Sugar 4g
Protein 7g	Fat 4g
Carbohydrate ...15g	Saturates 1g

 10 MINS   25 MINS

SERVES 4

INGREDIENTS

6 oz cellophane noodles

1 tbsp vegetable oil

1 garlic clove, crushed

2 tsp grated fresh gingerroot

24 raw tiger prawns or jumbo shrimp, peeled and deveined

1 red bell pepper, seeded and thinly sliced

1 green bell pepper, seeded and thinly sliced

1 onion, chopped

2 tbsp light soy sauce

juice of 1 orange

2 tsp wine vinegar

pinch of brown sugar

⅔ cup fish stock

1 tbsp cornstarch

2 tsp water

orange slices, to garnish

1 Cook the noodles in a pan of boiling water for 1 minute. Drain well, rinse under cold water, and then drain again.

2 Heat the oil in a wok and stir-fry the garlic and ginger for 30 seconds.

3 Add the shrimp and stir-fry for 2 minutes. Remove with a draining spoon and keep warm.

4 Add the bell peppers and onion to the wok and stir-fry for 2 minutes. Stir in the soy sauce, orange juice, vinegar, sugar, and stock. Return the shrimp to the wok and cook for 8-10 minutes until cooked through.

5 Blend the cornstarch with the water and stir into the wok. Bring to a boil, add the noodles, and cook for 1-2 minutes. Garnish and serve.

VARIATION

Lime or lemon juice and slices may be used instead of the orange. Use 3-5½ tsp of these juices.

Sweet & Sour Noodles

This delicious dish combines sweet and sour flavors with rice noodles, jumbo shrimp, and vegetables to make a satisfying meal.

NUTRITIONAL INFORMATION

Calories	352	Sugars	........14g
Protein	........23g	Fat	..........17g
Carbohydrate	...29g	Saturates	.......3g

10 MINS   10 MINS

SERVES 4

INGREDIENTS

3 tbsp fish sauce

2 tbsp distilled white vinegar

2 tbsp sugar

2 tbsp tomato paste

2 tbsp sunflower oil

3 garlic cloves, crushed

12 oz rice noodles, soaked in boiling water
    for 5 minutes

8 scallions, sliced

1¼ cups grated carrot

1¼ cups bean sprouts

2 eggs, beaten

8 oz peeled jumbo shrimp

½ cup chopped peanuts

1 tsp chili flakes, to garnish

1 Mix together the fish sauce, vinegar, sugar, and tomato paste.

2 Heat the sunflower oil in a large preheated wok.

3 Add the garlic to the wok and stir-fry for 30 seconds.

4 Drain the noodles thoroughly and add them to the wok together with the fish sauce and tomato paste mixture; mix well to combine.

5 Add the scallions, carrot, and bean sprouts to the wok and stir-fry for 2–3 minutes.

6 Move the contents of the wok to one side, add the beaten eggs to the empty part of the wok, and cook until the egg sets. Add the noodles, shrimp, and peanuts to the wok and mix well. Transfer to warm serving dishes and garnish with chili flakes. Serve hot.

COOK'S TIP

If you don't have any dried chili flakes in the cupboard, dust the noodles with ground red pepper.

Noodles with Shrimp

This is a simple dish containing egg noodles and large shrimp, which give the dish a wonderful flavor, texture, and color.

NUTRITIONAL INFORMATION

Calories 142   Sugars 0.4g
Protein ....11g   Fat 7g
Carbohydrate ....11g Saturates 1g

5 MINS   10 MINS

SERVES 4

INGREDIENTS

8 oz thin egg noodles

2 tbsp peanut oil

1 garlic clove, crushed

½ tsp ground star anise

1 bunch scallions, cut into 2-inch pieces

24 raw jumbo shrimp, peeled with tails intact

2 tbsp light soy sauce

2 tsp lime juice

lime wedges, to garnish

1 Blanch the noodles in a saucepan of boiling water for about 2 minutes.

2 Drain the noodles well, rinse under cold water, and drain thoroughly again; keep warm and set aside until required.

3 Heat the peanut oil in a preheated wok or large skillet until almost smoking.

4 Add the crushed garlic and ground star anise to the wok and stir-fry for 30 seconds.

5 Add the scallions and jumbo shrimp to the wok and stir-fry for 2-3 minutes.

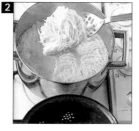

6 Stir in the light soy sauce, lime juice, and noodles and mix well.

7 Cook the mixture in the wok for about 1 minute until thoroughly heated through and all the ingredients are thoroughly incorporated.

8 Spoon the noodle and shrimp mixture into a warm serving dish. Transfer to serving bowls, garnish with lime wedges, and serve immediately.

COOK'S TIP

If fresh egg noodles are available, these require very little cooking: simply place in boiling water for about 3 minutes, then drain and toss in oil. Noodles can be boiled and eaten plain, or stir-fried with meat and vegetables for a light meal or snack.

Noodles with Chili & Shrimp

This is a simple dish to prepare that is packed with flavor, making it an ideal choice for special occasions.

NUTRITIONAL INFORMATION

Calories 259	Sugars 9g
Protein 28g	Fat 8g
Carbohydrate ...20g	Saturates 1g

 10 MINS   5 MINS

SERVES 4

INGREDIENTS

9 oz thin cellophane noodles

2 tbsp sunflower oil

1 onion, sliced

2 red chilies, seeded and very finely chopped

4 lime leaves, thinly shredded

1 tbsp fresh cilantro

2 tbsp sugar

2 tbsp fish sauce

1 lb raw jumbo shrimp, peeled

1 Place the noodles in a large bowl. Pour over enough boiling water to cover the noodles and leave to stand for 5 minutes. Drain thoroughly and set aside until required.

COOK'S TIP

If you cannot buy raw jumbo shrimp, use cooked shrimp instead and cook them with the noodles for 1 minute only, just to heat through.

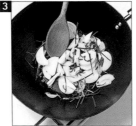  

2 Heat the sunflower oil in a large preheated wok or skillet until it is really hot.

3 Add the onion, red chilies, and lime leaves to the wok and stir-fry for 1 minute.

4 Add the cilantro, sugar, fish sauce, and shrimp to the wok or skillet and stir-fry for a further 2 minutes or until the shrimp turn pink.

5 Add the drained noodles to the wok, toss to mix well, and stir-fry for 1–2 minutes, or until heated through.

6 Transfer the noodles and shrimp to warm serving bowls and serve immediately.

Chili-Shrimp Noodles

Cellophane or "glass" noodles are made from mung bean flour. They are sold dried, so they need soaking before use.

NUTRITIONAL INFORMATION

Calories 152	Sugars 2g	
Protein 11g	Fat 8g	
Carbohydrate ...10g	Saturates 1g	

25 MINS   10 MINS

SERVES 4

INGREDIENTS

2 tbsp light soy sauce

1 tbsp lime or lemon juice

1 tbsp fish sauce

4 oz firm tofu, cut into chunks

4 oz cellophane noodles

2 tbsp sesame oil

4 shallots, sliced finely

2 garlic cloves, crushed

1 small red chili, seeded and finely chopped

2 celery stalks, finely sliced

2 carrots, finely sliced

4 oz cooked, peeled shrimp

1 cup bean sprouts

TO GARNISH

celery leaves

fresh chilies

1 Mix together the light soy sauce, lime or lemon juice, and fish sauce in a small bowl. Add the tofu cubes and toss them until coated in the mixture; cover and set aside for 15 minutes.

2 Put the noodles into a large bowl and cover with warm water. Leave them to soak for about 5 minutes, then drain well.

3 Heat the sesame oil in a wok or large skillet. Add the shallots, garlic, and red chili and stir-fry for 1 minute.

4 Add the sliced celery and carrots to the wok or pan and stir-fry for a further 2–3 minutes.

5 Tip the drained noodles into the wok or skillet and cook, stirring, for 2 minutes. Add the shrimp, bean sprouts, and tofu, along with the soy sauce mixture. Cook over a medium high heat for 2–3 minutes until heated through.

6 Transfer the mixture in the wok to a serving dish and garnish with celery leaves and chilies.

Noodles with Cod & Mango

Fish and fruit are tossed with a trio of bell peppers in this spicy dish served with noodles for a quick, healthy meal.

NUTRITIONAL INFORMATION

Calories ....274 Sugars 11g
Protein ....25g Fat 8g
Carbohydrate ...26g Saturates 1g

 10 MINS   25 MINS

SERVES 4

INGREDIENTS

9 oz egg noodles

1 lb skinless cod fillet

1 tbsp paprika

2 tbsp sunflower oil

1 red onion, sliced

1 orange bell pepper, seeded and sliced

1 green bell pepper, seeded and sliced

3½ oz baby corn cobs, halved

1 mango, sliced

1 cup bean sprouts

2 tbsp tomato catsup

2 tbsp soy sauce

2 tbsp medium sherry

1 tsp cornstarch

  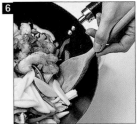

1 Place the egg noodles in a large bowl and cover with boiling water; leave to stand for about 10 minutes.

2 Rinse the cod fillet and pat dry with paper towels. Cut the cod flesh into thin strips.

3 Place the cod strips in a large bowl. Add the paprika and toss well to coat the fish.

4 Heat the sunflower oil in a large preheated wok.

5 Add the onion, bell peppers, and baby corn cobs to the wok and stir-fry for about 5 minutes.

6 Add the cod to the wok together with the sliced mango and stir-fry for a further 2–3 minutes, or until the fish is tender.

7 Add the bean sprouts to the wok and toss well to combine.

8 Mix together the tomato catsup, soy sauce, sherry, and cornstarch. Add the mixture to the wok and cook, stirring occasionally, until the juices thicken.

9 Drain the noodles thoroughly and transfer to warm serving bowls. Transfer the cod and mango stir-fry to separate serving bowls and serve the dish immediately.

Oyster Sauce Noodles

Chicken and noodles are cooked and then tossed in oyster sauce and egg in this Chinese-style recipe.

NUTRITIONAL INFORMATION

Calories	278	Sugars	.........2g
Protein	........30g	Fat	..........12g
Carbohydrate	...13g	Saturates	.......3g

5 MINS   25 MINS

SERVES 4

I N G R E D I E N T S

9 oz egg noodles

1 lb chicken thighs

2 tbsp peanut oil

¾ cup sliced carrots

3 tbsp oyster sauce

2 eggs

3 tbsp cold water

1 Place the egg noodles in a large bowl or dish. Pour enough boiling water over the noodles to cover and leave to stand for 10 minutes.

2 Meanwhile, remove the skin from the chicken thighs. Cut the chicken flesh into small pieces, using a sharp knife.

VARIATION

Oyster sauce is sold in bottles in the Chinese-food section of supermarkets. Flavor the eggs with soy sauce or hoisin sauce as an alternative to the oyster sauce, if you prefer.

3 Heat the peanut oil in a large preheated wok or skillet, swirling the oil around the bottom of the wok until it is really hot.

4 Add the pieces of chicken and the carrot slices to the wok and stir-fry for about 5 minutes.

5 Drain the noodles thoroughly. Add the noodles to the wok and stir-fry for a

further 2–3 minutes, or until the noodles are heated through.

6 Beat together the oyster sauce, eggs, and 3 tablespoons of cold water. Drizzle the mixture over the noodles and stir-fry for a further 2–3 minutes, or until the eggs set.

7 Transfer the mixture in the wok to warm serving bowls and serve hot.

Fried Rice with Prawns

Use either large or jumbo shrimp for this rice dish. This is an ideal dish to serve as part of a Chinese meal.

NUTRITIONAL INFORMATION

Calories	599	Sugars	.........0g
Protein	........26g	Fat	..........16g
Carbohydrate	...94g	Saturates	.......3g

 5 MINS   35 MINS

SERVES 4

I N G R E D I E N T S

1½ cups long-grain rice

2 eggs

4 tsp cold water

salt and pepper

3 tbsp sunflower oil

4 scallions, thinly sliced diagonally

1 garlic clove, crushed

1½ cups thinly sliced closed-cap or button mushrooms

2 tbsp oyster or anchovy sauce

7-oz can water chestnuts, drained and sliced

9 oz peeled shrimp, defrosted if frozen

½ bunch watercress, roughly chopped

watercress sprigs, to garnish (optional)

1 Cook the rice in boiling salted water for 10-12 minutes until tender; drain well, and keep warm.

2 Beat each egg separately with 2 teaspoons of cold water and salt and pepper.

3 Heat 2 teaspoons of sunflower oil in a wok or large skillet, swirling it around until really hot. Pour in the first egg, swirl it around, and leave to cook undisturbed until set. Transfer to a plate or board and repeat with the second egg. Cut the omelets into 1-inch squares.

4 Heat the remaining oil in the wok and when really hot add the scallions and garlic and stir-fry for 1 minute. Add the mushrooms and continue to cook for a further 2 minutes.

5 Stir in the oyster or anchovy sauce and seasoning. Add the water chestnuts and shrimp and stir-fry for 2 minutes.

6 Stir in the cooked rice and stir-fry for 1 minute, then add the watercress and omelet squares and stir-fry for a further 1-2 minutes until piping hot. Serve at once garnished with sprigs of watercress, if liked.

Crab Fried Rice

Canned crabmeat is used in this recipe for convenience, but fresh white crabmeat can be used — quite deliciously — in its place.

NUTRITIONAL INFORMATION

Calories ....225 Sugars 1g
Protein ....12g Fat 11g
Carbohydrate ...20g Saturates 2g

 5 MINS   25 MINS

SERVES 4

INGREDIENTS

¾ cup long-grain rice

2 tbsp peanut oil

½ cup white crabmeat, drained if canned

1 leek, sliced

1½ cups bean sprouts

2 eggs, beaten

1 tbsp light soy sauce

2 tsp lime juice

1 tsp sesame oil

salt

sliced lime, to garnish

1 Cook the rice in a saucepan of boiling salted water for 15 minutes. Drain well, rinse under cold running water, and drain again thoroughly.

2 Heat the peanut oil in a preheated wok until it is really hot.

3 Add the crabmeat, leek, and bean sprouts to the wok and stir-fry for 2-3 minutes. Remove the mixture from the wok with a draining spoon and set aside until required.

4 Add the eggs to the wok and cook, stirring occasionally, for 2-3 minutes, until they begin to set.

5 Stir the rice and the crabmeat, leek, and bean sprout mixture into the eggs in the wok.

6 Add the soy sauce and lime juice to the mixture in the wok. Cook for 1 minute, stirring to combine. Sprinkle with the sesame oil.

7 Transfer the crab fried rice to a serving dish, garnish with the sliced lime, and serve immediately.

COOK'S TIP

To prepare fresh crab, twist off the claws and legs, crack with a heavy knife and pick out the meat with a skewer. Discard the gills and pull out the under shell; discard the stomach sac. Pull the soft meat from the shell. Cut open the body section and prise out the meat with a skewer.

Rice with Crab & Mussels

Shellfish makes an ideal partner for rice. Mussels and crab add flavor and texture to this spicy dish.

NUTRITIONAL INFORMATION

Calories	336	Sugars	.........4g
Protein	........32g	Fat	..........10g
Carbohydrate	...33g	Saturates	.......1g

 🦀 🦀 🦀

 20 MINS   ⏱ 10 MINS

SERVES 4

I N G R E D I E N T S

1½ cups long-grain rice

6 oz white crabmeat, fresh, canned, or frozen (defrosted if frozen), or 8 crab sticks, defrosted if frozen

2 tbsp sesame or sunflower oil

1-inch piece gingerroot, grated

4 scallions, thinly sliced diagonally

4 oz snow peas, cut into 2 or 3 pieces

½ tsp turmeric

1 tsp ground cumin

2 x 7-oz jars mussels, well drained, or 12 oz frozen mussels, defrosted

1 x 15-oz can bean sprouts, well drained

salt and pepper

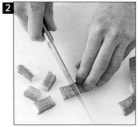  

1 Cook the rice in boiling salted water, stir well, cover the wok tightly, and simmer for 12–13 minutes.

2 Extract the crabmeat, if using fresh crab (see right). Flake the crabmeat or cut the crab sticks into 3 or 4 pieces.

3 Heat the oil in a preheated wok and stir-fry the ginger and scallions for a minute or so. Add the snow peas and continue to cook for a further minute.

Sprinkle the turmeric, cumin, and seasoning over the vegetables and mix well.

4 Add the crabmeat and mussels and stir-fry for 1 minute. Stir in the cooked rice and bean sprouts and stir-fry for 2 minutes, or until hot and well mixed.

5 Adjust the seasoning to taste and serve immediately.

Aromatic Seafood Rice

This is one of those easy, delicious meals where the rice and fish are cooked together in one pan. Remove the whole spices before serving.

NUTRITIONAL INFORMATION

Calories 380	Sugar 2g	
Protein 40g	Fats 13g	
Carbohydrates ...26g	Saturates 5g	

  20 MINS   25 MINS

SERVES 4

I N G R E D I E N T S

1¼ cups basmati rice

2 tbsp ghee or vegetable oil

1 onion, peeled and chopped

1 garlic clove, peeled and crushed

1 tsp cumin seeds

½-1 tsp ground red chili

4 cloves

1 cinnamon stick or a piece of cassia bark

2 tsp curry paste

8 oz peeled shrimp

1 lb 2 oz white fish fillets, such as monkfish, cod, or haddock, skinned and boned and cut into bite-sized pieces

salt and pepper

2½ cups boiling water

⅓ cup frozen peas

⅓ cup frozen corn kernels

1-2 tbsp lime juice

2 tbsp toasted shredded coconut

cilantro sprigs and lime slices, to garnish

1 Place the rice in a strainer and wash well under cold running water until the water runs clear; drain well.

2 Heat the ghee or oil in a saucepan. Add the onion, garlic, spices, and curry paste and fry very gently for 1 minute.

3 Stir in the rice and mix well until coated in the spiced oil. Add the shrimp and white fish and season well with salt and pepper. Stir lightly, then pour in the boiling water.

4 Cover and cook gently for 10 minutes, without uncovering the pan. Add the peas and corn, cover, and continue cooking for a further 8 minutes. Remove from the heat and allow to stand for 10 minutes.

5 Uncover the pan, fluff up the rice with a fork, and transfer to a warm serving platter.

6 Sprinkle the dish with the lime juice and toasted coconut, and serve garnished with cilantro sprigs and lime slices.

Indian Cod with Tomatoes

Quick and easy — cod steaks are cooked in a rich tomato and coconut sauce to produce tender, succulent results.

NUTRITIONAL INFORMATION

Calories 194	Sugars 6g
Protein 21g	Fat 9g
Carbohydrate 7g	Saturates 1g

 5 MINS   25 MINS

SERVES 4

INGREDIENTS

3 tbsp vegetable oil

4 cod steaks, about 1 inch thick

salt and pepper

1 onion, finely chopped

2 garlic cloves, crushed

1 red bell pepper, seeded and chopped

1 tsp ground coriander

1 tsp ground cumin

1 tsp ground turmeric

½ tsp garam masala

1 x 14-oz can chopped tomatoes

⅔ cup coconut milk

1-2 tbsp chopped fresh cilantro or parsley

VARIATION

The mixture can also be flavored with 1 tablespoon of curry powder or curry paste (mild, medium, or hot, according to personal preference) instead of the mixture of spices in step 2, if wished.

  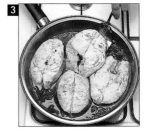

1 Heat the oil in a skillet. Add the fish steaks, season with salt and pepper, and fry until browned on both sides (but not cooked through); remove from the pan and reserve.

2 Add the onion, garlic, red bell pepper, and spices and cook very gently for 2 minutes, stirring frequently. Add the tomatoes, bring to a boil, and simmer for 5 minutes.

3 Add the fish steaks to the pan and simmer gently for 8 minutes, or until the fish is cooked through.

4 Remove from the pan and keep warm on a serving dish. Add the coconut milk and cilantro or parsley to the pan and reheat gently.

5 Spoon the sauce over the cod steaks and serve immediately.

Flounder Fillets with Grapes

Fish is ideal for a quick meal, especially when cut into strips as in this recipe — it takes only minutes to cook.

NUTRITIONAL INFORMATION

Calories 226   Sugars 6g
Protein ....23g   Fat 9g
Carbohydrate ....9g   Saturates 4g

5 MINS   10 MINS

SERVES 4

I N G R E D I E N T S

1 lb 2 oz flounder fillets, skinned

4 scallions, white and green parts, sliced diagonally

½ cup dry white wine

1 tbsp cornstarch

2 tbsp skim milk

2 tbsp chopped fresh dill

¼ cup heavy cream

4½ oz seedless green grapes

1 tsp lemon juice

salt and pepper

fresh dill sprigs, to garnish

TO SERVE

basmati rice

zucchini ribbons

1 Cut the flounder fillets into strips about 1¾ inches long and put into a skillet with the scallions, wine, and seasoning.

2 Bring to a boil, cover, and simmer for 4 minutes. Carefully transfer the fish to a warm serving dish; cover and keep warm.

3 Mix the cornstarch and milk then add to the pan with the dill and cream. Bring to a boil, and boil, stirring, for 2 minutes until thickened.

4 Add the grapes and lemon juice and heat through gently for 1–2 minutes, then pour over the fish. Garnish with dill and serve with rice and zucchini ribbons.

COOK'S TIP

Dill has a fairly strong anise seed flavor that goes very well with fish. The feathery leaves are particularly attractive when used as a garnish.

Flounder with Mushrooms

The moist texture of broiled fish is complemented by the texture of the mushrooms in this simple entertaining dish.

NUTRITIONAL INFORMATION

Calories	243	Sugars	........2g
Protein	........30g	Fat	..........13g
Carbohydrate	....2g	Saturates	......3g

10 MINS   20 MINS

SERVES 4

INGREDIENTS

4 × 5½ oz white-skinned flounder fillets

2 tbsp lime juice

celery salt and pepper

⅓ cup low-fat spread

4 cups mixed small mushrooms, such as button, oyster, shiitake, chanterelle or morel, sliced or quartered

4 tomatoes, skinned, seeded, and chopped

basil leaves, to garnish

mixed salad, to serve

1 Line a broiler rack with baking parchment and place the fish on top.

2 Sprinkle the lime juice over and season with celery salt and pepper.

3 Place under a preheated medium broiler and cook for 7–8 minutes without turning, until just cooked; keep warm.

4 Meanwhile, gently melt the low-fat spread in a nonstick skillet. Add the mushrooms and fry for 4–5 minutes over a low heat until tender.

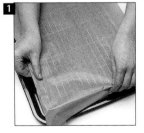  

5 Gently heat the tomatoes in a small saucepan.

6 Spoon the mushrooms, with any pan juices, and the tomatoes over the flounder.

7 Garnish the broiled flounder with the basil leaves and serve with a mixed salad.

COOK'S TIP

Mushrooms are ideal in a low-fat diet, because they are packed full of flavor and do not contain any fat. More "meaty" types of mushroom, such as crimini, will take slightly longer to cook.

Delicately Spiced Trout

The firm, sweet flesh of the trout is enhanced by the sweet-spicy flavor of the marinade and cooking juices.

NUTRITIONAL INFORMATION

Calories ....374 Sugars 13g
Protein ....38g Fat 19g
Carbohydrate ...14g Saturates 3g

45 MINS   20 MINS

SERVES 4

INGREDIENTS

4 trout, each weighing 6–9 oz, drawn

3 tbsp oil

1 tsp fennel seeds

1tsp onion seeds

1 garlic clove, crushed

⅔ cup coconut milk or fish stock

3 tbsp tomato paste

⅓ cup golden raisins

½ tsp garam masala

TO GARNISH

¼ cup chopped cashew nuts

lemon wedges

sprigs of fresh cilantro

MARINADE

4 tbsp lemon juice

2 tbsp chopped fresh cilantro

1 tsp ground cumin

½ tsp salt

½ tsp ground black pepper

1 Slash the trout skin in several places on both sides with a sharp knife.

2 To make the marinade, mix all the ingredients together in a bowl.

3 Put the trout in a shallow dish and pour the marinade over. Leave to marinate for 30–40 minutes; turn the fish over during the marinating time.

4 Heat the oil in a Balti pan or wok and fry the fennel seeds and onion seeds until they start popping.

5 Add the crushed garlic, coconut milk or fish stock, and tomato paste and bring the mixture in the wok to a boil.

6 Add the golden raisins, garam masala, and trout with the juices from the marinade. Cover and simmer for 5 minutes. Turn the trout over and simmer for a further 10 minutes.

7 Serve garnished with the nuts, lemon and cilantro sprigs.

Lemony Monkfish Skewers

A simple basting sauce is brushed over these tasty barbecued kabobs. When served with crusty bread, they make a perfect light meal.

NUTRITIONAL INFORMATION

Calories 191	Sugars 2g
Protein 21g	Fat 11g
Carbohydrate 1g	Saturates 1g

 10 MINS   15 MINS

SERVES 4

I N G R E D I E N T S

1 lb monkfish tail

2 zucchini

1 lemon

12 cherry tomatoes

8 bay leaves

S A U C E

3 tbsp olive oil

2 tbsp lemon juice

1 tsp chopped, fresh thyme

½ tsp lemon pepper

salt

TO SERVE

green salad leaves

fresh, crusty bread

1 Cut the monkfish into 2-inch chunks.

VARIATION

Use flounder fillets instead of the monkfish, if you prefer. Allow 2 fillets per person, and skin and cut each fillet lengthways in half. Roll up each piece and thread them onto the skewers.

2 Cut the zucchini into thick slices and the lemon into wedges.

3 Thread the monkfish, zucchini, lemon, tomatoes, and bay leaves onto 4 skewers.

4 To make the basting sauce, combine the oil, lemon juice, thyme, lemon pepper, and salt to taste in a small bowl.

5 Brush the basting sauce liberally all over the fish, lemon, tomatoes, and bay leaves on the skewers.

6 Cook the skewers on the barbecue for about 15 minutes over medium-hot coals, basting them frequently with the sauce, until the fish is cooked through. Transfer the skewers to plates and serve with green salad leaves and wedges of crusty bread.

Smoky Fish Skewers

The combination of fresh and smoked fish gives these barbecued kabobs a pronounced flavor. Choose thick fish fillets to get good-sized pieces.

NUTRITIONAL INFORMATION

Calories	221	Sugars	0g
Protein	33g	Fat	10g
Carbohydrate	0g	Saturates	1g

4 HOURS   10 MINS

SERVES 4

INGREDIENTS

12 oz smoked cod fillet

12 oz cod fillet

8 raw large shrimp

8 bay leaves

fresh dill, to garnish (optional)

MARINADE

4 tbsp sunflower oil, plus a little for brushing

2 tbsp lemon or lime juice

grated peel of ½ lemon or lime

¼ tsp dried dill

salt and pepper

1 Skin both types of cod and cut the flesh into bite-size pieces. Peel the shrimp, leaving just the tail.

2 To make the marinade, combine the oil, lemon or lime juice and peel, dill, and salt and pepper to taste in a shallow, nonmetallic dish.

3 Place the prepared fish in the marinade and stir together until the fish is well coated on all sides; leave the fish to marinate for 1–4 hours.

4 Thread the fish onto 4 skewers, alternating the 2 types of cod with the shrimp and bay leaves.

5 Cover the rack with lightly oiled kitchen foil and place the fish skewers on top of the foil.

6 Barbecue the fish skewers over hot coals for 5-10 minutes, basting with any remaining marinade, turning once.

7 Garnish the skewers with fresh dill (if using) and serve immediately.

COOK'S TIP

Cod fillet can be flaky, so choose the thicker end that is easier to cut into chunky pieces. Cook the fish on foil rather directly on the rack, so if the fish breaks away from the skewer, it is not wasted.

Oriental Shellfish Kabobs

These shellfish and vegetable kabobs are ideal for serving at parties. They are quick and easy to prepare and take next to no time to cook.

NUTRITIONAL INFORMATION

Calories	93	Sugars	.........1g
Protein	........15g	Fat	...........2g
Carbohydrate	....2g	Saturates	.....0.3g

🍤 2½ HOURS 🕐 5 MINS

MAKES 12

INGREDIENTS

12 oz raw jumbo shrimp, peeled leaving tails intact

12 oz scallops, cleaned, trimmed, and halved (quartered if large)

1 bunch scallions, sliced into 1-inch pieces

1 red bell pepper, seeded and cubed

3½ oz baby corn cobs, trimmed and sliced into ½-inch pieces

3 tbsp dark soy sauce

½ tsp cayenne pepper

½ tsp ground ginger

1 tbsp sunflower oil

1 red chili, seeded and sliced, to garnish

DIP

4 tbsp dark soy sauce

4 tbsp dry sherry

2 tsp honey

1-inch piece gingerroot, peeled and grated

1 scallion, trimmed and very finely sliced

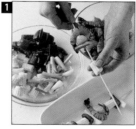  

1 Divide the shrimp, scallops, scallions, bell pepper, and baby corn into 12 portions and thread onto the skewers (soaked for 10 minutes in water to prevent them from burning). Cover the ends with foil so they do not burn and place in a shallow dish.

2 Mix the soy sauce, cayenne, and ground ginger and coat the kabobs; cover and chill for about 2 hours.

3 Preheat the broiler to hot. Arrange the kabobs on the rack, brush with oil, and cook for 2–3 minutes on each side until the shrimp turn pink, the scallops become opaque, and the vegetables soften.

4 Mix together the dip ingredients. Remove the foil and transfer the kabobs to a warm serving platter. Garnish with sliced chili and serve with the dip.

Scallop Skewers

Because the scallops are marinated, it is not essential that they are fresh; frozen shellfish are fine for cooking on a barbecue.

NUTRITIONAL INFORMATION

Calories	182	Sugars	.........0g
Protein	........29g	Fat	...........7g
Carbohydrate	....0g	Saturates	......1g

 30 MINS   10 MINS

SERVES 4

INGREDIENTS

grated peel and juice of 2 limes

2 tbsp finely chopped lemongrass, or 1 tbsp lemon juice

2 garlic cloves, crushed

1 green chili, seeded and chopped

16 scallops, with corals

2 limes, each cut into 8 segments

2 tbsp sunflower oil

1 tbsp lemon juice

salt and pepper

TO SERVE

1 cup arugula leaves

3 cups mixed salad greens

1 Soak 8 skewers in warm water for at least 10 minutes before you use them to prevent the food from sticking.

2 Combine the lime juice and peel, lemongrass, garlic, and chili together in a mortar and pestle or spice grinder to make a paste.

3 Thread 2 scallops onto each of the soaked skewers. Cover the ends with foil to prevent them from burning.

4 Alternate the scallops with the lime segments.

5 Whisk together the oil, lemon juice, and salt and pepper for the dressing.

6 Coat the scallops with the spice paste and place over medium-hot coals, basting occasionally.

7 Cook for 10 minutes, turning once.

8 Toss the arugula, mixed salad greens, and dressing together well; put into a serving bowl.

9 Serve the scallops piping hot, 2 skewers on each plate, with the salad.

Meat Dishes

A whole variety of ways in which meat can be cooked is included in this chapter to create a sumptuous selection of dishes. Barbecues, stir-fries, roasts, and casseroles are

combined to offer a wealth of textures and flavors. Classic and traditional recipes feature alongside more exotic dishes from all around the world, incorporating exciting new ingredients alongside family favorites such as pork and lamb chops. The dishes in this chapter range from easy, economic midweek suppers to sophisticated and elegant main courses for special occasions.

Creamed Strips of Sirloin

This quick-and-easy dish tastes superb and makes a delicious main course for a dinner party.

NUTRITIONAL INFORMATION

Calories ....796 Sugars 2g
Protein ....29g Fat 63g
Carbohydrate ...26g Saturates 39g

 15 MINS   30 MINS

SERVES 4

INGREDIENTS

6 tbsp butter

1 lb sirloin steak, trimmed and cut
  into thin strips

2¼ cups sliced button mushrooms

1 tsp mustard

pinch of freshly grated gingerroot

2 tbsp dry sherry

⅔ cup heavy cream

salt and pepper

4 slices hot toast, cut into triangles,
  to serve

PASTA

1 lb dried rigatoni

2 tbsp olive oil

2 fresh basil sprigs

½ cup butter

COOK'S TIP

Dried pasta will keep for up
to 6 months. Keep it in the
package and reseal it once you
have opened it, or transfer the
pasta to an airtight jar.

1 Melt the butter in a large skillet and gently fry the steak over a low heat, stirring frequently, for 6 minutes. Using a draining spoon, transfer the steak to a baking dish and keep warm.

2 Add the sliced mushrooms to the skillet and cook for 2–3 minutes in the juices remaining in the pan. Add the mustard, ginger, and salt and pepper. Cook for 2 minutes, then add the sherry and cream. Cook for a further 3 minutes, then pour the cream sauce over the steak.

3 Bake the steak and cream mixture in a preheated oven at 375°F for 10 minutes.

4 Meanwhile, cook the pasta. Bring a large saucepan of lightly salted water to the boil. Add the rigatoni, olive oil, and one of the basil sprigs and boil rapidly for 10 minutes until tender, but still firm to the bite. Drain the pasta and transfer to a warm serving plate. Toss the pasta with the butter and garnish with a sprig of basil.

5 Serve the creamed steak strips with the pasta and triangles of warm toast.

Beef & Spaghetti Surprise

This delicious Sicilian recipe originated as a handy way of using up leftover cooked pasta.

NUTRITIONAL INFORMATION

Calories	797	Sugars	.........7g
Protein	........31g	Fat	..........60g
Carbohydrate	...35g	Saturates	......16g

30 MINS   1½ HOURS

SERVES 4

I N G R E D I E N T S

⅔ cup olive oil, plus extra for brushing

2 eggplants

12 oz ground beef

1 onion, chopped

2 garlic cloves, crushed

2 tbsp tomato paste

14-oz can chopped tomatoes

1 tsp Worcestershire sauce

1 tsp chopped fresh marjoram or oregano,
    or ½ tsp dried marjoram or oregano

½ cup pitted black olives, sliced

1 green, red, or yellow bell pepper, cored,
    seeded, and chopped

6 oz dried spaghetti

1 cup freshly grated Parmesan cheese

salt and pepper

fresh oregano or parsley sprigs,
    to garnish

1 Brush an 8-inch springform round cake pan with oil, line the base with baking parchment, and brush with oil.

2 Slice the eggplants. Heat a little oil in a pan and fry the eggplant, in batches, for 3–4 minutes, or until browned on both sides. Add more oil, as necessary. Drain on paper towels.

3 Put the ground beef, onion, and garlic in a saucepan and cook over a medium heat, stirring occasionally, until browned. Add the tomato paste, tomatoes, Worcestershire sauce, marjoram or oregano, and salt and pepper to taste. Leave to simmer, stirring occasionally, for 10 minutes. Add the olives and bell pepper and cook for a further 10 minutes.

4 Bring a pan of salted water to the boil. Add the spaghetti and 1 tbsp oil and cook for 8–10 minutes until tender, but still firm to the bite; drain and pour the spaghetti into a bowl. Add the meat mixture and cheese and toss with 2 forks.

5 Arrange eggplant slices over the bottom and up the sides of the pan. Add the spaghetti, pressing down firmly, and then cover with the rest of the eggplant slices. Bake in a preheated oven at 400°F for 40 minutes. Leave to stand for 5 minutes, then invert onto a serving dish; discard the baking parchment. Garnish with the fresh herbs and serve.

Beef & Pasta Bake

The combination of Italian and Indian ingredients makes a surprisingly delicious recipe. Marinate the steak in advance to save time.

NUTRITIONAL INFORMATION

Calories	1050	Sugars	4g
Protein	47g	Fat	81g
Carbohydrate	37g	Saturates	34g

6¼ HOURS   1¼ HOURS

SERVES 4

INGREDIENTS

2 lb steak, cut into cubes

⅔ cup beef stock

1 lb dried macaroni

1¼ cups heavy cream

½ tsp garam masala

salt

fresh cilantro and slivered almonds,
    to garnish

KORMA PASTE

½ cup blanched almonds

6 garlic cloves

1-inch piece fresh gingerroot,
    coarsely chopped

6 tbsp beef stock

1 tsp ground cardamom

4 cloves, crushed

1 tsp cinnamon

2 large onions, chopped

1 tsp coriander seeds

2 tsp ground cumin seeds

pinch of cayenne pepper

6 tbsp of sunflower oil

1 To make the korma paste, grind the almonds finely using a mortar and pestle. Put the ground almonds and the rest of the korma paste ingredients into a food processor or blender and process to make a very smooth paste.

2 Put the steak in a shallow dish and spoon the korma paste over, turning to coat the steak well. Leave in the refrigerator to marinate for 6 hours.

3 Transfer the steak and korma paste to a large saucepan, and simmer over a low heat, adding a little beef stock if required, for 35 minutes.

4 Meanwhile, bring a large saucepan of lightly salted water to the boil. Add the macaroni and cook for 10 minutes until tender, but still firm to the bite. Drain the pasta thoroughly and transfer to a deep Dutch oven. Add the steak, heavy cream and garam masala.

5 Bake in a preheated oven at 400°F for 30 minutes. Remove the Dutch oven from the oven and allow to stand for about 10 minutes. Garnish with fresh cilantro and serve.

Fresh Spaghetti & Meatballs

This well-loved Italian dish is popular around the world. Make the most of it by using high-quality steak for the meatballs.

45 MINS   1¼ HOURS

SERVES 4

I N G R E D I E N T S

2½ cups brown bread crumbs

⅔ cup milk

2 tbsp butter

¼ cup whole-wheat flour

1 cup beef stock

14-oz can chopped tomatoes

2 tbsp tomato paste

1 tsp sugar

1 tbsp finely chopped fresh tarragon

1 large onion, chopped

1 lb ground steak

1 tsp paprika

4 tbsp olive oil

1 lb fresh spaghetti

salt and pepper

fresh tarragon sprigs, to garnish

1 Place the bread crumbs in a bowl, add the milk, and set aside to soak for about 30 minutes.

2 Melt half of the butter in a pan. Add the flour and cook, stirring constantly, for 2 minutes. Gradually stir in the beef stock and cook, stirring constantly, for a further 5 minutes. Add the tomatoes, tomato paste, sugar, and tarragon. Season well and simmer for 25 minutes.

3 Mix the onion, steak, and paprika into the bread crumbs and season to taste. Shape the mixture into 14 meatballs.

4 Heat the oil and remaining butter in a skillet and fry the meatballs, turning, until brown all over. Place in a deep Dutch oven, pour the tomato sauce over, cover and bake in a preheated oven at 350°F for 25 minutes.

5 Bring a large saucepan of lightly salted water to a boil. Add the fresh spaghetti, bring back to the boil, and cook for about 2–3 minutes, or until tender, but still firm to the bite.

6 Meanwhile, remove the meatballs from the oven and allow them to cool for 3 minutes. Serve the meatballs and their sauce with the spaghetti, garnished with tarragon sprigs.

Meatballs in Red Wine Sauce

A different twist is given to this traditional pasta dish with a rich, but subtle, sauce.

NUTRITIONAL INFORMATION

Calories 811   Sugars 7g
Protein . . . . .30g   Fat 43g
Carbohydrate . . .76g   Saturates 12g

  45 MINS   🕐 1½ HOURS

SERVES 4

INGREDIENTS

⅔ cup milk

2½ cups white bread crumbs

2 tbsp butter

9 tbsp olive oil

3 cups sliced oyster mushrooms

¼ cup whole-wheat flour

1 cup beef stock

⅔ cup red wine

4 tomatoes, skinned and chopped

1 tbsp tomato paste

1 tsp brown sugar

1 tbsp finely chopped fresh basil

12 shallots, chopped

1 lb ground steak

1 tsp paprika

1 lb dried egg tagliarini

salt and pepper

fresh basil sprigs, to garnish

1 Pour the milk into a bowl and soak the bread crumbs in the milk for 30 minutes.

2 Heat half of the butter and 4 tbsp of the oil in a pan. Fry the mushrooms for 4 minutes, then stir in the flour and cook for 2 minutes. Add the stock and wine and simmer for 15 minutes. Add the tomatoes, tomato paste, sugar, and basil; season and simmer for 30 minutes.

3 Mix the shallots, steak, and paprika with the bread crumbs and season to taste. Shape the mixture into 14 meatballs.

4 Heat 4 tbsp of the remaining oil and the remaining butter in a large skillet. Fry the meatballs, turning frequently, until brown all over. Transfer to a deep Dutch oven, pour the red wine and the mushroom sauce over, cover, and bake in a preheated oven at 350°F for 30 minutes.

5 Bring a pan of salted water to a boil. Add the pasta and the remaining oil and cook for 8–10 minutes, or until tender; drain and transfer to a serving dish. Remove the casserole from the oven and cool for 3 minutes. Pour the meatballs and sauce onto the pasta, garnish, and serve.

Pork Chops with Sage

The fresh taste of sage is the perfect ingredient to counteract the richness of pork.

NUTRITIONAL INFORMATION

Calories	364	Sugars 5g
Protein	........34g	Fat 19g
Carbohydrate	...14g	Saturates 7g

10 MINS   15 MINS

SERVES 4

I N G R E D I E N T S

2 tbsp all-purpose flour

1 tbsp chopped fresh sage, or 1 tsp dried

4 lean boneless pork chops, trimmed of excess fat

2 tbsp olive oil

1 tbsp butter

2 red onions, sliced into rings

1 tbsp lemon juice

2 tsp sugar

4 plum tomatoes, quartered

salt and pepper

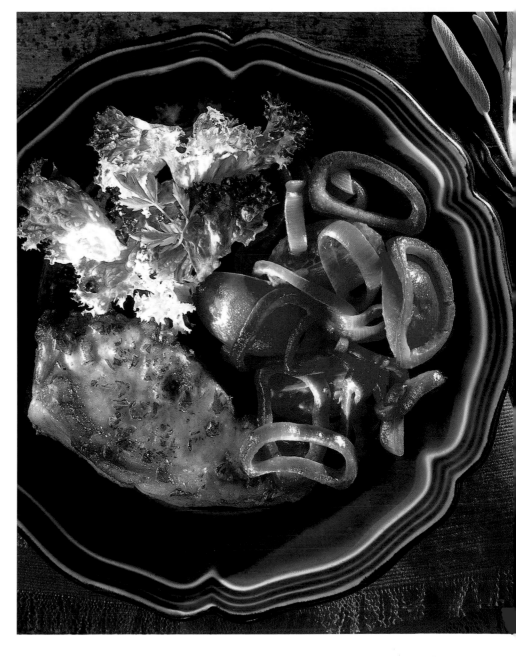

1 Mix the flour, sage, and salt and pepper to taste on a plate. Lightly dust the pork chops on both sides with the seasoned flour.

2 Heat the oil and butter in a skillet. Add the chops and cook them for 6–7 minutes on each side until cooked through. Drain the chops, reserving the pan juices; keep warm.

3 Toss the onion in the lemon juice and fry along with the sugar and tomatoes for 5 minutes until tender.

4 Serve the pork with the tomato and onion mixture and a green salad.

Pasta & Pork in Cream Sauce

This unusual and attractive dish is extremely delicious. Make the Italian Red Wine Sauce well in advance to reduce the preparation time.

NUTRITIONAL INFORMATION

Calories 735	Sugars 4g	
Protein 31g	Fat 52g	
Carbohydrate ...37g	Saturates 19g	

45 MINS   35 MINS

SERVES 4

INGREDIENTS

1 lb pork tenderloin, thinly sliced

4 tbsp olive oil

3 cups sliced button mushrooms

1 cup Italian Red Wine Sauce (see page 15)

1 tbsp lemon juice

pinch of saffron

12 oz dried orecchioni

4 tbsp heavy cream

12 quail eggs (see Cook's Tip)

salt

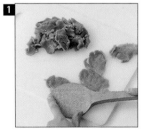

1 Pound the slices of pork between 2 sheets of plastic wrap until wafer thin, then cut into strips.

2 Heat the olive oil in a large skillet. Add the pork and stir-fry for 5 minutes. Add the mushrooms to the pan and stir-fry for a further 2 minutes.

3 Pour the Italian Red Wine Sauce over, lower the heat and simmer gently for 20 minutes.

4 Meanwhile, bring a large saucepan of lightly salted water to a boil. Add the lemon juice, saffron, and orecchioni and cook for 8–10 minutes until tender, but still firm to the bite. Drain the pasta and keep warm.

5 Stir the cream into the pan with the pork and heat gently for a few minutes.

6 Boil the quail eggs for 3 minutes, cool them in cold water, and remove the shells.

7 Transfer the pasta to a large, warm serving plate, top with the pork and the sauce and garnish with the eggs. Serve immediately.

COOK'S TIP

In this recipe, the quail eggs are soft-cooked). As they are extremely difficult to shell when warm, it is important that they are thoroughly cooled first. Otherwise, they will break up unattractively.

Pork with Fennel & Juniper

The addition of juniper and fennel to the pork chops gives an unusual and delicate flavor to this dish.

NUTRITIONAL INFORMATION

Calories ....277 Sugars 0.4g
Protein ....32g Fat 16g
Carbohydrate ...0.4g Saturates 5g

2¼ HOURS   15 MINS

SERVES 4

I N G R E D I E N T S

½ fennel bulb

1 tbsp juniper berries

about 2 tbsp olive oil

finely grated peel and juice of 1 orange

4 pork chops, each about 5 oz

fresh bread and a crisp salad, to serve

1 Finely chop the fennel bulb, discarding the green parts.

2 Grind the juniper berries in a mortar and pestle. Mix the crushed juniper berries with the fennel flesh, olive oil, and orange peel.

3 Using a sharp knife, score a few cuts all over each chop.

COOK'S TIP

Juniper berries are most commonly associated with gin, but they are often added to meat dishes in Italy for a delicate citrus flavor. They can be bought dried from most health-food stores and some larger supermarkets.

4 Place the pork chops in a roasting pan or a baking dish. Spoon the fennel and juniper mixture over the chops.

5 Pour the orange juice over the top of each chop, cover, and marinate in the refrigerator for about 2 hours.

6 Cook the pork chops under a preheated broiler, for 10–15 minutes, depending on the thickness of the meat, or until the meat is tender and cooked through, turning occasionally.

7 Transfer the pork chops to serving plates and serve with a crisp, fresh salad and plenty of fresh bread to mop up the cooking juices.

Pork Cooked in Milk

This traditional dish of boned pork cooked with garlic and milk can be served hot or cold.

20 MINS   1¾ HOURS

SERVES 4

INGREDIENTS

1 lb 12 oz leg of pork, boned

1 tbsp oil

2 tbsp butter

1 onion, chopped

2 garlic cloves, chopped

½ cup diced pancetta

5 cups milk

1 tbsp green peppercorns, crushed

2 fresh bay leaves

2 tbsp marjoram

2 tbsp thyme

1 Using a sharp knife, remove the fat from the pork. Shape the meat into a neat form, tying it in place with a piece of string.

2 Heat the oil and butter in a large pan. Add the onion, garlic, and pancetta to the pan and cook for 2–3 minutes.

3 Add the pork to the pan and cook, turning occasionally, until it is browned all over.

4 Pour the milk over, add the peppercorns, bay leaves, marjoram, and thyme and cook over a low heat for 1¼–1½ hours, or until tender; watch the

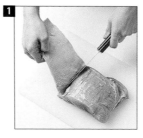  

liquid carefully for the last 15 minutes of cooking time because it tends to reduce very quickly and can burn. If the liquid reduces and the pork is still not tender, add another ½ cup milk and continue cooking. Reserve the cooking liquid (as the milk reduces naturally in this dish, it forms a thick and creamy sauce, which curdles slightly but tastes very delicious).

5 Remove the pork from the saucepan. Using a sharp knife, cut the meat into slices. Transfer the pork slices to serving plates and serve immediately with the reserved cooking liquid.

Pork with Lemon & Garlic

This is a simplified version of a traditional dish from the Marche region of Italy. Pork tenderloin pockets are stuffed with prosciutto and herbs.

NUTRITIONAL INFORMATION

Calories	428	Sugars 2g
Protein	........31g	Fat 32g
Carbohydrate	....4g	Saturates 4g

25 MINS   1 HOUR

SERVES 4

I N G R E D I E N T S

1 lb pork tenderloin

½ cup chopped almonds

2 tbsp olive oil

3½ oz raw prosciutto, finely chopped

2 garlic cloves, chopped

1 tbsp fresh oregano, chopped

finely grated peel of 2 lemons

4 shallots, finely chopped

¾ cup ham or chicken stock

1 tsp sugar

1 Using a sharp knife, cut the pork tenderloin into 4 equal pieces. Place the pork between sheets of waxed paper and pound each piece with a meat mallet or the end of a rolling pin to flatten it.

2 Cut a horizontal slit in each piece of pork to make a pocket.

3 Place the almonds on a cookie sheet. Lightly toast the almonds under a medium-hot broiler for 2–3 minutes, or until golden.

4 Mix the almonds with 1 tbsp oil, prosciutto, garlic, oregano, and the finely grated peel from 1 lemon. Spoon the mixture into the pockets of the pork.

5 Heat the remaining oil in a large skillet. Add the shallots and cook for 2 minutes.

6 Add the pork to the skillet and cook for 2 minutes on each side, or until browned all over.

7 Add the ham or chicken stock to the pan. Bring to a boil, cover, and leave to simmer for 45 minutes, or until the pork is tender. Remove the meat from the pan; set aside and keep warm.

8 Add the lemon peel and sugar to the pan and boil for 3–4 minutes, or until reduced and syrupy. Pour the lemon sauce over the pork and serve immediately.

Neapolitan Pork Chops

An Italian version of broiled pork steaks, this dish is easy to make and delicious to eat.

NUTRITIONAL INFORMATION

Calories	353	Sugars	.........3g
Protein	........39g	Fat	..........20g
Carbohydrate	....4g	Saturates	.......5g

 10 MINS   25 MINS

SERVES 4

I N G R E D I E N T S

2 tbsp olive oil

1 garlic clove, chopped

1 large onion, sliced

14-oz can tomatoes

2 tsp yeast extract

4 pork loin chops, each about 4 oz

¾ cup pitted black olives

2 tbsp fresh basil, shredded

freshly grated Parmesan cheese, to serve

1 Heat the oil in a large skillet. Add the onions and garlic and cook, stirring, for 3–4 minutes, or until they just begin to soften.

2 Add the tomatoes and yeast extract to the skillet and leave to simmer for about 5 minutes, or until the sauce starts to thicken.

COOK'S TIP

Parmesan is a mature and exceptionally hard cheese produced in Italy. You only need to add a little because it has a very strong flavor.

3 Cook the pork chops under a preheated broiler for 5 minutes on both sides (until the meat is cooked through); set the pork aside and keep warm.

4 Add the olives and fresh shredded basil to the sauce in the skillet and stir quickly to combine.

5 Transfer the chops to warm serving plates. Top the steaks with the sauce, sprinkle with freshly grated Parmesan cheese, and serve immediately.

Roman Pan-Fried Lamb

Chunks of tender lamb, pan-fried with garlic and stewed in red wine are a real Roman dish.

NUTRITIONAL INFORMATION

Calories ....299 Sugars 1g
Protein ....31g Fat 16g
Carbohydrate ....1g Saturates 7g

 15 MINS   50 MINS

SERVES 4

INGREDIENTS

1 tbsp oil

1 tbsp butter

1 lb 5 oz shoulder or leg of lamb,
   cut into 1-inch chunks

4 garlic cloves, peeled

3 sprigs thyme, stems removed

6 canned anchovy fillets

⅔ cup red wine

⅔ cup lamb or vegetable stock

1 tsp sugar

½ cup black olives, pitted and halved

2 tbsp chopped parsley, to garnish

mashed potato, to serve

1 Heat the oil and butter in a large skillet. Add the lamb and cook for 4–5 minutes, stirring, until the meat is browned all over.

2 Using a mortar and pestle, grind together the garlic, thyme, and anchovies to make a smooth paste.

3 Add the wine and lamb or vegetable stock to the skillet. Stir in the garlic and anchovy paste together with the sugar.

4 Bring the mixture to a boil. Reduce the heat, cover, and simmer for 30–40 minutes, or until the lamb is tender; for the last 10 minutes of the cooking time, remove the lid to let the sauce to reduce slightly.

5 Stir the olives into the sauce and mix to combine.

6 Transfer the lamb and the sauce to a serving bowl and garnish. Serve with creamy mashed potatoes.

COOK'S TIP

Rome is the capital of both the region of Lazio and Italy and thus has become a focal point for specialties from all over Italy. Food from this region tends to be fairly simple and quick to prepare, all with plenty of herbs and seasonings for really robust flavors.

Lamb Chops with Rosemary

A classic combination of flavors, this dish would make a perfect Sunday lunch. Serve with tomato and onion salad and jacket potatoes.

NUTRITIONAL INFORMATION

Calories ....560 Sugars 1g
Protein ....48g Fat 40g
Carbohydrate ....1g Saturates 13g

1¼ HOURS   15 MINS

SERVES 4

INGREDIENTS

8 lamb chops

5 tbsp olive oil

2 tbsp lemon juice

1 garlic clove, crushed

½ tsp lemon pepper

salt

8 sprigs rosemary

baked potatoes, to serve

SALAD

4 tomatoes, sliced

4 scallions, sliced diagonally

DRESSING

2 tbsp olive oil

1 tbsp lemon juice

1 clove garlic, chopped

¼ tsp fresh rosemary, finely chopped

1 Trim the lamb chops by cutting away the flesh with a sharp knife to expose the tips of the bones.

2 Place the oil, lemon juice, garlic, lemon pepper, and salt in a shallow, nonmetallic dish and whisk with a fork to combine.

3 Lay the sprigs of rosemary in the dish and place the lamb on top. Leave to marinate for at least 1 hour, turning the lamb chops once.

4 Remove the chops from the marinade and wrap a little kitchen foil around the bones to stop them from burning.

5 Place the rosemary sprigs on the rack and place the lamb on top. Barbecue for 10–15 minutes, turning once.

6 Meanwhile make the salad and dressing. Arrange the tomatoes on a serving dish and scatter the scallions on top. Place all the ingredients for the dressing in a screw-top jar, shake well, and pour over the salad. Serve with the lamb chops and baked potatoes.

COOK'S TIP

Choose medium to small baking potatoes if you want to cook baked potatoes on the barbecue. Scrub them well, prick with a fork, and wrap in buttered foil. Bury them in the hot coals and barbecue for 50–60 minutes.

Lamb with Olives

This is a very simple dish, and the chili adds a bit of spiciness. It is quick to prepare and makes an ideal supper dish.

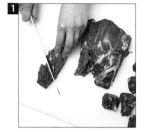

NUTRITIONAL INFORMATION

Calories 577	Sugars 1g	
Protein 62g	Fat 33g	
Carbohydrate 1g	Saturates 10g	

15 MINS   1½ HOURS

SERVES 4

INGREDIENTS

2 lb 12 oz boned leg of lamb

⅓ cup olive oil

2 garlic cloves, crushed

1 onion, sliced

1 small red chili, cored, seeded, and finely chopped

¾ cup dry white wine

1 cup pitted black olives

salt

chopped fresh parsley, to garnish

1 Using a sharp knife, cut the lamb into 1-inch cubes.

2 Heat the oil in a skillet and fry the garlic, onion and chili for 5 minutes.

3 Add the meat and wine and cook for a further 5 minutes.

4 Stir in the olives, then transfer the mixture to a Dutch oven. Place in a preheated oven at 350°F and cook for 80 minutes, or until the meat is tender. Season with salt to taste, and serve garnished with chopped fresh parsley.

Lamb with Bay & Lemon

These lamb chops quickly become more elegant when the bone is removed to shape noisettes.

NUTRITIONAL INFORMATION

Calories ....268 Sugars 0.2g
Protein ....24g Fat 16g
Carbohydrate ...0.2g Saturates 7g

10 MINS   35 MINS

SERVES 4

INGREDIENTS

4 lamb chops

1 tbsp oil

1 tbsp butter

⅔ cup white wine

⅔ cup lamb or vegetable stock

2 bay leaves

pared peel of 1 lemon

salt and pepper

1 Using a sharp knife, carefully remove the bone from each lamb chop, keeping the meat intact. Alternatively, ask the butcher to prepare the lamb noisettes for you.

2 Shape the meat into rolls and secure with a piece of string.

3 In a large skillet, heat together the oil and butter until the mixture starts to froth.

4 Add the lamb noisettes to the skillet and cook for 2–3 minutes on each side, or until browned all over.

5 Remove the skillet from the heat; drain off all of the excess fat and discard.

6 Return the skillet to the heat. Add the wine, stock, bay leaves, and lemon peel to the skillet and cook for 20–25 minutes, or until the lamb is tender. Season the lamb noisettes and sauce to taste with a little salt and pepper.

7 Transfer to serving plates. Remove the string from each noisette and serve with the sauce.

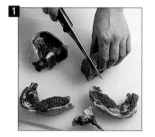

COOK'S TIP

The butcher at your supermarket will give you good advice on how to prepare the lamb noisettes, if you are wary of preparing them yourself.

Barbecued Butterfly Lamb

The appearance of the lamb as it is opened out to cook on the barbecue gives this dish its name. Marinate the lamb in advance if possible.

NUTRITIONAL INFORMATION

Calories 733	Sugars 6g	
Protein 69g	Fat 48g	
Carbohydrate 6g	Saturates 13g	

  6¼ HOURS   1 HOUR

SERVES 4

I N G R E D I E N T S

boned leg of lamb, about 4 lb

8 tbsp balsamic vinegar

grated peel and juice of 1 lemon

⅔ cup sunflower oil

4 tbsp chopped fresh mint

2 garlic cloves, crushed

2 tbsp soft brown sugar

salt and pepper

TO SERVE

broiled vegetables

mixed salad greens

1 Open out the boned leg of lamb so its shape resembles a butterfly. Thread 2 or 3 skewers through the meat to make it easier to turn on the barbecue.

2 Combine the balsamic vinegar, lemon peel and juice, oil, mint, garlic, sugar, and salt and pepper to taste in a nonmetallic dish large enough to hold the lamb.

3 Place the lamb in the dish and turn it over a few times so the meat is coated on both sides with the marinade. Leave to marinate for at least 6 hours or preferably overnight, turning occasionally.

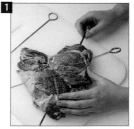  

4 Remove the lamb from the marinade and reserve the liquid for basting.

5 Place the rack about 6 inches above the coals and barbecue the lamb for about 30 minutes on each side, turning once and basting frequently with the marinade.

6 Transfer the lamb to a chopping board and remove the skewers. Cut the lamb into slices across the grain and serve.

COOK'S TIP

If you prefer, cook the lamb for half the cooking time in a preheated oven at 350°F, then finish off on the barbecue.

Veal in a Rose-Petal Sauce

This spectacular dish is equally delicious whether you use veal or pork tenderloin. Make sure the roses are free from blemishes and pesticides.

NUTRITIONAL INFORMATION

Calories 810	Sugars 2g
Protein 31g	Fat 56g
Carbohydrate . . .49g	Saturates 28g

 10 MINS   35 MINS

SERVES 4

INGREDIENTS

1 lb dried fettuccine

7 tbsp olive oil

1 tsp chopped fresh oregano

1 tsp chopped fresh marjoram

¾ cup butter

1 lb veal tenderloin, thinly sliced

⅔ cup rose-petal vinegar
    (see Cook's Tip)

⅔ cup fish stock

¼ cup grapefruit juice

¼ cup heavy cream

salt

TO GARNISH

12 pink grapefruit segments

12 pink peppercorns

rose petals

fresh herb leaves

1 Bring a large saucepan of lightly salted water to a boil. Add the fettuccine and 1 tablespoon of the oil and cook for 8–10 minutes, or until tender, but still firm to the bite. Drain and transfer to a warm serving dish. Sprinkle 2 tablespoons of the olive oil, the oregano, and marjoram over.

2 Melt 4 tbsp of the butter with the remaining oil in a large skillet. Add the veal and cook over a low heat for 6 minutes. Remove the veal from the pan and place on top of the pasta.

3 Add the vinegar and fish stock to the pan and bring to a boil. Boil vigorously until reduced by two-thirds. Add the grapefruit juice and cream and simmer over a low heat for 4 minutes. Dice the remaining butter and add to the pan, one piece at a time, whisking constantly until it has been completely incorporated.

4 Pour the sauce around the veal, garnish with grapefruit segments, pink peppercorns, the rose petals (washed), and your favorite herb leaves.

COOK'S TIP

To make rose-petal vinegar, infuse the petals of 8 pesticide-free roses in ⅔ cup white-wine vinegar for 48 hours. Prepare well in advance to reduce the preparation time.

Vitello Tonnato

Veal dishes are the specialty of Lombardy, with this dish being one of the more sophisticated. Serve cold with seasonal salads.

NUTRITIONAL INFORMATION

Calories	654	Sugars	.........1g
Protein	........49g	Fat	..........47g
Carbohydrate	....1g	Saturates	.......8g

30 MINS   1¼ HOURS

SERVES 4

INGREDIENTS

1 lb 10 oz boned leg of veal, rolled

2 bay leaves

10 black peppercorns

2–3 cloves

½ tsp salt

2 carrots, sliced

1 onion, sliced

2 celery stalks, sliced

about 3 cups stock or water

⅔ cup dry white wine (optional)

3 oz canned tuna, well drained

1½-oz can anchovy fillets, drained

⅔ cup olive oil

2 tsp bottled capers, drained

2 egg yolks

1 tbsp lemon juice

salt and pepper

TO GARNISH

capers

lemon wedges

fresh herbs

1 Put the veal in a saucepan with the bay leaves, peppercorns, cloves, salt, and vegetables. Add sufficient stock or water and the wine (if using) to barely cover the veal. Bring to a boil, remove any scum from the surface, then cover the pan and simmer gently for about 1 hour, or until tender. Leave in the water until cool, then drain thoroughly; if time allows, chill the veal to make it easier to carve.

2 For the tuna sauce: thoroughly mash the tuna with 4 anchovy fillets, 1 tablespoon of oil, and the capers. Add the egg yolks and press through a strainer or purée in a food processor or blender until smooth.

3 Stir in the lemon juice, then gradually whisk in the rest of the oil a few drops at a time until the sauce is smooth and has the consistency of thick cream; season with salt and pepper to taste.

4 Slice the veal thinly and arrange on a platter in overlapping slices. Spoon the sauce over the veal to cover, then cover the dish and chill overnight.

5 Before serving, uncover the veal carefully. Arrange the remaining anchovy fillets and the capers in a decorative pattern on top. Garnish with lemon wedges and sprigs of fresh herbs.

Neapolitan Veal Chops

The delicious combination of apple, onion, and mushroom perfectly complements the delicate flavor of veal.

NUTRITIONAL INFORMATION

Calories ....1071 Sugars 13g
Protein ....74g   Fat 59g
Carbohydrate ...66g   Saturates 16g

20 MINS   45 MINS

SERVES 4

INGREDIENTS

¾ cup plus 2 tbsp butter

4 x 9-oz veal chops, trimmed

1 large onion, sliced

2 apples, peeled, cored, and sliced

2½ cups button mushrooms

1 tbsp chopped fresh tarragon

8 black peppercorns

1 tbsp sesame seeds

14 oz dried marille

7 tbsp extra virgin olive oil

¾ cup mascarpone cheese

2 large beef tomatoes, cut in half

leaves of 1 fresh basil sprig

salt and pepper

fresh basil leaves, to garnish

1 Melt 4 tbsp of the butter in a skillet. Fry the veal over a low heat for 5 minutes on each side; transfer to a dish and keep warm.

2 Fry the onion and apples in the pan until lightly browned. Transfer to a dish, place the veal on top, and keep warm.

3 Melt the remaining butter in the skillet. Gently fry the mushrooms, tarragon, and peppercorns over a low heat for 3 minutes; sprinkle the sesame seeds over.

4 Bring a pan of salted water to a boil. Add the pasta and 1 tbsp of oil. Cook for 8–10 minutes, or until tender, but still firm to the bite. Drain; transfer to a plate.

5 Broil or fry the tomatoes and basil for 2–3 minutes.

6 Top the pasta with the mascarpone cheese and sprinkle the remaining olive oil over. Place the onions, apples, and veal chops on top of the pasta. Spoon the mushrooms, peppercorns, and pan juices onto the chops. Place the tomatoes and basil leaves around the edge and place in a preheated oven at 300°F for 5 minutes.

7 Season to taste with salt and pepper, garnish with fresh basil leaves, and serve immediately.

Veal Italienne

This dish is really superb if made with tender veal. However, if veal is unavailable, use pork or turkey scallops instead.

NUTRITIONAL INFORMATION

Calories	592	Sugars	.........5g
Protein	........44g	Fat	..........23g
Carbohydrate	...48g	Saturates	.......9g

25 MINS   1 HR 20 MINS

SERVES 4

I N G R E D I E N T S

4 tbsp butter

1 tbsp olive oil

5 cups potatoes, cubed

4 veal scallops, weighing 6 oz each

1 onion, cut into 8 wedges

2 garlic cloves, crushed

2 tbsp all-purpose flour

2 tbsp tomato paste

⅔ cup red wine

1¼ cups chicken stock

8 ripe tomatoes, peeled, seeded, and diced

¼ cup black olives, halved

2 tbsp chopped fresh basil

salt and pepper

fresh basil leaves, to garnish

1 Heat the butter and oil in a large skillet. Add the potato cubes and cook for 5-7 minutes, stirring frequently, until they begin to brown.

2 Remove the potatoes from the skillet with a draining spoon and set aside.

3 Place the veal in the skillet and cook for 2-3 minutes on each side until sealed; remove from the pan and set aside.

4 Stir the onion and garlic into the skillet and cook for 2-3 minutes.

5 Add the flour and tomato paste and cook for 1 minute, stirring. Gradually blend in the red wine and chicken stock, stirring to make a smooth sauce.

6 Return the potatoes and veal to the skillet. Stir in the tomatoes, olives, and chopped basil and season with salt and pepper.

7 Transfer to a casserole dish and cook in a preheated oven at 350°F for 1 hour, or until the potatoes and veal are cooked through. Garnish with basil leaves and serve.

COOK'S TIP

For a quicker cooking time and really tender meat, pound the meat with a meat mallet to flatten it slightly before cooking.

Turkey & Italian Sausage

Anchovies are often used to enhance flavor, particularly in meat dishes. Either veal or turkey scallops can be used for this pan-fried dish.

NUTRITIONAL INFORMATION

Calories ....233 Sugars 1g
Protein ....28g Fat 13g
Carbohydrate ....1g Saturates 1g

 10 MINS   20 MINS

SERVES 4

I N G R E D I E N T S

1 tbsp olive oil

6 canned anchovy fillets, drained

1 tbsp capers, drained

1 tbsp fresh rosemary, stalks removed

finely grated peel and juice of 1 orange

3 oz Italian sausage, diced

3 tomatoes, skinned and chopped

4 turkey or veal scallops, each about 4 oz

salt and pepper

crusty bread or cooked polenta, to serve

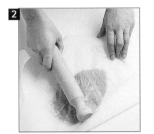

1 Heat the oil in a large skillet. Add the anchovies, capers, fresh rosemary, orange peel and juice, Italian sausage, and tomatoes to the pan and cook for 5–6 minutes, stirring occasionally.

2 Meanwhile, place the turkey or veal scallops between sheets of waxed paper. Pound the meat with a meat mallet or the end of a rolling pin to flatten it.

3 Add the meat to the mixture in the skillet. Season to taste with salt and pepper, cover, and cook for 3–5 minutes on each side, slightly longer if the meat is thicker.

4 Transfer to serving plates and serve with fresh crusty bread or cooked polenta, if you prefer.

VARIATION

Use four minute steaks, slightly flattened, instead of the turkey or veal. Cook them for 4–5 minutes on top of the sauce in the pan.

Liver with Wine Sauce

Liver is popular in Italy and is served in many ways. Tender calf liver is the best type to use for this recipe, but you can use lamb liver.

NUTRITIONAL INFORMATION

Calories	435	Sugars	.........2g
Protein	........30g	Fat	..........31g
Carbohydrate	....4g	Saturates	......12g

25 MINS   20 MINS

SERVES 4

INGREDIENTS

4 slices calf liver or 8 slices lamb liver,
    about 1 lb 2 oz in total

all-purpose flour, for coating

1 tbsp olive oil

2 tbsp butter

4 oz lean bacon, cut into narrow strips

1 garlic clove, crushed

1 onion, chopped

1 celery stalk, thinly sliced

⅔ cup red wine

⅔ cup beef stock

good pinch of ground allspice

1 tsp Worcestershire sauce

1 tsp chopped fresh sage, or ½ tsp
    dried sage

3–4 tomatoes, peeled, quartered, and
    seeded

salt and pepper

fresh sage leaves, to garnish

new potatoes or sautéed potatoes, to serve

1 Wipe the liver with paper towels, season with salt and pepper to taste, and then coat lightly in flour, shaking off any excess.

2 Heat the oil and butter in a pan and fry the liver until well sealed on both sides and just cooked through; take care not to overcook. Remove the liver from the pan, cover, and keep warm, but do not let it dry out.

3 Add the bacon to the fat left in the pan, with the garlic, onion, and celery. Fry gently until soft.

4 Add the red wine, beef stock, allspice, Worcestershire sauce, sage, and salt and pepper to taste. Bring to a boil and simmer for 3–4 minutes.

5 Cut each tomato segment in half. Add to the sauce and continue to cook for 2–3 minutes.

6 Serve the liver on a little of the sauce, with the remainder spooned over. Garnish with fresh sage leaves and serve with tiny new potatoes or sautéed potatoes.

Chicken & Poultry

For the poultry-lover there are pasta dishes, risottos, and baked dishes in this chapter, incorporating a variety of healthy and colorful ingredients. For those who enjoy Asian

cuisine, there are a number of spicy dishes; alternatively there are rich Italian sauces and old favorites, such as more traditional casseroles. All of these recipes are mouthwatering and quick and easy to prepare. They are also extremely wholesome, offering a comprehensive range of tastes. Anyone on a low-fat diet should choose lean cuts of meat and look out for low-fat ground meat to enjoy the dishes featured here.

Garlic & Herb Chicken

There is a delicious surprise of creamy herb-and-garlic soft cheese hidden inside these chicken rolls!

NUTRITIONAL INFORMATION

Calories 272   Sugars 4g
Protein . . . . .29g   Fat 13g
Carbohydrate . . . .4g   Saturates 6g

20 MINS   25 MINS

SERVES 4

INGREDIENTS

4 boneless chicken breast halves,
   skin removed

½ cup full-fat soft cheese, flavored
   with herbs and garlic

8 slices prosciutto

⅔ cup red wine

⅔ cup chicken stock

1 tbsp brown sugar

1 Using a sharp knife, make a horizontal slit along the length of each chicken breast half to form a pocket.

2 Beat the cheese with a wooden spoon to soften it. Spoon the cheese into the pocket in the chicken pieces.

3 Wrap 2 slices of prosciutto around each chicken breast and secure firmly in place with a piece of string.

4 Pour the wine and chicken stock into a large skillet and bring to a boil. When the mixture is just starting to boil, add the sugar, and stir well to dissolve.

5 Add the chicken breasts to the mixture in the skillet. Leave to simmer for 12–15 minutes, or until the chicken is tender and the juices run clear when a

skewer is inserted into the thickest part of the meat.

6 Remove the chicken from the pan; set aside and keep warm.

7 Reheat the sauce and boil until reduced and thickened. Remove the string from the chicken and cut into slices. Pour the sauce over the chicken to serve.

VARIATION
Try adding 2 finely chopped sun-dried tomatoes to the soft cheese in step 2, if you prefer.

Chicken with Vegetables

This dish combines succulent chicken with tasty vegetables, flavored with wine and olives.

NUTRITIONAL INFORMATION

Calories	.470	Sugars	.7g
Protein	.29g	Fat	.34g
Carbohydrate	.7g	Saturates	.16g

 20 MINS   1½ HOURS

SERVES 4

I N G R E D I E N T S

4 chicken breast halves, part boned

2 tbsp butter

2 tbsp olive oil

1 large onion, finely chopped

2 garlic cloves, crushed

2 bell peppers, red, yellow, or green, cored, seeded, and cut into large pieces

3 cups sliced or quartered large closed-cap mushrooms

6 oz tomatoes, peeled and halved

⅔ cup dry white wine

1 cup pitted green olives

4–6 tbsp heavy cream

salt and pepper

chopped flat-leaf parsley, to garnish

1 Season the chicken with salt and pepper to taste. Heat the oil and butter in a skillet. Add the chicken and fry until browned all over; remove the chicken from the pan.

2 Add the onion and garlic to the skillet and fry gently until just beginning to soften. Add the bell peppers to the pan with the mushrooms and continue to cook for a few minutes longer, stirring occasionally.

3 Add the tomatoes and plenty of seasoning to the pan and then transfer the vegetable mixture to a Dutch oven. Place the chicken on the bed of vegetables.

4 Add the wine to the skillet and bring to a boil. Pour the wine over the chicken and cover the Dutch oven tightly. Cook in a preheated oven at 350°F for 50 minutes.

5 Add the olives to the chicken and stir in lightly, then pour on the cream. Re-cover the Dutch oven and return to the oven for 10–20 minutes, or until the chicken is very tender.

6 Adjust the seasoning and serve the pieces of chicken, surrounded by the vegetables and sauce, with pasta or tiny new potatoes. Sprinkle with chopped parsley to garnish.

Rich Chicken Casserole

This casserole is packed with the sunshine flavors of Italy. Sweet sun-dried tomatoes add a wonderful richness.

NUTRITIONAL INFORMATION

Calories ....320 Sugars 8g
Protein ....34g Fat 17g
Carbohydrate ....8g Saturates 4g

 15 MINS   1¼ HOURS

SERVES 4

INGREDIENTS

8 chicken thighs

2 tbsp olive oil

1 red onion, sliced

2 garlic cloves, crushed

1 large red bell pepper, thickly sliced

thinly pared peel and juice of 1 small
    orange

½ cup chicken stock

14-oz can chopped tomatoes

½ cup sun-dried tomatoes, thinly sliced

1 tbsp chopped fresh thyme

½ cup pitted black olives

salt and pepper

orange peel and thyme sprigs, to garnish

crusty fresh bread, to serve

1 In a heavy or nonstick large skillet, fry the chicken without fat over a fairly high heat, turning occasionally until golden brown. Using a draining spoon, drain off any excess fat from the chicken and transfer to a Dutch oven.

2 Add the oil to the pan and fry the onion, garlic, and bell pepper over a medium heat for 3–4 minutes; transfer the vegetables to the Dutch oven.

3 Add the orange peel and juice, chicken stock, canned tomatoes, and sun-dried tomatoes to the Dutch oven and stir to combine.

4 Bring to a boil, then cover the Dutch oven and simmer very gently over a low heat for about 1 hour, stirring occasionally. Add the chopped fresh thyme and pitted black olives, then adjust the seasoning with salt and pepper to taste.

5 Scatter orange peel and thyme over the casserole to garnish. Serve with crusty bread.

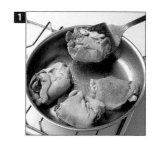

COOK'S TIP

Sun-dried tomatoes have a dense texture and concentrated taste, and add intense flavor to slowly cooked casseroles.

Pasta & Chicken Medley

Strips of cooked chicken are tossed with colored pasta, grapes, and carrot sticks in a pesto-flavored dressing.

NUTRITIONAL INFORMATION

Calories	609	Sugars	.....11g
Protein	......26g	Fat	........38g
Carbohydrate	...45g	Saturates	.....6g

30 MINS   10 MINS

SERVES 2

I N G R E D I E N T S

4–5 oz dried pasta shapes, such as
   twists or bows

1 tbsp oil

2 tbsp mayonnaise

2 tsp bottled pesto sauce

1 tbsp sour cream or plain
   fromage blanc

6 oz cooked skinless, boneless
   chicken meat

1–2 celery stalks

1 cup black grapes
   (preferably seedless)

1 large carrot, trimmed

salt and pepper

celery leaves, to garnish

V I N A I G R E T T E

1 tbsp wine vinegar

3 tbsp extra-virgin olive oil

salt and pepper

1 To make the vinaigrette, whisk all the ingredients together until smooth.

2 Cook the pasta with the oil for 8–10 minutes in plenty of boiling salted water until just tender; drain thoroughly, rinse, and drain again. Transfer to a bowl and stir in 1 tablespoon of the dressing while hot; set aside until cool.

3 Combine the mayonnaise, pesto sauce, and sour cream or fromage blanc in a bowl and season to taste.

4 Cut the chicken into narrow strips. Cut the celery diagonally into narrow slices. Reserve a few grapes for garnish, halve the rest and remove any seeds. Cut the carrot into narrow julienne strips.

5 Add the chicken, the celery, the halved grapes, the carrot, and the mayonnaise mixture to the pasta and toss thoroughly. Check the seasoning, adding more salt and pepper if necessary.

6 Arrange the pasta mixture on 2 plates and garnish with the reserved black grapes and the celery leaves.

Pasta with Chicken Sauce

Spinach ribbon noodles, topped with a rich tomato sauce and creamy chicken, make a very appetizing dish.

NUTRITIONAL INFORMATION

Calories . . . . . . .995 Sugars 8g
Protein . . . . .36g Fat 74g
Carbohydrate . . .50g Saturates 34g

🍲 15 MINS   🕐 45 MINS

SERVES 4

I N G R E D I E N T S

9 oz fresh green tagliatelle

1 tbsp olive oil

salt

fresh basil leaves, to garnish

T O M A T O   S A U C E

2 tbsp olive oil

1 small onion, chopped

1 garlic clove, chopped

14-oz can chopped tomatoes

2 tbsp chopped fresh parsley

1 tsp dried oregano

2 bay leaves

2 tbsp tomato paste

1 tsp sugar

salt and pepper

C H I C K E N   S A U C E

4 tbsp unsalted butter

2¾ cups boned chicken breasts
   skinned and cut into thin strips

¾ cup blanched almonds

1¼ cups heavy cream

salt and pepper

1 To make the tomato sauce, heat the oil in a pan over a medium heat. Add the onion and fry until translucent. Add the garlic and fry for 1 minute. Stir in the tomatoes, parsley, oregano, bay leaves, tomato paste, sugar, and salt and pepper to taste. Bring to a boil and simmer, uncovered, for 15–20 minutes until reduced by half. Remove the pan from the heat and discard the bay leaves.

2 To make the chicken sauce, melt the butter in a skillet over a medium heat. Add the chicken and almonds and stir-fry for 5–6 minutes, or until the chicken is cooked through.

3 Meanwhile, bring the cream to a boil in a small pan over a low heat and boil for about 10 minutes until reduced by almost half. Pour the cream over the chicken and almonds, stir, and season to taste with salt and pepper; set aside and keep warm.

4 Bring a large pan of lightly salted water to a boil. Add the tagliatelle and olive oil and cook for 8–10 minutes until tender, but still firm to the bite; drain and transfer to a warm serving dish. Spoon the tomato sauce over and arrange the chicken sauce along the center. Garnish with the basil leaves and serve immediately.

Chicken Pepperonata

All the sunshine colors and flavours of Italy are combined in this easy dish, ideal for a midweek family meal.

NUTRITIONAL INFORMATION

Calories	328	Sugars	.........7g
Protein	........35g	Fat	..........15g
Carbohydrate	...13g	Saturates	.......4g

 15 MINS    40 MINS

SERVES 4

I N G R E D I E N T S

8 skinless chicken thighs

2 tbsp whole-wheat flour

2 tbsp olive oil

1 small onion, thinly sliced

1 garlic clove, crushed

1 each large red, yellow, and green bell
    peppers, thinly sliced

14-oz can chopped tomatoes

1 tbsp chopped oregano

salt and pepper

fresh oregano, to garnish

crusty whole-wheat bread,
    to serve

1 Remove the skin from the chicken thighs and toss the thighs in the flour.

2 Heat the oil in a wide skillet and fry the chicken quickly until sealed and lightly browned; remove from the pan.

3 Add the onion to the pan and gently fry until soft. Add the garlic, bell peppers, tomatoes, and oregano, then bring to a boil, stirring.

4 Arrange the chicken over the vegetables. Season well with salt and pepper, then cover the pan tightly, and simmer for 20–25 minutes, or until the chicken is completely cooked and tender.

5 Season with salt and pepper to taste, garnish with oregano, and serve with crusty whole-wheat bread.

COOK'S TIP

For extra flavor, halve the bell peppers and broil under a preheated broiler until the skins are charred. Leave to cool, then remove the skins and seeds. Slice the bell peppers thinly and use in the recipe.

Chicken with Orange Sauce

The refreshing combination of chicken and orange sauce makes this a perfect dish for a warm summer evening.

NUTRITIONAL INFORMATION

Calories	797	Sugars	.......28g
Protein	........59g	Fat	.........25g
Carbohydrate	...77g	Saturates	.......6g

15 MINS   25 MINS

SERVES 4

INGREDIENTS

2 tbsp canola oil

3 tbsp olive oil

4 x 8-oz boneless chicken breast halves

⅔ cup orange brandy

2 tbsp all-purpose flour

⅔ cup freshly squeezed orange juice

¼ cup zucchini cut into matchstick strips

¼ cup red bell pepper cut into matchstick strips

¼ cup finely shredded leek

14 oz dried whole-wheat spaghetti

3 large oranges, peeled and cut into segments

peel of 1 orange cut into very fine strips

2 tbsp chopped fresh tarragon

⅔ cup fromage blanc or ricotta cheese

salt and pepper

fresh tarragon leaves, to garnish

1 Heat the canola oil and 1 tablespoon of the olive oil in a skillet. Add the chicken and cook quickly until golden brown. Add the orange brandy and cook for 3 minutes. Sprinkle the flour over and cook for 2 minutes.

2 Lower the heat and add the orange juice, zucchini, bell pepper, and leek and season. Simmer for 5 minutes until the sauce has thickened.

3 Meanwhile, bring a pan of salted water to a boil. Add the spaghetti and

1 tablespoon of the olive oil and cook for 10 minutes. Drain the spaghetti, transfer to a serving dish and drizzle the remaining oil over.

4 Add half of the orange segments, half of the orange peel, the tarragon, and fromage blanc or ricotta cheese to the sauce in the pan and cook for 3 minutes.

5 Place the chicken on top of the pasta, pour a little sauce over, garnish with orange segments, peel, and tarragon. Serve immediately.

Skewered Chicken Spirals

These unusual chicken kabobs have a wonderful Italian flavor, and the bacon helps keep them moist during cooking.

NUTRITIONAL INFORMATION

Calories 231	Sugars 1g	
Protein 29g	Fat 13g	
Carbohydrate 1g	Saturates 5g	

15 MINS   10 MINS

SERVES 4

I N G R E D I E N T S

4 skinless, boneless chicken breast halves

1 garlic clove, crushed

2 tbsp tomato paste

4 slices smoked bacon

large handful of fresh basil leaves

oil for brushing

salt and pepper

1 Spread out a piece of chicken between 2 sheets of plastic wrap and beat firmly with a rolling pin to flatten the chicken to an even thickness; repeat with the remaining chicken breast halves.

2 Mix the garlic and tomato paste and spread over the chicken. Lay a bacon slice over each, then scatter with the basil; season with salt and pepper.

3 Roll up each piece of chicken firmly, then cut into thick slices.

4 Thread the slices onto 4 skewers, making sure the skewer holds the chicken pieces in spiral shapes.

5 Brush lightly with oil and cook on a preheated hot barbecue or under a broiler for about 10 minutes, turning once. Serve hot with a green salad.

Chicken Scallops

Served in scallop shells, this makes a stylish presentation for a starter or a light lunch.

NUTRITIONAL INFORMATION

Calories ....532 Sugars 3g
Protein ....25g Fat 34g
Carbohydrate ...33g Saturates 14g

  20 MINS 🕐 25 MINS

SERVES 4

I N G R E D I E N T S

6 oz short-cut macaroni, or other
    short pasta shapes
3 tbsp vegetable oil, plus extra for brushing
1 onion, finely chopped
3 slices unsmoked bacon, chopped
1½ cups sliced or chopped button
    mushrooms
¾ cup diced cooked chicken
¾ cup crème fraîche or sour cream
4 tbsp dry bread crumbs
½ cup grated sharp cheddar cheese
salt and pepper
flat-leaf parsley sprigs, to garnish

1 Cook the pasta in a large pan of boiling salted water, to which you have added 1 tablespoon of the oil, for 8–10 minutes, or until tender. Drain the pasta, return to the pan, and cover.

2 Heat the broiler to medium. Heat the remaining oil in a pan over medium heat and fry the onion until it is translucent. Add the chopped bacon and mushrooms and cook for 3–4 minutes, stirring once or twice.

3 Stir in the pasta, chicken, and crème fraîche or sour cream and season to taste with salt and pepper.

4 Brush 4 large scallop shells with oil. Spoon in the chicken mixture and smooth to make neat mounds.

5 Mix together the bread crumbs and cheese, sprinkle over the top of the shells. Press the topping lightly into the chicken mixture and broil for 4–5 minutes until golden brown and bubbling. Garnish with sprigs of flat-leaf parsley and serve hot.

Chicken & Balsamic Vinegar

A rich caramelized sauce, flavoured with balsamic vinegar and wine, adds a piquant flavor. The chicken needs to be marinated overnight.

NUTRITIONAL INFORMATION

Calories ....148 Sugars 0.2g
Protein ....11g Fat 8g
Carbohydrate ...0.2g Saturates 3g

 10 MINS   35 MINS

SERVES 4

INGREDIENTS

4 chicken thighs, boned

2 garlic cloves, crushed

¾ cup red wine

3 tbsp white-wine vinegar

1 tbsp oil

1 tbsp butter

6 shallots

3 tbsp balsamic vinegar

2 tbsp fresh thyme

salt and pepper

cooked polenta or rice, to serve

1 Using a sharp knife, make a few slashes in the skin of the chicken. Brush the chicken with the crushed garlic and place in a nonmetallic dish.

2 Pour the wine and white-wine vinegar over the chicken and season with salt and pepper to taste. Cover and leave to marinate in the refrigerator overnight.

3 Remove the chicken pieces with a draining spoon, draining well; reserve the marinade.

4 Heat the oil and butter in a skillet. Add the shallots and cook for 2–3 minutes, or until they begin to soften.

5 Add the chicken pieces to the pan and cook for 3-4 minutes, turning, until browned all over. Reduce the heat and add half of the reserved marinade. Cover and cook for 15–20 minutes, adding more marinade when necessary.

6 Once the chicken is tender, add the balsamic vinegar and thyme, and cook for a further 4 minutes.

7 Transfer the chicken and marinade to serving plates and serve with polenta or rice.

COOK'S TIP

To make the chicken pieces look a little neater, use wooden skewers to hold them together or secure them with a piece of string.

Chicken with Green Olives

Olives are a popular flavoring for poultry and game in the Apulia region of Italy, where this recipe originates.

NUTRITIONAL INFORMATION

Calories . . . . .614 Sugars 6g

Protein . . . . .34g Fat 30g

Carbohydrate . . .49g Saturates 11g

 15 MINS   1½ HOURS

SERVES 4

INGREDIENTS

3 tbsp olive oil

2 tbsp butter

4 chicken breast halves, part boned

1 large onion, finely chopped

2 garlic cloves, crushed

2 red, yellow, or green bell peppers, cored, seeded, and cut into large pieces

3½ cups sliced or quartered button mushrooms

6 oz tomatoes, skinned and halved

⅔ cup dry white wine

1½ cups pitted green olives

4–6 tbsp heavy cream

14 oz dried pasta

salt and pepper

chopped flat leaf parsley, to garnish

1 Heat 2 tbsp of the oil and the butter in a skillet. Add the chicken breasts and fry until golden brown all over; remove the chicken from the pan.

2 Add the onion and garlic to the pan and fry over a medium heat until beginning to soften. Add the bell peppers and mushrooms and cook for 2–3 minutes.

3 Add the tomatoes and season to taste with salt and pepper. Transfer the vegetables to a Dutch oven and arrange the chicken on top.

4 Add the wine to the pan and bring to a boil. Pour the wine over the chicken; cover and cook in a preheated oven at 350°F for 50 minutes.

5 Add the olives to the Dutch oven and mix in. Pour in the cream, cover, and return to the oven for 10–20 minutes.

6 Meanwhile, bring a large pan of lightly salted water to a boil. Add the pasta and the remaining oil and cook for 8–10 minutes or until tender, but still firm to the bite. Drain the pasta well and transfer to a serving dish.

7 Arrange the chicken on top of the pasta, spoon the sauce over, garnish with the parsley, and serve immediately. Alternatively, place the pasta in a large serving bowl and serve separately.

Broiled Chicken

This Italian-style dish is richly flavored with pesto sauce, a mixture of basil, olive oil, pine nuts, and Parmesan cheese.

NUTRITIONAL INFORMATION

Calories	787	Sugars	.........6g
Protein	........45g	Fat	..........38g
Carbohydrate	...70g	Saturates	.......9g

🧈 10 MINS   🕐 25 MINS

SERVES 4

I N G R E D I E N T S

8 part-boned chicken thighs

olive oil for brushing

1⅔ cups strained puréed tomatoes

½ cup bottled green or red
   pesto sauce

12 slices French bread

1 cup freshly grated
   Parmesan cheese

½ cup pine nuts or slivered almonds

salad leaves, to serve

1 Arrange the chicken in a single layer in a wide flameproof dish and brush lightly with oil. Place under a preheated broiler for about 15 minutes, turning occasionally, until golden brown.

COOK'S TIP

Although leaving the skin on the chicken means that it will have a higher fat content, many people like the rich taste and crispy skin, especially when it is blackened on the barbecue. The skin also keeps in the cooking juices.

2 Pierce the chicken with a skewer to test if it is cooked through – the juices will run clear, not pink, when it is ready.

3 Pour off any excess fat. Warm the tomatoes and half the pesto sauce in a small pan and pour over the chicken. Broil for a few more minutes, turning until coated.

4 Meanwhile, spread the remaining pesto onto the slices of bread. Arrange the bread over the chicken and sprinkle with the Parmesan cheese. Scatter the pine nuts over the cheese. Broil for 2–3 minutes, or until browned and bubbling. Serve with salad leaves.

Chicken Cacciatora

This is a popular Italian classic in which browned chicken quarters are cooked in a tomato and bell pepper sauce.

NUTRITIONAL INFORMATION

Calories 397	Sugars 4g	
Protein 37g	Fat 17g	
Carbohydrate . . .22g	Saturates 4g	

 20 MINS   1 HOUR

SERVES 4

I N G R E D I E N T S

1 roasting chicken, about 3 lb 5 oz,
   cut into 6 or 8 serving pieces

1 cup all-purpose flour

3 tbsp olive oil

⅔ cup dry white wine

1 green bell pepper, seeded and sliced

1 red bell pepper, seeded and sliced

1 carrot, finely chopped

1 celery stalk, finely chopped

1 garlic clove, crushed

7-oz can of chopped tomatoes

salt and pepper

1 Rinse and pat dry the chicken pieces with paper towels. Lightly dust them with seasoned flour.

2 Heat the oil in a large skillet. Add the chicken and fry over a medium heat until browned all over; remove from the pan and set aside.

3 Drain off all but 2 tablespoons of the fat in the pan. Add the wine and stir for a few minutes. Then add the bell peppers, carrots, celery, and garlic and season with salt and pepper to taste. Simmer together for about 15 minutes.

4 Add the tomatoes to the pan. Cover and simmer for 30 minutes, stirring often, until the chicken is completely cooked through.

5 Check the seasoning before serving piping hot.

Pan-Cooked Chicken

Artichokes are a familiar ingredient in Italian cookery. In this dish, they are used to delicately flavor chicken.

NUTRITIONAL INFORMATION

Calories 296	Sugars 2g	
Protein 27g	Fat 15g	
Carbohydrate 7g	Saturates 6g	

 15 MINS   55 MINS

SERVES 4

INGREDIENTS

4 chicken breast halves, part boned

2 tbsp butter

2 tbsp olive oil

2 red onions, cut into wedges

2 tbsp lemon juice

⅔ cup dry white wine

⅔ cup chicken stock

2 tsp all-purpose flour

14-oz can artichoke halves,
    drained and halved

salt and pepper

chopped fresh parsley, to garnish

1 Season the chicken with salt and pepper to taste. Heat the oil and 1 tablespoon of the butter in a large skillet. Add the chicken and fry for 4–5 minutes on each side until lightly golden; remove from the pan using a draining spoon.

2 Toss the onion in the lemon juice, and add to the skillet. Gently fry, stirring, for 3–4 minutes until just beginning to soften.

3 Return the chicken to the pan. Pour in the wine and stock and bring to a boil. Cover and simmer gently for 30 minutes.

4 Remove the chicken from the pan, reserving the cooking juices, and keep warm. Bring the juices to a boil, and boil rapidly for 5 minutes.

5 Blend the remaining butter with the flour to form a paste. Reduce the juices to a simmer and spoon the paste into the skillet, stirring until the juices are thickened.

6 Adjust the seasoning according to taste, stir in the artichoke hearts, and cook for a further 2 minutes. Pour the mixture over the chicken and garnish with chopped parsley.

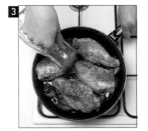

Mustard-Baked Chicken

Chicken pieces are cooked in a succulent, mild mustard sauce, then coated in poppy seeds and served on a bed of fresh pasta shells.

NUTRITIONAL INFORMATION

Calories 652   Sugars 5g
Protein . . . . .51g   Fat 31g
Carbohydrate . . .46g   Saturates 12g

10 MINS   35 MINS

SERVES 4

I N G R E D I E N T S

8 chicken pieces, about 4 oz each

4 tbsp butter, melted

4 tbsp mild mustard (see Cook's Tip)

2 tbsp lemon juice

1 tbsp brown sugar

1 tsp paprika

3 tbsp poppy seeds

14 oz fresh pasta shells

1 tbsp olive oil

salt and pepper

1 Arrange the chicken pieces in a single layer in a large baking dish.

2 Mix together the butter, mustard, lemon juice, sugar, and paprika in a bowl and season with salt and pepper to taste. Brush the mixture over the upper

COOK'S TIP

Dijon is the type of mustard most often used in cooking, because it has a clean and mildly spicy flavor. German mustard has a sweet-sour taste, with Bavarian mustard being slightly sweeter. American mustard is mild and sweet.

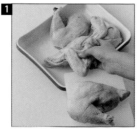

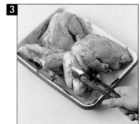

surfaces of the chicken pieces and bake in a preheated oven at 400°F for 15 minutes.

3 Remove the dish from the oven and carefully turn the chicken pieces over. Coat the upper surfaces of the chicken with the remaining mustard mixture, sprinkle the chicken pieces with poppy seeds, and return to the oven for a further 15 minutes.

4 Meanwhile, bring a large saucepan of lightly salted water to a boil. Add the pasta shells and olive oil and cook for 8–10 minutes, or until tender, but still firm to the bite.

5 Drain the pasta thoroughly and arrange on a warmed serving dish. Top the pasta with the chicken, pour the sauce over, and serve immediately.

Chicken & Lobster on Penne

While this is certainly a treat to get the taste buds tingling,
it is not as extravagant as it sounds.

NUTRITIONAL INFORMATION

Calories . . . . . . .696 Sugars 4g
Protein . . . . .59g Fat 32g
Carbohydrate . . .45g Saturates 9g

 20 MINS   30 MINS

SERVES 6

I N G R E D I E N T S

butter for greasing

6 boneless chicken breast halves

1 lb dried penne rigate

6 tbsp extra-virgin olive oil

1 cup freshly grated
   Parmesan cheese

salt

F I L L I N G

4 oz lobster meat, chopped

2 shallots, very finely chopped

2 figs, chopped

1 tbsp Marsala wine

2 tbsp bread crumbs

1 extra-large egg, beaten

salt and pepper

VARIATION

For a less expensive
version, substitute
crabmeat for the lobster.

  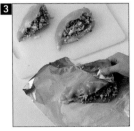

1 Grease 6 pieces of foil large enough to enclose each chicken piece and lightly grease a cookie sheet.

2 Place all of the filling ingredients into a mixing bowl and blend together thoroughly with a spoon.

3 Cut a pocket in each chicken piece with a sharp knife and fill with the lobster mixture. Wrap each chicken piece in foil and place the bundles on the greased cookie sheet. Bake in a preheated oven at 400°F for 30 minutes.

4 Meanwhile, bring a large pan of lightly salted water to a boil. Add the pasta and 1 tablespoon of the olive oil and cook for about 10 minutes, or until tender but still firm to the bite; drain the pasta thoroughly and transfer to a large serving plate. Sprinkle the remaining olive oil and the grated Parmesan cheese over; set aside and keep warm.

5 Carefully remove the foil from around the chicken pieces. Slice the chicken very thinly, arrange over the pasta, and serve immediately.

Chicken Marengo

Napoleon's chef was ordered to cook a sumptuous meal on the eve of the battle of Marengo — this feast of flavors was the result.

NUTRITIONAL INFORMATION

Calories 521	Sugars 6g
Protein 47g	Fat 19g
Carbohydrate . . .34g	Saturates 8g

 20 MINS   50 MINS

SERVES 4

INGREDIENTS

8 chicken pieces

2 tbsp olive oil

1¼ cups strained puréed tomatoes

1 cup white wine

2 tsp Italian seasoning

3 tbsp butter, melted

2 garlic cloves, crushed

8 slices white bread

1½ cups mixed mushrooms,
    such as button, oyster and ceps

⅓ cup chopped black olives

1 tsp sugar

fresh basil, to garnish

1 Using a sharp knife, remove the bone from each of the chicken pieces.

2 Heat 1 tbsp of oil in a large skillet. Add the chicken pieces and cook for 4–5 minutes, turning occassionally, or until browned all over.

3 Add the tomatoes, wine, and Italian seasoning to the skillet. Bring to a boil and then leave to simmer for 30 minutes, or until the chicken is tender and the juices run clear when a skewer is inserted into the thickest part of the meat.

4 Mix the melted butter and crushed garlic together. Lightly toast the slices of bread and brush with the garlic butter.

5 Add the remaining oil to a separate skillet and cook the mushrooms for 2–3 minutes, or until just browned.

6 Add the olives and sugar to the chicken mixture and warm through.

7 Transfer the chicken and sauce to serving plates. Serve with the bruschetta (fried bread) and fried mushrooms.

Italian Chicken Spirals

These little foil rolls retain all the natural juices of the chicken while cooking conveniently over the pasta as it boils.

NUTRITIONAL INFORMATION

Calories	367	Sugars	.........1g
Protein	........33g	Fat	..........12g
Carbohydrate	...35g	Saturates	.......2g

🍗 🍗 🍗

🧈 20 MINS   🕐 20 MINS

SERVES 4

I N G R E D I E N T S

4 skinless, boneless chicken breast halves

1 cup fresh basil leaves

2 tbsp hazelnuts

1 garlic clove, crushed

9 oz whole-wheat pasta spirals

2 sun-dried tomatoes or fresh tomatoes

1 tbsp lemon juice

1 tbsp olive oil

1 tbsp capers

½ cup black olives

1 Beat the chicken breast halves with a rolling pin to flatten evenly.

2 Place the basil and hazelnuts in a food processor and process until finely chopped. Mix with the garlic and salt and pepper to taste.

3 Spread the basil mixture over the chicken breasts and roll up from one short end to enclose the filling. Wrap the chicken roll tightly in foil so it holds its shape; seal the ends well.

4 Bring a pan of lightly salted water to a boil and cook the pasta for 8–10 minutes, or until tender, but still firm to the bite. Meanwhile, place the chicken rolls in a steamer or colander set over the pan, cover tightly, and steam for 10 minutes.

5 Using a sharp knife, dice the tomatoes.

6 Drain the pasta and return to the pan with the lemon juice, olive oil, tomatoes, capers, and olives; heat through.

7 Pierce the chicken with a skewer to make sure the juices run clear, but not pink; this shows that the chicken is cooked through. Slice the chicken, arrange over the pasta and serve.

COOK'S TIP

Sun-dried tomatoes have a wonderful, rich flavor but if they're unavailable, use fresh tomatoes instead.

Slices of Duck with Pasta

A raspberry and honey sauce superbly counterbalances the richness of the duck breast meat.

NUTRITIONAL INFORMATION

Calories ......686 Sugars 15g
Protein ....62g Fat 20g
Carbohydrate ...70g Saturates 7g

 15 MINS   25 MINS

SERVES 4

INGREDIENTS

4 x 9 oz boned duck breast halves

2 tbsp butter

⅓ cup finely chopped carrots

4 tbsp finely chopped shallots

1 tbsp lemon juice

⅔ cup meat stock

4 tbsp honey

¾ cup fresh or thawed frozen raspberries

¼ cup all-purpose flour

1 tbsp Worcestershire sauce

14 oz fresh linguine

1 tbsp olive oil

salt and pepper

TO GARNISH

fresh raspberries

fresh sprig of flat-leaf parsley

1 Trim and score the duck breast halves with a sharp knife and season well all over. Melt the butter in a skillet. Add the duck breasts and fry all over until lightly colored.

2 Add the carrots, shallots, lemon juice, and half the meat stock and simmer over a low heat for 1 minute. Stir in half of the honey and half of the raspberries.

Sprinkle half of the flour over and cook, stirring constantly, for 3 minutes. Season with pepper to taste and add the Worcestershire sauce.

3 Stir in the remaining stock and cook for 1 minute. Stir in the remaining honey and remaining raspberries and sprinkle over the remaining flour. Cook for a further 3 minutes.

4 Remove the duck breast halves from the pan, but leave the sauce to continue simmering over a very low heat.

5 Meanwhile, bring a large saucepan of lightly salted water to a boil. Add the linguine and olive oil and cook for 8–10 minutes, or until tender, but still firm to the bite. Drain and divide between 4 plates.

6 Slice the duck breast lengthways into ¼ inch thick pieces. Pour a little sauce over the pasta and arrange the sliced duck in a fan shape on top of it. Garnish with raspberries and flat-leaf parsley and serve immediately.

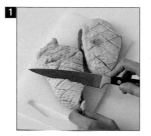

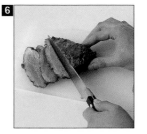

Pesto-Baked Partridge

Partridge has a more delicate flavor than many game birds and this subtle sauce complements it perfectly.

NUTRITIONAL INFORMATION

Calories 895	Sugars 5g	
Protein 79g	Fat 45g	
Carbohydrate . . .45g	Saturates 18g	

 15 MINS   40 MINS

SERVES 4

I N G R E D I E N T S

8 partridge pieces, about 4 oz each

4 tbsp butter, melted

4 tbsp Dijon mustard

2 tbsp lime juice

1 tbsp brown sugar

6 tbsp pesto sauce

1 lb dried rigatoni

1 tbsp olive oil

1⅓ cups freshly grated
   Parmesan cheese

salt and pepper

1 Arrange the partridge pieces, smooth side down, in a single layer in a large baking dish.

2 Mix together the butter, Dijon mustard, lime juice, and brown sugar in a bowl; season to taste. Brush this mixture over the partridge pieces and bake in a preheated oven at 400°F for 15 minutes.

3 Remove the dish from the oven and coat the partridge pieces with 3 tbsp of the pesto sauce. Return to the oven and bake for a further 12 minutes.

4 Remove the dish from the oven and carefully turn the partridge pieces over. Coat the top of the partridges with the remaining mustard mixture and return to the oven for a further 10 minutes.

5 Meanwhile, bring a large pan of lightly salted water to a boil. Add the rigatoni and olive oil and cook for 8–10 minutes until tender, but still firm to the bite; drain and transfer to a serving dish. Toss the pasta with the remaining pesto sauce and the Parmesan cheese.

6 Serve the partridge with the pasta, pouring the cooking juices over.

VARIATION

You can also prepare young pheasant in the same way.

Pasta & Rice

Pasta and rice are quick and easy to cook and, when combined with other ingredients, can produce an endless variety of dishes. To cook pasta, bring a pan of lightly salted water to a boil. Add the pasta and 1 tbsp olive oil; do not

cover but bring the water to a rolling boil. When the pasta is tender, but firm to the bite, drain and toss with butter, olive oil, or sauce. As a rough guide, fresh

unfilled pasta will take three minutes; filled fresh 10 minutes to cook. Dried pasta will take 10–15 minutes. To cook a good-quality rice like basmati, soak it for 20–30 minutes to prevent the grains from sticking to each other. Drain and add the grains to gently boiling, lightly salted water, stir once, and cook until tender, but firm to the bite; this will take up to 20 minutes. Allow 2¾ oz per person.

Spaghetti Sauce

An authentic recipe takes about 4 hours to cook and should be left over night to let the flavors mingle. This version, however, is much quicker.

NUTRITIONAL INFORMATION

Calories 591	Sugars 7g
Protein 29g	Fat 24g
Carbohydrate ...64g	Saturates 9g

 20 MINS   1 HR 5 MINS

SERVES 4

I N G R E D I E N T S

1 tbsp olive oil

1 onion, finely chopped

2 garlic cloves, chopped

1 carrot, scraped and chopped

1 celery stalk, chopped

1⅓ cup diced pancetta or streaky bacon

12 oz lean ground beef

14-oz can chopped tomatoes

2 tsp dried oregano

½ cup red wine

2 tbsp tomato paste

salt and pepper

1½ lb fresh spaghetti, or 12 oz
    dried spaghetti

1 Heat the oil in a large skillet. Add the onions and cook for 3 minutes.

2 Add the garlic, carrot, celery, and pancetta or bacon and sauté for 3–4 minutes, or until just beginning to brown.

3 Add the beef and cook over a high heat for another 3 minutes, or until all of the meat is brown.

4 Stir in the tomatoes, oregano, and red wine and bring to a boil. Reduce the heat and leave to simmer for about 45 minutes.

5 Stir in the tomato paste and season with salt and pepper.

6 Cook the spaghetti in a pan of boiling water for 8–10 minutes until tender, but still has bite; drain thoroughly.

7 Transfer the spaghetti to a serving plate and pour the bolognese sauce over. Toss to mix well and serve hot.

VARIATION

Try adding 1 oz dried porcini, soaked for 10 minutes in 2 tablespoons of warm water, to the sauce in step 4, if you wish.

Pasta Carbonara

Lightly cooked eggs and pancetta are combined with cheese to make this rich, classic Italian sauce.

NUTRITIONAL INFORMATION

Calories 547	Sugars 1g	
Protein 21g	Fat 31g	
Carbohydrate ...49g	Saturates 14g	

 15 MINS   20 MINS

SERVES 4

INGREDIENTS

1 tbsp olive oil

3 tbsp butter

⅔ cup diced pancetta or
   unsmoked bacon

3 eggs, beaten

2 tbsp milk

1 tbsp thyme, stems removed

1½ lb fresh conchigoni rigati or
   12 oz dried

½ cup grated Parmesan cheese

salt and pepper

1 Heat the oil and butter in a skillet until the mixture is just beginning to froth.

2 Add the pancetta or bacon to the pan and cook for 5 minutes, or until browned all over.

3 Mix together the eggs and milk in a small bowl. Stir in the thyme and season to taste with salt and pepper.

4 Cook the pasta in a saucepan of boiling water for 8–10 minutes until tender, but still has bite; drain thoroughly.

5 Add the cooked, drained pasta to the skillet with the eggs and cook over a high heat for about 30 seconds, or until the eggs just begin to cook and set; do not overcook the eggs or they will become rubbery.

6 Add half of the grated Parmesan cheese, stirring to combine.

7 Transfer the pasta to a serving plate, pour the sauce over, and toss to mix well.

8 Sprinkle the rest of the grated Parmesan over the top and serve immediately.

VARIATION

For an extra-rich carbonara sauce, stir in 4 tablespoons heavy cream with the eggs and milk in step 3. Follow the same cooking method.

Three-Cheese Macaroni

Based on a traditional family favorite, this baked pasta dish has plenty of flavor. Serve with a crisp salad for a family supper.

NUTRITIONAL INFORMATION

Calories 672   Sugars 10g
Protein ....31g   Fat 44g
Carbohydrate ...40g   Saturates 23g

30 MINS   45 MINS

SERVES 4

INGREDIENTS

2½ cups Béchamel Sauce
  (see page 14)

8 oz macaroni

1 egg, beaten

1 cup grated sharp cheddar cheese

1 tbsp wholegrain mustard

2 tbsp chopped fresh chives

4 tomatoes, sliced

1 cup grated brick cheese

½ cup crumbled blue cheese

2 tbsp sunflower seeds

salt and pepper

snipped fresh chives, to garnish

1 Make the Béchamel Sauce, put into a bowl, and cover with plastic wrap to prevent a skin forming; set aside.

2 Bring a saucepan of salted water to a boil and cook the macaroni for 8–10 minutes, or until just tender. Drain well and place in a baking dish.

3 Stir the beaten egg, cheddar, mustard, chives, and seasoning into the Béchamel Sauce and spoon over the macaroni, making sure it is well covered. Top with a layer of sliced tomatoes.

4 Sprinkle the brick and blue cheeses and sunflower seeds over. Put on a cookie sheet and bake in a preheated oven at 375°F for 25–30 minutes, or until bubbling and golden. Garnish with chives and serve immediately.

Macaroni & Corn Fritters

These vegetarian fritters can be filled with your favorite vegetables — a delicious alternative is shredded parsnips with 1 tablespoon mustard.

NUTRITIONAL INFORMATION

Calories 702   Sugars 4g
Protein . . . . .13g   Fat 50g
Carbohydrate . . .55g   Saturates 23g

15 MINS   40 MINS

SERVES 4

INGREDIENTS

2 corn cobs

4 tbsp butter

1 cup cored, seeded, and finely diced
  red bell pepper

10 oz dried short-cut macaroni

⅔ cup heavy cream

¼ cup all-purpose flour

4 egg yolks

4 tbsp olive oil

salt and pepper

TO SERVE

oyster mushrooms

fried leeks

1 Bring a saucepan of water to a boil. Add the corn cobs and cook for about 8 minutes; drain thoroughly and refresh under cold running water for 3 minutes. Carefully cut away the kernels onto paper towels and set aside to dry.

2 Melt 2 tbsp of the butter in a skillet. Add the bell peppers and cook over a low heat for 4 minutes. Drain and pat dry with paper towels.

3 Bring a large saucepan of lightly salted water to a boil. Add the macaroni and cook for about 12 minutes, or until tender, but still firm to the bite. Drain the macaroni thoroughly and leave to cool in cold water until required.

4 Beat together the cream, flour, a pinch of salt, and the egg yolks in a bowl until smooth. Add the corn and bell peppers to the cream and egg mixture.

Drain the macaroni and then toss into the corn and cream mixture; season with pepper to taste.

5 Heat the remaining butter with the oil in a large skillet. Drop spoonfuls of the mixture into the pan and press down until the mixture forms a flat fritter. Fry until golden on both sides, frying until all the mixture is used. Serve immediately with oyster mushrooms and fried leeks.

Italian Tomato Sauce & Pasta

Fresh tomatoes make a delicious Italian-style sauce that goes especially well with pasta.

NUTRITIONAL INFORMATION

Calories .... .304	Sugars 8g	
Protein 15g	Fat .... .14g	
Carbohydrate ...31g	Saturates 5g	

   10 MINS   25 MINS

SERVES 2

INGREDIENTS

1 tbsp olive oil

1 small onion, finely chopped

1–2 cloves garlic, crushed

2½ cups peeled and chopped tomatoes

2 tsp tomato paste

2 tbsp water

10½–12 oz dried pasta shapes

¾ cup diced lean bacon

½ cup sliced mushrooms

1 tbsp chopped fresh parsley, or 1 tsp
   chopped fresh cilantro

2 tbsp sour cream or plain fromage
   blanc (optional)

salt and pepper

COOK'S TIP

Sour cream contains
18–20% fat, so if you are
following a low-fat diet leave
it out of this recipe or substitute
a low-fat alternative.

1 To make the tomato sauce, heat the oil in a saucepan and fry the onion and garlic gently until soft.

2 Add the tomatoes, tomato paste, water, and salt and pepper to taste to the mixture in the pan and bring to a boil. Cover and simmer gently for 10 minutes.

3 Meanwhile, cook the pasta in a saucepan of boiling salted water for 8–10 minutes, or until just tender; drain

the pasta thoroughly and transfer to warm serving dishes.

4 Heat the bacon gently in a skillet until the fat runs. Add the mushrooms and continue cooking for 3–4 minutes; drain off any excess oil.

5 Add the bacon and mushrooms to the tomato mixture, together with the parsley or cilantro and the sour cream or fromage blanc, if using. Reheat and serve with the pasta.

Pasta with Green Vegetables

The different shapes and textures of the vegetables make a mouthwatering presentation in this light and summery dish.

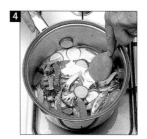

NUTRITIONAL INFORMATION

Calories 517	Sugars 5g
Protein 17g	Fat 32g
Carbohydrate . . .42g	Saturates 18g

🍲 10 MINS   🕐 25 MINS

SERVES 4

I N G R E D I E N T S

8 oz gemelli or other pasta shapes

1 tbsp olive oil

2 tbsp chopped fresh parsley

2 tbsp freshly grated Parmesan

salt and pepper

S A U C E

1 head of green broccoli, cut into flowerets

2 zucchini, sliced

8 oz asparagus spears, trimmed

4 oz snow peas, trimmed

1 cup frozen peas

2 tbsp butter

3 tbsp vegetable stock

5 tbsp heavy cream

large pinch of freshly grated nutmeg

1 Cook the pasta in a large pan of salted boiling water, adding the olive oil, for 8–10 minutes, or until tender. Drain the pasta in a colander, return to the pan, cover, and keep warm.

2 Steam the broccoli, zucchini, asparagus spears, and snow peas over a pan of boiling, salted water until just beginning to soften. Remove from the heat and plunge into cold water to prevent further cooking; drain and set aside.

3 Cook the peas in boiling, salted water for 3 minutes, then drain. Refresh in cold water and drain again.

4 Put the butter and vegetable stock in a pan over a medium heat. Add all of the vegetables, except for the asparagus spears, and toss carefully with a wooden spoon to heat through, taking care not to break them up. Stir in the cream and leave the sauce to heat through. Season with salt and pepper and nutmeg.

5 Transfer the pasta to a warmed serving dish and stir in the chopped parsley. Spoon the sauce over and sprinkle with the freshly grated Parmesan. Arrange the asparagus spears on top. Serve hot.

Pasta with Garlic & Broccoli

Broccoli coated in a garlic-flavored cream sauce, served on herb tagliatelle. Try sprinkling with toasted pine nuts to add extra crunch.

NUTRITIONAL INFORMATION

Calories 538	Sugars 4g	
Protein 23g	Fat 29g	
Carbohydrate ...50g	Saturates 17g	

 5 MINS   5 MINS

SERVES 4

INGREDIENTS

1 lb 2 oz broccoli

1¼ cups full-fat garlic-and-herb
  soft cheese

4 tbsp milk

12 oz fresh herb tagliatelle

¼ cup grated Parmesan cheese

chopped fresh chives, to garnish

1 Cut the broccoli into even-sized flowerets. Cook the broccoli in a saucepan of boiling salted water for 3 minutes; drain thoroughly.

2 Put the soft cheese into a saucepan and heat gently, stirring, until melted. Add the milk and stir until well combined.

3 Add the broccoli to the cheese mixture and stir to coat.

4 Meanwhile, bring a large saucepan of salted water to a boil and add the tagliatelle. Stir and bring back to a boil. Reduce the heat slightly and cook the tagliatelle, uncovered, for 3–4 minutes until just tender.

5 Drain the tagliatelle thoroughly and divide among 4 warmed serving plates. Spoon the broccoli and cheese sauce on top. Sprinkle with grated Parmesan cheese, garnish with chopped chives and serve.

COOK'S TIP

A herb-flavored pasta goes particularly well with the broccoli sauce, but failing this, a tagliatelle verde or *paglia e fieno* (literally "straw and hay" – thin green and yellow noodles) will fit the bill.

Pasta & Bean Casserole

A satisfying winter dish, this is a slowly cooked, one-pot meal. The beans need to be soaked overnight so prepare them well in advance.

NUTRITIONAL INFORMATION

Calories	377	Sugars	........5g
Protein	........10g	Fat	.........18g
Carbohydrate	...43g	Saturates	.......5g

30 MINS · 3½ HOURS

SERVES 6

INGREDIENTS

1¼ cups dried navy beans, soaked
   overnight and drained

8 oz dried penne

6 tbsp olive oil

3½ cups vegetable stock

2 large onions, sliced

2 garlic cloves, chopped

2 bay leaves

1 tsp dried oregano

1 tsp dried thyme

5 tbsp red wine

2 tbsp tomato paste

2 celery stalks, sliced

1 fennel bulb, sliced

1¼ cups sliced mushrooms

8 oz tomatoes, sliced

1 tsp dark brown sugar

4 tbsp dry white bread crumbs

salt and pepper

salad greens and crusty bread,
   to serve

1 Put the navy beans in a large saucepan and add sufficient cold water to cover. Bring to a boil and continue to boil vigorously for 20 minutes; drain, set aside, and keep warm.

2 Bring a large saucepan of lightly salted water to a boil. Add the penne and 1 tbsp of the olive oil and cook for about 3 minutes. Drain the pasta thoroughly, then set aside and keep warm.

3 Put the beans in a large Dutch oven. Add the vegetable stock and stir in the remaining olive oil, the onions, garlic, bay leaves, oregano, thyme, wine, and tomato paste. Bring to a boil, then cover and cook in a preheated oven at 350°F for 2 hours.

4 Add the penne, celery, fennel, mushrooms, and tomatoes to the Dutch oven and season to taste with salt and pepper. Stir in the brown sugar and sprinkle the bread crumbs over. Cover the Dutch oven and cook in the oven for 1 hour.

5 Serve the pasta and bean casserole hot with salad greens and crusty bread.

Pasta & Vegetable Sauce

A Mediterranean mixture of red bell peppers, garlic, and zucchini cooked in olive oil and tossed with pasta.

NUTRITIONAL INFORMATION

Calories . . . . .341 Sugars 8g
Protein . . . . .13g Fat 20g
Carbohydrate . . .30g Saturates 8g

 15 MINS   20 MINS

SERVES 4

INGREDIENTS

3 tbsp olive oil

1 onion, sliced

2 garlic cloves, chopped

3 red bell peppers, seeded and cut
    into strips

3 zucchini, sliced

14-oz can chopped tomatoes

3 tbsp sun-dried tomato paste

2 tbsp chopped fresh basil

8 oz fresh pasta spirals

1 cup grated Gruyère Swiss cheese

salt and pepper

fresh basil sprigs, to garnish

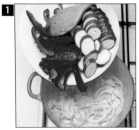

1 Heat the oil in a heavy-based saucepan or Dutch oven. Add the onion and garlic and cook, stirring occasionally, until softened. Add the bell peppers and zucchini and fry for 5 minutes, stirring occasionally.

2 Add the tomatoes, sun-dried tomato paste, basil, and seasoning. Cover and cook for 5 minutes.

3 Meanwhile, bring a large saucepan of salted water to a boil and add the pasta. Stir and bring back to a boil.

Reduce the heat slightly and cook, uncovered, for 3 minutes, or until just tender. Drain thoroughly and add to the vegetables; toss gently to mix well.

4 Put the mixture into a shallow baking dish and sprinkle the cheese over.

5 Cook under a preheated broiler for 5 minutes until the cheese is golden. Garnish with basil sprigs and serve.

COOK'S TIP

Be careful not to overcook fresh pasta — it should be "al dente" (retaining some "bite"). It takes only a few minutes to cook as it is still full of moisture.

Basil & Pine Nut Pesto

Delicious stirred into pasta, soups, and salad dressings, pesto is available in most supermarkets, but making your own gives a concentrated flavor.

NUTRITIONAL INFORMATION

Calories	321	Sugars	.........1g
Protein	........11g	Fat	..........17g
Carbohydrate	...32g	Saturates	.......4g

 15 MINS 10 MINS

SERVES 4

I N G R E D I E N T S

about 40 fresh basil leaves,
  washed and dried

3 garlic cloves, crushed

2 tbsp pine nuts

½ cup finely grated Parmesan cheese

2–3 tbsp extra-virgin olive oil

salt and pepper

1½ lb fresh pasta, or
  12 oz dried pasta

1 Rinse the basil leaves and pat them dry with paper towels.

2 Put the basil leaves, garlic, pine nuts, and grated Parmesan cheese into a food processor and blend for about 30 seconds or until smooth. Alternatively, pound all of the ingredients by hand, using a mortar and pestle.

3 If you are using a food processor, keep the motor running and slowly add the olive oil. Alternatively, add the oil drop by drop while stirring briskly. Season with salt and pepper to taste.

4 Cook the pasta in a saucepan of boiling water allowing 3–4 minutes for fresh pasta or 8–10 minutes for dried, or until it is cooked through, but still has "bite"; drain the pasta thoroughly in a colander.

5 Transfer the pasta to a serving plate and serve with the pesto. Toss to mix well and serve hot.

COOK'S TIP

You can store pesto in the refrigerator for about 4 weeks. Cover the surface of the pesto with olive oil before sealing the container or bottle, to prevent the basil from oxidizing and turning black.

Spaghetti Olio e Aglio

This easy and satisfying Roman dish originated as a cheap meal for poor people, but has now become a favorite in restaurants and trattorias.

NUTRITIONAL INFORMATION

Calories 515	Sugars 1g
Protein 8g	Fat 33g
Carbohydrate . . .50g	Saturates 5g

 5 MINS   5 MINS

SERVES 4

INGREDIENTS

½ cup olive oil

3 garlic cloves, crushed

1 lb fresh spaghetti

3 tbsp roughly chopped fresh parsley

salt and pepper

1 Reserve 1 tablespoon of the olive oil and heat the remainder in a medium saucepan. Add the garlic and a pinch of salt and cook over a low heat, stirring constantly, until golden brown; remove the pan from the heat. Do not allow the garlic to burn because it will taint its flavor. (If it does burn, you will have to start all over again!)

2 Meanwhile, bring a large saucepan of lightly salted water to a boil. Add the spaghetti and remaining olive oil to the pan and cook for 2–3 minutes, or until tender, but still firm to the bite. Drain the spaghetti thoroughly and return to the pan.

3 Add the oil and garlic mixture to the spaghetti and toss to coat thoroughly. Season with pepper, add the chopped fresh parsley, and toss to coat again.

4 Transfer the spaghetti to a warm serving dish and serve immediately.

COOK'S TIP

Oils produced by different countries, mainly Italy, Spain, and Greece, have their own characteristic flavors. Some produce an oil that has a hot, peppery taste, while others have a "green" flavour.

Vegetables & Tofu

This is a simple, clean-tasting dish of green vegetables, tofu and pasta, lightly tossed in olive oil.

NUTRITIONAL INFORMATION

Calories 400	Sugars 5g	
Protein 19g	Fat 17g	
Carbohydrate ...46g	Saturates 5g	

25 MINS   20 MINS

SERVES 4

INGREDIENTS

8 oz asparagus

4 oz snow peas

8 oz green beans

1 leek

8 oz shelled small fava beans

10 oz dried fusilli

2 tbsp olive oil

2 tbsp butter or margarine

1 garlic clove, crushed

1½ cups tofu, cut into 1-inch cubes

⅓ cup pitted green olives in
   brine, drained

salt and pepper

freshly grated Parmesan, to serve

1 Cut the asparagus into 2-inch pieces. Finely slice the snow peas diagonally and slice the green beans into 1-inch pieces. Finely slice the leek.

2 Bring a large saucepan of water to a boil and add the asparagus, green beans, and fava beans. Bring back to a boil and cook for 4 minutes until just tender. Drain well and rinse in cold water; set aside.

3 Bring a large saucepan of salted water to the boil and cook the fusilli for 8–9 minutes until just tender; drain well. Toss in 1 tablespoon of the oil and season well.

4 Meanwhile, in a wok or large skillet, heat the remaining oil and the butter or margarine and gently fry the leek, garlic, and tofu for 1–2 minutes until the vegetables have just softened.

5 Stir in the snow peas and cook for 1 minute.

6 Add the boiled vegetables and olives to the pan and heat through for 1 minute. Carefully stir in the pasta and seasoning. Cook for 1 minute and pile into a warmed serving dish. Serve sprinkled with Parmesan.

Tagliatelle with Pumpkin

This unusual pasta dish comes from the Emilia Romagna region of Italy. When pumpkin is out of season use butternut squash.

NUTRITIONAL INFORMATION

Calories	454	Sugars	.........4g
Protein	.........9g	Fat	..........33g
Carbohydrate	...33g	Saturates	......12g

 15 MINS   35 MINS

SERVES 4

INGREDIENTS

1 lb 2 oz pumpkin or butternut
   squash

2 tbsp olive oil

1 onion, finely chopped

2 garlic cloves, crushed

4–6 tbsp chopped fresh parsley

good pinch of ground or freshly grated
   nutmeg

about 1 cup chicken or vegetable
   stock

4 oz prosciutto, cut into narrow strips

9 oz tagliatelle, green or white
   (fresh or dried)

⅔ cup heavy cream

salt and pepper

freshly grated Parmesan, to serve

1 Peel the pumpkin or squash and scoop out the seeds and membrane. Cut the flesh into ½-inch dice.

2 Heat the olive oil in a pan and gently fry the onion and garlic until softened. Add half of the parsley and fry for 1–2 minutes.

3 Add the pumpkin or squash and continue to cook for 2–3 minutes. Season well with salt and pepper and nutmeg.

4 Add half of the stock and bring to a boil. Cover and simmer for about 10 minutes, or until the pumpkin is tender, adding more stock as necessary. Add the prosciutto and continue to cook for 2 minutes, stirring frequently.

5 Meanwhile, cook the tagliatelle in a large saucepan of boiling salted water, allowing 3–4 minutes for fresh pasta or 8–10 minutes for dried. Drain thoroughly and turn into a warmed dish.

6 Add the cream to the ham mixture and heat gently. Season and spoon over the pasta. Sprinkle with the remaining parsley and grated Parmesan separately.

Pasta with Cheese & Broccoli

Some of the simplest and most satisfying dishes are made with pasta, such as this delicious combination of tagliatelle with two-cheese sauce.

NUTRITIONAL INFORMATION

Calories	624	Sugars	.........2g
Protein	........22g	Fat	..........45g
Carbohydrate	...34g	Saturates	......28g

5 MINS   15 MINS

SERVES 4

INGREDIENTS

10 oz dried tagliatelle tricolore
(plain, spinach- and tomato-flavored
noodles)

8 oz broccoli, broken into small
flowerets

1½ cups mascarpone cheese

1 cup crumbled blue cheese

1 tbsp chopped fresh oregano

2 tbsp butter

salt and pepper

sprigs of fresh oregano, to garnish

freshly grated Parmesan, to serve

1 Cook the tagliatelle in plenty of boiling salted water for 8–10 minutes, or until just tender.

2 Meanwhile, cook the broccoli flowerets in a small amount of lightly salted, boiling water; avoid overcooking the broccoli, so it retains much of its color and texture.

3 Heat the mascarpone and blue cheeses together gently in a large saucepan until they are melted. Stir in the oregano and season with salt and pepper to taste.

4 Drain the pasta thoroughly. Return it to the saucepan and add the butter, tossing the tagliatelle to coat it. Drain the broccoli well and add to the pasta with the sauce, tossing gently to mix.

5 Divide the pasta between 4 warmed serving plates. Garnish with sprigs of fresh oregano and serve with freshly grated Parmesan.

Spicy Tomato Tagliatelle

A deliciously fresh and slightly spicy tomato sauce with pasta to make an excellent dish for lunch or a light supper.

NUTRITIONAL INFORMATION

Calories	306	Sugars	.........7g
Protein	.........8g	Fat	..........12g
Carbohydrate	...45g	Saturates	.......7g

15 MINS   35 MINS

SERVES 4

I N G R E D I E N T S

3 tbsp butter

1 onion, finely chopped

1 garlic clove, crushed

2 small red chilies,
    seeded and diced

1 lb fresh tomatoes, skinned,
    seeded, and diced

¾ cup vegetable stock

2 tbsp tomato paste

1 tsp sugar

salt and pepper

1½ lb fresh green and white
    tagliatelle, or 12 oz dried

VARIATION

Try topping your pasta dish with ½ cup diced pancetta or unsmoked bacon, dry-fried for 5 minutes until crispy.

1 Melt the butter in a large saucepan. Add the onion and garlic and cook for 3–4 minutes, or until softened.

2 Add the chilies to the pan and continue cooking for about 2 minutes.

3 Add the tomatoes and stock, reduce the heat, and leave to simmer for 10 minutes, stirring.

4 Pour the sauce into a food processor and blend for 1 minute until smooth.

Alternatively, push the sauce through a strainer.

5 Return the sauce to the pan and add the tomato paste, sugar, and salt and pepper to taste. Gently reheat over a low heat until piping hot.

6 Cook the tagliatelle in a pan of boiling water for 8–10 minutes, or until it is tender, but still has "bite"; drain the tagliatelle. Transfer to serving plates and serve with the tomato sauce.

Pasta & Cheese Puddings

These delicious pasta puddings are served with a sauce flavored by tomatoes and a bay-leaf.

NUTRITIONAL INFORMATION

Calories 517   Sugars 8g
Protein . . . . .19g   Fat 27g
Carbohydrate . . .47g   Saturates 13g

 45 MINS   50 MINS

SERVES 4

INGREDIENTS

1 tbsp butter or margarine,
    softened

½ cup dried white bread crumbs

6 oz tricolor spaghetti

1¼ cups Béchamel Sauce (see page 14)

1 egg yolk

1 cup grated Gruyère cheese

salt and pepper

fresh flat-leaf parsley, to garnish

TOMATO SAUCE

2 tsp olive oil

1 onion, finely chopped

1 bay leaf

⅔ cup dry white wine

⅔ cup strained puréed tomatoes

1 tbsp tomato paste

1 Grease four ¾-cup molds or ramekins with the butter or margarine. Evenly coat the insides with half of the bread crumbs.

2 Break the spaghetti into 2-inch pieces. Bring a saucepan of lightly salted water to a boil and cook the spaghetti for 5–6 minutes, or until just tender; drain well and put in a bowl.

3 Mix the Béchamel Sauce, egg yolk, cheese, and seasoning into the cooked pasta and pack into the molds.

4 Sprinkle with the remaining bread crumbs and place the molds on a cookie sheet. Bake in a preheated oven at 425°F for 20 minutes until golden; leave to stand for 10 minutes.

5 Meanwhile, make the sauce. Heat the oil in a pan and fry the onion and bay leaf for 2–3 minutes, or until just softened.

6 Stir in the wine, tomatoes, tomato paste, and seasoning. Bring to a boil and simmer for 20 minutes, or until thickened; discard the bay leaf.

7 Run a spatula around the inside of the molds. Turn onto serving plates, garnish, and serve with the tomato sauce.

Tagliatelle with Garlic Butter

Pasta is not difficult to make yourself, just a little time consuming. The resulting pasta only takes a couple of minutes to cook and tastes wonderful.

NUTRITIONAL INFORMATION

Calories 642   Sugars 2g
Protein . . . . .16g   Fat 29g
Carbohydrate . . .84g   Saturates 13g

45 MINS   5 MINS

SERVES 4

INGREDIENTS

3¼ cups hard white flour,
    plus extra for dredging

2 tsp salt

4 eggs, beaten

3 tbsp olive oil

5 tbsp butter, melted

3 garlic cloves, finely chopped

2 tbsp chopped fresh parsley

pepper

1 Sift the flour into a large bowl and stir in the salt.

2 Make a well in the middle of the dry ingredients and add the eggs and 2 tablespoons of oil. Using a wooden spoon, stir in the eggs, gradually drawing in the flour. After a few minutes the dough will be too stiff to use a spoon and you will need to use your fingers.

3 Once all of the flour has been incorporated, turn out the dough onto a floured surface and knead for about 5 minutes, or until smooth and elastic: if you find the dough is too wet, add a little more flour and continue kneading. Cover with plastic wrap and leave to rest for at least 15 minutes.

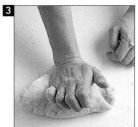

4 The basic dough is now ready; roll out the pasta thinly and create the pasta shapes required. This can be done by hand or using a pasta machine. Results from a machine are usually neater and thinner, but not necessarily better.

5 To make the tagliatelle by hand, fold the thinly rolled pasta sheets into thirds and cut out long, thin stips, about ½ inch wide.

6 To cook, bring a pan of water to a boil and add 1 tbsp of oil and the pasta. It will take 2–3 minutes to cook, and the texture should have a slight bite to it; drain.

7 Mix together the butter, garlic, and parsley. Stir into the pasta, season with a little pepper to taste, and serve immediately.

COOK'S TIP

Generally allow about 5 oz fresh pasta, or about 3 oz dried pasta per person.

Fettuccine & Walnut Sauce

This mouthwatering dish makes an excellent light, vegetarian lunch for four or a good first course for six.

NUTRITIONAL INFORMATION

Calories	...... .833	Sugars	.... .5g
Protein	.... .20g	Fat	.... .66g
Carbohydrate	...44g	Saturates	......15g

15 MINS · 10 MINS

SERVES 6

I N G R E D I E N T S

2 thick slices whole-wheat
   bread, crusts removed

1¼ cups milk

2½ cups shelled walnuts

2 garlic cloves, crushed

1 cup pitted black olives

⅔ cup freshly grated
   Parmesan cheese

8 tbsp extra-virgin olive oil

⅔ cup heavy cream

1 lb fresh fettuccine

salt and pepper

2–3 tbsp chopped fresh parsley

1 Put the bread in a shallow dish, pour the milk over, and set aside to soak until the liquid has been absorbed.

2 Spread the walnuts out on a cookie sheet and toast in a preheated oven at 375°F for about 5 minutes, or until golden; set aside to cool.

3 Put the soaked bread, walnuts, garlic, olives, Parmesan cheese, and 6 tablespoons of the olive oil in a food processor and work to make a purée. Season to taste with salt and pepper and stir in the cream.

4 Bring a large pan of lightly salted water to a boil. Add the fettuccine and 1 tablespoon of the remaining oil and cook for 2–3 minutes, or until tender but still firm to the bite. Drain the fettuccine thoroughly and toss with the remaining olive oil.

5 Divide the fettuccine between individual serving plates and spoon the walnut sauce on top. Sprinkle the fresh parsley over and serve.

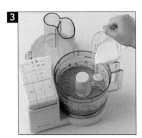

COOK'S TIP

Parmesan quickly loses its pungency and "bite". It is better to buy small quantities and grate it yourself. Wrapped in foil, it will keep in the refrigerator for several months.

Fettuccine all'Alfredo

This simple, traditional dish can be made with any long pasta, but is especially good with flat noodles, such as fettuccine or tagliatelle.

NUTRITIONAL INFORMATION

Calories 627	Sugars 2g
Protein 18g	Fat 41g
Carbohydrate ...51g	Saturates 23g

5 MINS   10 MINS

SERVES 4

I N G R E D I E N T S

2 tbsp butter

1 cup heavy cream

1 lb fresh fettuccine

1 tbsp olive oil

1 cup freshly grated Parmesan
    cheese, plus extra to serve

pinch of freshly grated nutmeg

salt and pepper

fresh parsley sprigs, to garnish

1 Put the butter and ²⁄₃ cup of the cream in a large saucepan and bring the mixture to a boil over a medium heat. Reduce the heat and simmer gently for about 1¹⁄₂ minutes, or until slightly thickened.

2 Meanwhile, bring a large pan of lightly salted water to a boil. Add the

fettuccine and olive oil and cook for 2–3 minutes until tender, but still firm to the bite. Drain the fettuccine thoroughly and then pour the cream sauce over.

3 Toss the fettuccine in the sauce over a low heat until thoroughly coated.

4 Add the remaining cream, the Parmesan cheese, and nutmeg to the fettuccine mixture and season to taste

with salt and pepper. Toss thoroughly to coat while gently heating through.

5 Transfer the fettuccine mixture to a warm serving plate and garnish with the fresh sprig of parsley. Serve immediately, handing out extra grated Parmesan cheese separately.

VARIATION

This classic Roman dish is often served with the addition of strips of ham and fresh peas. Add 2 cups shelled cooked peas and 6 oz ham strips with the Parmesan cheese in step 4.

Spaghetti with Ricotta Sauce

This makes a quick-and-easy first course, and is particularly ideal for the summer.

NUTRITIONAL INFORMATION

Calories 688   Sugars 5g
Protein . . . . .17g   Fat 51g
Carbohydrate . . .43g   Saturates 16g

15 MINS   20 MINS

SERVES 4

INGREDIENTS

12 oz spaghetti

3 tbsp olive oil

3 tbsp butter, cut into small pieces

2 tbsp chopped fresh parsley

SAUCE

1 cup freshly ground blanched almonds

½ cup ricotta cheese

large pinch of grated nutmeg

large pinch of ground cinnamon

⅔ cup crème fraîche or sour cream

½ cup chicken stock, hot

1 tbsp pine nuts

pepper

cilantro leaves, to garnish

COOK'S TIP

To toss spaghetti and coat it with a sauce or dressing, use the 2 largest forks you can find. Holding one fork in each hand, ease the prongs under the spaghetti from each side and lift them toward the center. Repeat evenly until the pasta is well coated.

1 Cook the spaghetti in a large pan of boiling salted water, to which you have added 1 tablespoon of the oil, for 8–10 minutes, or until tender. Drain the pasta in a colander, return to the pan, and toss with the butter and parsley; cover the pan and keep warm.

2 To make the sauce, mix together the ground almonds, ricotta, nutmeg, cinnamon, and crème fraîche to make a

thick paste. Gradually pour on the remaining oil, stirring constantly until it is well blended. Gradually pour on the hot stock, stirring all the time, until the sauce is smooth.

3 Transfer the spaghetti to warmed serving dishes, pour on the sauce, and toss well. Sprinkle each serving with pine nuts and garnish with cilantro leaves. Serve warm.

Artichoke & Olive Spaghetti

The classic Italian flavors of artichoke hearts and black olives are a winning combination in this simple dish.

NUTRITIONAL INFORMATION

Calories 393   Sugars 11g
Protein . . . . .14g   Fat 11g
Carbohydrate . . .63g   Saturates 2g

20 MINS   35 MINS

SERVES 4

INGREDIENTS

2 tbsp olive oil

1 large red onion, chopped

2 garlic cloves, crushed

1 tbsp lemon juice

4 baby eggplant, quartered

2½ cups strained puréed tomatoes

2 tsp sugar

2 tbsp tomato paste

14-oz can artichoke hearts, drained
    and halved

¾ cup pitted black olives

12 oz dried wholewheat spaghetti

salt and pepper

sprigs of fresh basil, to garnish

olive bread, to serve

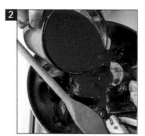

1 Heat 1 tablespoon of the oil in a large skillet and gently fry the onion, garlic, lemon juice, and eggplant for 4–5 minutes or until lightly browned.

2 Pour in the tomatoes and season with salt and pepper to taste. Add the sugar and tomato paste. Bring to the boil, reduce the heat, and simmer for 20 minutes.

3 Gently stir in the artichoke halves and olives and cook for 5 minutes.

4 Meanwhile, bring a large saucepan of lightly salted water to a boil and cook the spaghetti for 8–10 minutes, or until just tender. Drain well, toss in the remaining olive oil, and season with salt and pepper to taste.

5 Transfer the spaghetti to a warmed serving bowl and top with the vegetable sauce. Garnish with basil sprigs and serve with olive bread.

Chili & Bell Pepper Pasta

This roasted bell pepper and chili sauce is sweet and spicy — the perfect combination!

NUTRITIONAL INFORMATION

Calories	423	Sugars	.........5g
Protein	.........9g	Fat	..........27g
Carbohydrate	...38g	Saturates	.......4g

 25 MINS   30 MINS

SERVES 4

I N G R E D I E N T S

2 red bell peppers, halved and seeded

1 small red chili

4 tomatoes, halved

2 garlic cloves

¼ cup ground blanched almonds

7 tbsp olive oil

1½ lb fresh pasta, or 12 oz dried pasta

fresh oregano leaves, to garnish

1 Place the bell peppers, skin-side up, on a cookie sheet with the chili and tomatoes. Cook under a preheated broiler for 15 minutes, or until charred. After 10 minutes turn the tomatoes skin-side up. Place the bell peppers and chilies in a plastic bag and leave to sweat for 10 minutes.

2 Remove the skin from the bell peppers and chilies and slice the flesh into thin strips.

3 Peel the garlic, and peel and seed the tomatoes.

4 Place the almonds on a cookie sheet and place under the broiler for 2–3 minutes until golden.

5 Using a food processor, blend the bell pepper, chili, garlic, and tomatoes to make a purée. Keep the motor running and slowly add the olive oil to form a thick sauce. Alternatively, mash the mixture with a fork and beat in the olive oil, drop by drop.

6 Stir the toasted ground almonds into the mixture.

7 Warm the sauce in a saucepan until it is heated through.

8 Cook the pasta in a saucepan of boiling water for 8–10 minutes if using dried, or 3–5 minutes if using fresh. Drain the pasta thoroughly and transfer to a serving dish. Pour the sauce over and toss to mix. Garnish with the fresh oregano leaves.

VARIATION

Add 2 tablespoons of red-wine vinegar to the sauce and use as a dressing for a cold pasta salad, if you wish.

Tagliatelle & Garlic Sauce

This pasta dish can be prepared in a moment — the intense flavors are sure to make this a popular recipe.

NUTRITIONAL INFORMATION

Calories	501	Sugars	.........3g
Protein	........15g	Fat	..........31g
Carbohydrate	...43g	Saturates	......11g

🍲 15 MINS   🕐 20 MINS

SERVES 4

INGREDIENTS

2 tbsp walnut oil

1 bunch scallions, sliced

2 garlic cloves, thinly sliced

3 cups sliced mushrooms

1 lb 2 oz fresh green and white
tagliatelle

8 oz frozen chopped leaf spinach,
thawed and drained

½ cup full-fat soft cheese with
garlic and herbs

4 tbsp light cream

½ cup chopped, unsalted
pistachio nuts

2 tbsp shredded fresh basil

salt and pepper

sprigs of fresh basil, to garnish

Italian bread, to serve

1 Gently heat the oil in a wok or skillet and fry the scallions and garlic for 1 minute or until just softened. Add the mushrooms, stir well, cover, and cook gently for 5 minutes, or until softened.

2 Meanwhile, bring a large saucepan of lightly salted water to a boil and cook the pasta for 3–5 minutes, or until just tender. Drain the pasta thoroughly and return to the saucepan.

3 Add the spinach to the mushrooms and heat through for 1–2 minutes. Add the cheese and allow to melt slightly. Stir in the cream and continue to heat without boiling.

4 Pour the mixture over the pasta, season to taste, and mix well. Heat gently, stirring, for 2–3 minutes.

5 Pile into a warmed serving bowl and sprinkle the pistachio nuts and shredded basil over. Garnish with basil sprigs and serve with Italian bread.

Pasta with Nuts & Cheese

Simple and inexpensive, this tasty pasta dish is prepared very quickly and suitable for family meals.

NUTRITIONAL INFORMATION

Calories 531	Sugars 4g	
Protein 20g	Fat 35g	
Carbohydrate . . .35g	Saturates 16g	

 10 MINS   30 MINS

SERVES 4

INGREDIENTS

1 cup pine nuts

12 oz dried pasta shapes

2 zucchini, sliced

1¼ cups broccoli,
   broken into flowerets

1 cup full-fat soft cheese

⅔ cup milk

1 tbsp chopped fresh basil

1½ cups sliced button mushrooms

¾ cup crumbled blue cheese

salt and pepper

sprigs of fresh basil, to garnish

green salad, to serve

1 Scatter the pine nuts onto a cookie sheet and broil, turning occasionally, until lightly browned all over; set aside.

2 Cook the pasta in plenty of boiling salted water for 8–10 minutes, or until just tender.

3 Meanwhile, cook the zucchini and broccoli in a small amount of boiling, lightly salted water for about 5 minutes, or until just tender.

4 Put the soft cheese into a pan and heat gently, stirring constantly. Add the milk and stir to mix. Add the basil and mushrooms and cook gently for 2–3 minutes. Stir in the blue cheese and season to taste.

5 Drain the pasta and the vegetables and mix together. Pour the cheese and mushroom sauce over and add the pine nuts. Toss gently to mix. Garnish with basil sprigs and serve with a green salad.

Macaroni & Tuna Fish Layer

A layer of tuna fish with garlic, mushrooms, and red bell pepper is sandwiched between two layers of macaroni with a crunchy topping.

NUTRITIONAL INFORMATION

Calories	691	Sugars	. . . . .10g
Protein	. . . . .41g	Fat	. . . . .33g
Carbohydrate	. . .62g	Saturates	. . . . . .15g

20 MINS   50 MINS

SERVES 2

INGREDIENTS

1¼ cups dried macaroni

2 tbsp oil

1 garlic clove, crushed

¾ cup sliced button mushrooms

½ red bell pepper, thinly sliced

7-oz can of tuna fish in brine,
    drained and flaked

½ tsp dried oregano

salt and pepper

SAUCE

2 tbsp butter or margarine

1 tbsp all-purpose flour

1 cup milk

2 tomatoes, sliced

2 tbsp dried bread crumbs

¼ cup grated sharp cheddar or
    Parmesan cheese

VARIATION

Replace the tuna with chopped cooked chicken, beef, pork, or ham, or with 3–4 sliced hard-cooked eggs.

1 Cook the macaroni in boiling salted water, with 1 tablespoon of the oil added, for 10–12 minutes, or until tender. Drain, rinse, and drain thoroughly.

2 Heat the remaining oil in a saucepan or skillet and fry the garlic, mushrooms, and bell pepper until soft. Add the tuna, oregano, and seasonings and heat through.

3 Grease a baking dish (about 1 quart capacity). Add half of the cooked macaroni; cover with the tuna mixture, and then add the remaining macaroni.

4 To make the sauce, melt the butter or margarine in a saucepan. Stir in the flour and cook for 1 minute. Add the milk gradually and bring to a boil. Simmer for 1–2 minutes, stirring continuously, until thickened; season to taste. Pour the sauce over the macaroni.

5 Lay the sliced tomatoes over the sauce and sprinkle with the bread crumbs and cheese.

6 Place in a preheated oven at 400°F for about 25 minutes, or until piping hot and the top is well browned.

Pasta & Chili Tomatoes

The pappardelle and vegetables are tossed in a delicious chili and tomato sauce for a quick and economical family-style meal.

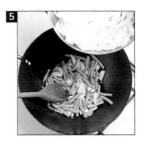

NUTRITIONAL INFORMATION

Calories	353	Sugars	.........7g
Protein	........10g	Fat	..........24g
Carbohydrate	...26g	Saturates	.......4g

 15 MINS　 20 MINS

SERVES 4

I N G R E D I E N T S

9 oz pappardelle

3 tbsp peanut oil

2 garlic cloves, crushed

2 shallots, sliced

8 oz sliced green beans

1½ cups cherry tomatoes, halved

1 tsp chili flakes

4 tbsp crunchy peanut butter

⅔ cup coconut milk

1 tbsp tomato paste

sliced scallions, to garnish

1 Cook the pappardelle in a large saucepan of boiling, lightly salted water for 5–6 minutes.

2 Heat the peanut oil in a large pan or preheated wok.

3 Add the garlic and shallots and stir-fry for 1 minute.

4 Drain the pappardelle thoroughly and set aside.

5 Add the green beans and drained pasta to the wok and stir-fry for 5 minutes.

6 Add the cherry tomatoes to the wok and mix well.

7 Mix together the chili flakes, peanut butter, coconut milk, and tomato paste.

8 Pour the chili mixture over the noodles, toss well to combine and heat through.

9 Transfer to warm serving dishes and garnish. Serve immediately.

VARIATION

Add slices of chicken or beef to the recipe and stir-fry with the beans and pasta in step 5 for a more substantial main meal.

Vermicelli & Clam Sauce

This recipe is quick to prepare and cook — it's so delicious it will be devoured even faster!

NUTRITIONAL INFORMATION

Calories 502   Sugars 2g
Protein ....27g   Fat 17g
Carbohydrate ...58g   Saturates 7g

 15 MINS   25 MINS

SERVES 4

INGREDIENTS

14 oz vermicelli, spaghetti, or other
   long pasta

1 tbsp olive oil

2 tbsp butter

2 tbsp Parmesan shavings, to garnish

sprig of basil, to garnish

SAUCE

1 tbsp olive oil

2 onions, chopped

2 garlic cloves, chopped

2 x 7-oz jars clams in brine

½ cup white wine

4 tbsp chopped fresh parsley

½ tsp dried oregano

pinch of freshly grated nutmeg

salt and pepper

1 Cook the pasta in a large pan of boiling salted water, adding the olive oil, for 8–10 minutes, or until tender. Drain the pasta in a colander and return to the pan. Add the butter, cover, and shake the pan; keep warm until required.

2 To make the clam sauce, heat the oil in a pan over a medium heat and fry the onion until it is translucent. Stir in the garlic and cook for 1 minute.

3 Strain the liquid from one jar of clams and pour it into the pan. Add the wine and stir well. Bring to simmering point and simmer for 3 minutes. Drain the brine from the second jar of clams and discard.

4 Add the shellfish and herbs to the pan and season with pepper to taste and the nutmeg. Lower the heat and cook until the sauce is heated through.

5 Transfer the pasta to a warmed serving dish and pour in the sauce.

6 Sprinkle with the Parmesan and garnish with the basil sprig. Serve hot.

Pasta & Squid Casserole

This pasta dish is easy to make and is a very hearty meal for a large number of guests.

NUTRITIONAL INFORMATION

Calories	237	Sugars 4g
Protein	........12g	Fat 11g
Carbohydrate	...19g	Saturates 2g

 15 MINS   35 MINS

SERVES 6

INGREDIENTS

8 oz short pasta shapes

1 tbsp olive oil

2 tbsp chopped fresh parsley

salt and pepper

SAUCE

12 oz cleaned squid,
 cut into ½-inch strips

6 tbsp olive oil

2 onions, sliced

1 cup fish stock

⅔ cup red wine

12 oz tomatoes, peeled
 and thinly sliced

2 tbsp tomato paste

1 tsp dried oregano

2 bay leaves

1 Cook the pasta for only 3 minutes in a large pan of boiling salted water, adding the oil. Drain in a colander, return to the pan, cover, and keep warm.

2 To make the sauce, heat the oil in a pan over medium heat and fry the onion until translucent. Add the squid and stock and simmer for 5 minutes. Pour in the wine and add the tomatoes, tomato paste, oregano, and bay leaves. Bring the sauce to a boil, season with salt and pepper to taste, and cook, uncovered, for 5 minutes.

3 Add the pasta, stir well, cover the pan and continue boiling for 10 minutes, or until the pasta and squid are almost tender; by this time the sauce should be thick and syrupy. If the sauce is too liquid, uncover the pan and continue cooking for a few minutes. Taste the sauce and adjust the seasoning if necessary.

4 Remove the bay leaves and stir in most of the parsley, reserving a little to garnish; transfer to a warmed serving dish. Sprinkle with the remaining parsley and serve hot. Serve with warm, crusty bread, such as ciabatta.

Spaghetti & Salmon Sauce

The smoked salmon ideally complements the spaghetti to make a very luxurious dish, suitable for a dinner party.

NUTRITIONAL INFORMATION

Calories	782	Sugars	.........3g
Protein	........20g	Fat	..........48g
Carbohydrate	...48g	Saturates	......27g

 10 MINS   15 MINS

SERVES 4

INGREDIENTS

1 lb 2 oz buckwheat spaghetti

2 tbsp olive oil

½ cup crumbled feta cheese

cilantro or parsley, to garnish

SAUCE

1¼ cups heavy cream

⅔ cup whiskey or brandy

4½ oz smoked salmon

large pinch of cayenne pepper

2 tbsp chopped cilantro or parsley

salt and pepper

1 Cook the spaghetti in a large saucepan of salted boiling water, adding 1 tablespoon of the olive oil, for 8–10 minutes, or until tender; drain in a colander. Return the pasta to the pan, sprinkle the remaining oil over, cover, and shake the pan. Set aside and keep warm until required.

2 In separate small saucepans, heat the cream and the whiskey or brandy to simmering point; do not let them boil.

3 Combine the cream with the whiskey or brandy.

4 Cut the smoked salmon into thin strips and add to the cream mixture. Season with a little black pepper and cayenne pepper to taste, then stir in the chopped cilantro or parsley.

5 Transfer the spaghetti to a warmed serving dish, pour the sauce over and toss thoroughly using 2 large forks. Scatter the crumbled cheese over the pasta and garnish with the cilantro or parsley. Serve at once.

Pasta & Mussel Sauce

Serve this aromatic seafood dish with plenty of fresh, crusty bread to soak up the delicious sauce.

NUTRITIONAL INFORMATION

Calories	735	Sugars	.........3g
Protein	........37g	Fat	..........46g
Carbohydrate	...41g	Saturates	......26g

 25 MINS 25 MINS

SERVES 6

I N G R E D I E N T S

14 oz pasta shells

1 tbsp olive oil

S A U C E

3½ quarts mussels, scrubbed

1 cup dry white wine

2 large onions, chopped

½ cup unsalted butter

6 large garlic cloves, finely chopped

5 tbsp chopped fresh parsley

1¼ cups heavy cream

salt and pepper

crusty bread, to serve

1 Pull off the "beards" from the mussels and rinse well in several changes of water: discard any mussels that refuse to close when tapped. Put the mussels in a large pan with the white wine and half of the onions. Cover the pan, shake, and cook over a medium heat for 2–3 minutes until the mussels open.

2 Remove the pan from the heat. Lift out the mussels with a draining spoon, reserving the liquid, and set aside until they are cool enough to handle; discard any mussels that have not opened.

3 Melt the butter in a pan over medium heat and fry the remaining onion for 3–4 minutes, or until translucent. Stir in the garlic and cook for 1 minute. Gradually pour in the reserved cooking liquor, stirring to blend thoroughly, then stir in the parsley and cream. Season to taste and bring to simmering point. Taste and adjust the seasoning if necessary.

4 Cook the pasta in a large pan of salted boiling water, adding the oil, for 8–10 minutes, or until tender. Drain the pasta in a colander, return to the pan, cover, and keep warm.

5 Remove the mussels from their shells, reserving a few shells for garnish. Stir the mussels into the cream sauce. Tip the pasta into a warmed serving dish, pour the sauce over and, using 2 large spoons, toss it together well. Garnish with a few of the reserved mussel shells. Serve hot, with warm, crusty bread.

Pasta & Sicilian Sauce

This Sicilian recipe of anchovies mixed with pine nuts and golden raisins in a tomato sauce is delicious with all types of pasta.

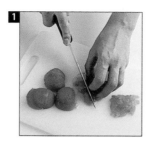

NUTRITIONAL INFORMATION

Calories ....286 Sugars 14g
Protein ....11g Fat 8g
Carbohydrate ...46g Saturates 1g

 25 MINS   30 MINS

SERVES 4

I N G R E D I E N T S

1 lb tomatoes, halved

¼ cup pine nuts

⅓ cup golden raisins

1¾-oz can anchovies, drained and
  halved lengthways

2 tbsp concentrated tomato paste

1½ lb fresh penne or 12 oz dried penne

1 Cook the tomatoes under a preheated broiler for about 10 minutes. Leave to cool slightly, then once cool enough to handle, peel off the skins and dice the flesh.

2 Place the pine nuts on a cookie sheet and lightly toast under the broiler for 2–3 minutes, or until golden brown.

3 Soak the golden raisins in a bowl of warm water for about 20 minutes; drain the golden raisins thoroughly.

4 Place the tomatoes, pine nuts, and golden raisins in a small saucepan and gently heat.

5 Add the anchovies and tomato paste, heating the sauce for a further 2–3 minutes, or until hot.

6 Cook the pasta in a saucepan of boiling water for 8–10 minutes, or until it is cooked through, but still has bite; drain thoroughly.

7 Transfer the pasta to a serving plate and serve with the hot Sicilian sauce.

VARIATION

Add 3 oz bacon, broiled for 5 minutes until crispy, then chopped, instead of the anchovies, if you prefer.

Spaghetti & Shellfish

Frozen shelled shrimp from the freezer can become the star ingredient in this colorful and delicious dish.

NUTRITIONAL INFORMATION

Calories	.510	Sugars	.38g
Protein	.33g	Fat	.24g
Carbohydrate	.44g	Saturates	.11g

35 MINS   30 MINS

SERVES 4

INGREDIENTS

8 oz spaghetti, broken into
   6-inch pieces

2 tbsp olive oil

1¼ cups chicken stock

1 tsp lemon juice

1 small cauliflower, cut into
   flowerets

2 carrots, sliced thinly

4 oz snow peas, trimmed

4 tbsp butter

1 onion, sliced

1½ cups zucchini, thinly sliced

1 garlic clove, chopped

12 oz frozen shelled shrimp,
   defrosted

2 tbsp chopped fresh parsley

¼ cup grated Parmesan cheese

salt and pepper

½ tsp paprika, to sprinkle

4 unshelled shrimp,
   to garnish (optional)

1 Cook the spaghetti in a large pan of boiling salted water, adding 1 tbsp of the oil, for 8–10 minutes, or until tender. Drain, then return to the pan and stir in the remaining oil; cover and keep warm.

2 Bring the chicken stock and lemon juice to a boil. Add the cauliflower and carrots and cook for 3–4 minutes until they are barely tender; remove with a draining spoon and set aside. Add the snow peas and cook for 1–2 minutes until they begin to soften. Remove with a draining spoon and add to the other vegetables; reserve the stock for future use.

3 Melt half of the butter in a skillet over a medium heat and fry the onion and zucchini for about 3 minutes. Add the garlic and shrimp and cook for a further 2–3 minutes until thoroughly heated through.

4 Stir in the reserved vegetables and heat through. Season with salt and pepper, then stir in the remaining butter.

5 Transfer the spaghetti to a warmed serving dish. Pour the sauce and parsley over. Toss well using 2 forks until thoroughly coated. Sprinkle with the grated cheese and paprika, and garnish with unshelled shrimp, if using. Serve immediately.

Pasta Vongole

Fresh clams are available from most good fish merchants. Or use canned clams, which are less messy to eat but not as attractive.

NUTRITIONAL INFORMATION

Calories	410	Sugars	.........1g
Protein	.......39g	Fat	..........9g
Carbohydrate	...39g	Saturates	.......1g

20 MINS   20 MINS

SERVES 4

INGREDIENTS

1½ lb fresh clams, or 1 x 10-oz can
   clams, drained

14 oz mixed seafood, such as
   shrimp, squid, and mussels,
   defrosted if frozen

2 tbsp olive oil

2 garlic cloves, finely chopped

⅔ cup white wine

⅔ cup fish stock

2 tbsp chopped tarragon

salt and pepper

1½ lb fresh pasta, or
   12 oz dried pasta

VARIATION

Red clam sauce can be made by adding 8 tablespoons of strained puréed tomatoes to the sauce along with the stock in step 4. Follow the same cooking method.

1 If you are using fresh clams, scrub them clean and discard any that are already open.

2 Heat the oil in a large skillet. Add the garlic and the clams to the pan and cook for 2 minutes, shaking the pan to insure all of the clams are coated in the oil.

3 Add the remaining seafood to the pan and cook for a further 2 minutes.

4 Pour the wine and stock over the mixed seafood and garlic and bring to a boil. Cover the pan, reduce the heat, and leave to simmer for 8–10 minutes, or until the shells open; discard any clams or mussels that do not open.

5 Meanwhile, cook the pasta in a saucepan of boiling water for 8–10 minutes, or until it is cooked through, but still has bite; drain the pasta thoroughly.

6 Stir the tarragon into the sauce and season with salt and pepper to taste.

7 Transfer the pasta to a serving plate and pour the sauce over. Serve immediately.

Spaghetti, Tuna & Parsley

This is a recipe to look forward to when parsley is at its most prolific, during its growing season.

NUTRITIONAL INFORMATION

Calories	.970	Sugars	.2g
Protein	.23g	Fat	.80g
Carbohydrate	.42g	Saturates	.18g

  10 MINS 15 MINS

SERVES 4

INGREDIENTS

1 lb 2 oz spaghetti

1 tbsp olive oil

2 tbsp butter

black olives, to serve (optional)

SAUCE

7-oz can tuna, drained

2-oz can anchovies, drained

1 cup olive oil

1 cup roughly chopped fresh
flat-leaf parsley

⅔ cup crème fraîche or sour cream

salt and pepper

1 Cook the spaghetti in a large saucepan of salted boiling water, adding the olive oil, for 8–10 minutes, or until tender; drain in a colander and return to the pan. Add the butter, toss thoroughly to coat, and keep warm until required.

2 Remove any bones from the tuna and flake into smaller pieces, using 2 forks. Put the tuna in a blender or food processor with the anchovies, olive oil, and parsley and process until the sauce is smooth. Pour in the crème fraîche and process for a few seconds to blend. Taste the sauce and season with salt and pepper.

3 Warm 4 plates. Shake the saucepan of spaghetti over a medium heat for a few minutes, or until it is thoroughly warmed through.

4 Pour the sauce over the spaghetti and toss quickly, using 2 forks. Serve immediately with a small dish of black olives, if liked.

Penne & Butternut Squash

The creamy, nutty flavor of squash complements the "al dente" texture of the pasta. This recipe is cooked in a microwave.

NUTRITIONAL INFORMATION

Calories 499	Sugars 4g	
Protein 20g	Fat 26g	
Carbohydrate . . .49g	Saturates 13g	

  15 MINS   30 MINS

SERVES 4

I N G R E D I E N T S

2 tbsp olive oil

1 garlic clove, crushed

1 cup fresh white bread crumbs

1 lb 2 oz peeled and seeded
   butternut squash

½ cup water

1 lb 2 oz fresh penne,
   or other pasta shape

1 tbsp butter

1 onion, sliced

½ cup cooked ham cut into strips

1 cup light cream

½ cup grated cheddar cheese

2 tbsp chopped fresh parsley

salt and pepper

COOK'S TIP

If the squash weighs more than is needed for this recipe, blanch the excess for 3–4 minutes on HIGH power in a covered bowl with a little water. Drain, cool, and place in a freezer bag. Store in the freezer for up to 3 months.

1 Mix together the oil, garlic, and bread crumbs and spread out on a large plate. Cook on HIGH power for 4–5 minutes, stirring every minute, until crisp and beginning to brown; set aside.

2 Dice the squash. Place in a large bowl with half of the water. Cover and cook on HIGH power for 8–9 minutes, stirring occasionally; leave to stand for 2 minutes.

3 Place the pasta in a large bowl. Add a little salt and pour boiling water to cover by 1 inch over. Cover and cook on HIGH power for 5 minutes, stirring once, until the pasta is just tender, but still firm to the bite. Leave to stand, covered, for 1 minute before draining.

4 Place the butter and onion in a large bowl. Cover and cook on HIGH power for 3 minutes.

5 Coarsely mash the squash, using a fork. Add to the onion with the pasta, ham, cream, cheese, parsley, and remaining water; season generously and mix well. Cover and cook on HIGH power for 4 minutes until heated through.

6 Serve the pasta sprinkled with the crisp garlic crumbs.

Sicilian Spaghetti Cake

Any variety of long pasta can be used for this popular dish from Sicily.

NUTRITIONAL INFORMATION

Calories ....876 Sugars 10g
Protein ....37g Fat 65g
Carbohydrate ...39g Saturates 18g

30 MINS   50 MINS

SERVES 4

INGREDIENTS

2 eggplant, about 1 lb 7 oz

⅔ cup olive oil

12 oz finely ground lean beef

1 onion, chopped

2 garlic cloves, crushed

2 tbsp tomato paste

14-oz can chopped tomatoes

1 tsp Worcestershire sauce

1 tsp chopped fresh oregano or marjoram,
    or ½ tsp dried oregano or marjoram

⅓ cup pitted sliced black olives

1 green, red, or yellow bell pepper, cored,
    seeded and chopped

6 oz spaghetti

1 cup grated Parmesan cheese

1 Brush an 8-inch springform cake pan with olive oil, place a disc of baking parchment in the base, and brush with oil. Trim the eggplants and cut into slanting slices, ¼ inch thick. Heat some of the oil in a skillet. Fry a few slices of eggplant at a time until lightly browned, turning once, and adding more oil as necessary; drain on paper towels.

2 Put the ground beef, onion, and garlic into a saucepan and cook, stirring frequently, until browned all over. Add the tomato paste, tomatoes, Worcestershire sauce, herbs, and seasoning and simmer for 10 minutes, stirring occasionally. Add the olives and bell pepper and cook for 10 minutes.

3 Bring a large saucepan of salted water to the boil. Cook the spaghetti for 8–10 minutes, or until just tender; drain thoroughly. Turn the spaghetti into a bowl and stir in the meat mixture and Parmesan, tossing together with 2 forks.

4 Lay overlapping slices of eggplant over the base of the cake pan and up the sides. Add the meat mixture, pressing it down, and cover with the remaining eggplant slices.

5 Stand the cake pan in a baking pan and cook in a preheated oven at 400°F for 40 minutes. Leave to stand for 5 minutes then loosen around the edges and invert onto a warmed serving dish, releasing the pan clip; remove the baking parchment. Serve immediately.

Vegetable Pasta Nests

These large pasta nests look impressive when presented filled with broiled mixed vegetables, and taste delicious.

NUTRITIONAL INFORMATION

Calories ....392 Sugars 1g
Protein ....6g Fat 28g
Carbohydrate ...32g Saturates 9g

25 MINS 40 MINS

SERVES 4

INGREDIENTS

6 oz spaghetti

1 eggplant, halved and sliced

1 zucchini, diced

1 red bell pepper, seeded and chopped
  diagonally

6 tbsp olive oil

2 garlic cloves, crushed

4 tbsp butter or margarine, melted

1 tbsp dry white bread crumbs

salt and pepper

fresh parsley sprigs, to garnish

1 Bring a large saucepan of water to a boil and cook the spaghetti for 8–10 minutes or until "al dente". Drain in a colander and set aside until required.

2 Place the eggplant, zucchini, and bell pepper on a cookie sheet.

3 Mix the oil and garlic together and pour over the vegetables, tossing to coat all over.

4 Cook under a preheated hot broiler for about 10 minutes, turning, until tender and lightly charred; set aside and keep warm.

5 Divide the spaghetti among 4 lightly greased Yorkshire pudding pans. Using 2 forks, curl the spaghetti to form nests.

6 Brush the pasta nests with melted butter or margarine and sprinkle with the bread crumbs. Bake in a preheated oven at 400°F for 15 minutes, or until lightly golden. Remove the pasta nests from the pans and transfer to serving plates. Divide the broiled vegetables between the pasta nests and season. Garnish and serve.

COOK'S TIP

"Al dente" means "to the bite" and describes cooked pasta that is not too soft, but still has a "bite" to it.

Pasticcio

A recipe that has both Italian and Greek origins, this dish may be served hot or cold, cut into thick, satisfying squares.

NUTRITIONAL INFORMATION

Calories ....590 Sugars 8g
Protein ....34g Fat 39g
Carbohydrate ...23g Saturates 16g

35 MINS   1¼ HOURS

SERVES 6

INGREDIENTS

8 oz fusilli, or other short
   pasta shapes
1 tbsp olive oil
4 tbsp heavy cream
salt
rosemary sprigs, to garnish

SAUCE

2 tbsp olive oil, plus extra for brushing
1 onion, thinly sliced
1 red bell pepper, cored, seeded,
   and chopped
2 garlic cloves, chopped
1 lb 6 oz lean ground beef
14-oz can chopped tomatoes
½ cup dry white wine
2 tbsp chopped fresh parsley
1¾-oz can anchovies, drained
   and chopped
salt and pepper

TOPPING

1¼ cups plain yogurt
3 eggs
pinch of freshly grated nutmeg
⅓ cup grated Parmesan cheese

1 To make the sauce, heat the oil in a large skillet and fry the onion and red bell pepper for 3 minutes. Stir in the garlic and cook for 1 minute more. Stir in the beef and cook, stirring frequently, until no longer pink.

2 Add the tomatoes and wine, stir well and bring to a boil. Simmer, uncovered, for 20 minutes, or until the sauce is fairly thick. Stir in the parsley and anchovies and season to taste.

3 Cook the pasta in a large pan of boiling salted water, adding the oil, for 8–10 minutes, or until tender. Drain the pasta in a colander, then transfer to a bowl. Stir in the cream and set aside.

4 To make the topping, beat together the yogurt and eggs and season with nutmeg and salt and pepper to taste.

5 Brush a shallow baking dish with oil. Spoon in half of the pasta and cover with half of the meat sauce. Repeat these layers, then spread the topping evenly over the final layer. Sprinkle the cheese on top.

6 Bake in a preheated oven at 375°F for 25 minutes, or until the topping is golden brown and bubbling. Garnish with sprigs of rosemary and serve with a selection of raw vegetable crudités.

Tagliatelle with Meatballs

There is an appetizing contrast of textures and flavors in this satisfying family dish.

 45 MINS   1 HR 5 MINS

SERVES 4

I N G R E D I E N T S

1 lb 2 oz ground lean beef

1 cup soft white bread crumbs

1 garlic clove, crushed

2 tbsp chopped fresh parsley

1 tsp dried oregano

large pinch of freshly grated nutmeg

¼ tsp ground coriander

½ cup grated Parmesan cheese

2–3 tbsp milk

all-purpose flour for dusting

4 tbsp olive oil

14 oz tagliatelle

2 tbsp butter, diced

salt and pepper

S A U C E

3 tbsp olive oil

2 large onions, sliced

2 celery stalks, thinly sliced

2 garlic cloves, chopped

14-oz can chopped tomatoes

4½-oz bottled sun-dried tomatoes, drained and chopped

2 tbsp tomato paste

1 tbsp dark brown sugar

⅔ cup white wine, or water

1. To make the sauce, heat the oil in a skillet and fry the onions and celery until translucent. Add the garlic and cook for 1 minute. Stir in the tomatoes, tomato paste, sugar, and wine, and season. Bring to the boil and simmer for 10 minutes.

2. Meanwhile, break up the meat in a bowl with a wooden spoon until it becomes a sticky paste. Stir in the bread crumbs, garlic, herbs, and spices. Stir in the cheese and enough milk to make a firm paste. Flour your hands, take large spoonfuls of the mixture and shape it into 12 balls. Heat 3 tbsp of the oil in a skillet and fry the meatballs for 5–6 minutes until browned.

3. Pour the tomato sauce over the meatballs. Lower the heat, cover the pan, and simmer for 30 minutes, turning once or twice. Add a little extra water if the sauce begins to dry.

4. Cook the pasta in a large saucepan of boiling salted water, adding the remaining oil, for 8–10 minutes, or until tender. Drain the pasta, then turn into a warmed serving dish, dot with the butter, and toss with 2 forks. Spoon the meatballs and sauce over the pasta and serve.

Tortelloni

These tasty little squares of pasta stuffed with mushrooms and cheese are surprisingly filling. This recipe makes 36 tortelloni.

NUTRITIONAL INFORMATION

Calories 360	Sugars 1g	
Protein 9g	Fat 21g	
Carbohydrate ...36g	Saturates 12g	

1¼ HOURS   25 MINS

SERVES 4

INGREDIENTS

about 10 oz fresh pasta, rolled out
  to thin sheets

5 tbsp butter

⅓ cup finely chopped shallots

3 garlic clove, crushed

⅔ cup wiped and finely chopped
  mushrooms

½ celery stalk, finely chopped

¼ cup finely grated Pecorino cheese
  plus extra to garnish

1 tbsp oil

salt and pepper

1 Using a serrated pasta cutter, cut 2-inch squares from the sheets of fresh pasta: to make 36 tortelloni you will need 72 squares. Once the pasta is cut, cover the squares with plastic wrap to stop them drying out.

2 Melt 3 tbsp of the butter in a skillet. Add the shallots, 1 crushed garlic clove, the mushrooms, and celery and cook for 4–5 minutes.

3 Remove the pan from the heat, stir in the cheese, and season with salt and pepper to taste.

4 Spoon ½ teaspoon of the mixture on to the middle of 36 pasta squares. Brush the edges of the squares with water and top with the remaining 36 squares. Press the edges together to seal; leave to rest for 5 minutes.

5 Bring a large pan of water to the boil, add the oil, and cook the tortelloni, in batches, for 2–3 minutes: the tortelloni will rise to the surface when cooked and the pasta should be tender with a slight bite. Remove from the pan with a draining spoon and drain thoroughly.

6 Meanwhile, melt the remaining butter in a pan. Add the remaining garlic and plenty of pepper and cook for 1–2 minutes. Transfer the tortelloni to serving plates and pour the garlic butter over. Garnish with grated pecorino cheese and serve immediately.

Tagliatelle & Chicken Sauce

Spinach ribbon noodles covered with a rich tomato sauce and topped with creamy chicken makes a very appetizing dish.

NUTRITIONAL INFORMATION

Calories	853	Sugars	.........6g
Protein	........32g	Fat	...........71g
Carbohydrate	...23g	Saturates	......34g

30 MINS   25 MINS

SERVES 4

INGREDIENTS

Basic Tomato Sauce (see page 14)

8 oz fresh green ribbon noodles

1 tbsp olive oil

salt

basil leaves, to garnish

CHICKEN SAUCE

4 tbsp unsalted butter

2¾ cups boned and skinned thinly sliced
   chicken breast

¾ cup blanched almonds

1¼ cups heavy cream

salt and pepper

basil leaves, to garnish

1 Make the tomato sauce and keep warm.

2 To make the chicken sauce, melt the butter in a pan over a medium heat and fry the chicken strips and almonds for 5–6 minutes, stirring frequently, until the chicken is cooked through.

3 Meanwhile, pour the cream into a small pan over a low heat. Bring it to the boil and boil for about 10 minutes, until reduced by almost half. Pour the

cream over the chicken and almonds, stir well, and season with salt and pepper to taste; set aside and keep warm.

4 Cook the pasta in a pan of boiling salted water, to which you have added the oil, for 8–10 minutes, or until tender. Drain, then return to the pan, cover, and keep warm.

5 Turn the pasta into a warmed serving dish and spoon the tomato sauce over it. Spoon the chicken and cream over the center, scatter the basil leaves over, and serve at once.

Sun-Dried Tomato Risotto

A Milanese risotto can be cooked in a variety of ways — but it always includes saffron. This version with sun-dried tomatoes has a tangy flavor.

NUTRITIONAL INFORMATION

Calories 558	Sugars 2g	
Protein 16g	Fat 19g	
Carbohydrate ...80g	Saturates 9g	

 10 MINS · 30 MINS

SERVES 4

INGREDIENTS

1 tbsp olive oil

2 tbsp butter

1 large onion, finely chopped

1¾ cups arborio (risotto) rice, washed

about 15 strands of saffron

²⁄₃ cup white wine

3¾ cups vegetable or chicken stock, hot

8 sun-dried tomatoes, cut into strips

¾ cup frozen peas, defrosted

1¾ oz prosciutto, shredded

½ cup grated Parmesan cheese

1 Heat the oil and butter in a large skillet. Add the onion and cook for 4–5 minutes, or until softened.

2 Add the rice and saffron to the skillet, stirring well to coat the rice in the oil, and cook for 1 minute.

3 Add the wine and stock slowly to the rice mixture in the pan, a ladleful at a time, stirring and making sure that all the liquid is absorbed before adding the next ladleful of liquid.

4 About half-way through adding the stock, stir in the sun-dried tomatoes.

5 When all of the wine and stock has been absorbed, the rice should be cooked. Test by tasting a grain — if it is still crunchy, add a little more water and continue cooking. It should take 15–20 minutes to cook.

6 Stir in the peas, prosciutto, and cheese. Cook for 2–3 minutes, stirring, until hot. Serve with extra Parmesan.

COOK'S TIP

The finished risotto should have moist, but separate grains. This is achieved by adding the hot stock a little at a time, only adding more when the last addition has been absorbed. Don't leave the risotto to cook by itself: it needs constant checking to see when more liquid is required.

Golden Chicken Risotto

Long-grain rice can be used instead of risotto rice, but it won't give you the traditional, creamy texture that is typical of Italian risottos.

NUTRITIONAL INFORMATION

Calories 701	Sugars 7g	
Protein 35g	Fat 26g	
Carbohydrate . . .88g	Saturates 8g	

10 MINS   30 MINS

SERVES 4

INGREDIENTS

2 tbsp sunflower oil

1 tbsp butter or margarine

1 leek, thinly sliced

1 large yellow bell pepper, diced

3 skinless, boneless chicken breast
   halves, diced

1¾ cups arborio (risotto) rice

a few strands of saffron

1½ quarts chicken stock

7-oz can corn kernels

½ cup toasted unsalted peanuts

½ cup grated Parmesan cheese

salt and pepper

1 Heat the sunflower oil and butter or margarine in a large saucepan. Fry the leek and bell pepper for 1 minute, then stir in the chicken and cook, stirring until golden brown.

2 Stir in the arborio (risotto) rice and cook for 2–3 minutes.

3 Stir in the saffron strands and salt and pepper to taste. Add the chicken stock, a little at a time, cover, and cook over a low heat, stirring occasionally, for about 20 minutes, or until the rice is tender and most of the liquid has been absorbed; do not let the risotto dry out — add more stock if necessary.

4 Stir in the corn kernels, peanuts, and Parmesan cheese, then season with salt and pepper to taste. Serve hot.

COOK'S TIP

Risottos can be frozen, before adding the Parmesan cheese, for up to 1 month, but remember to reheat this risotto thoroughly because it contains chicken.

Milanese Risotto

Italian rice is a round, short-grained variety with a nutty flavor, which is essential for a good risotto. Arborio is a good one to use.

NUTRITIONAL INFORMATION

Calories 631	Sugars 1g
Protein 16g	Fat 29g
Carbohydrate . . .77g	Saturates 17g

🍲 🍲 🍲

🥗 10 MINS   🕐 35 MINS

SERVES 4

I N G R E D I E N T S

2 good pinches of saffron threads

1 large onion, chopped finely

1–2 garlic cloves, crushed

6 tbsp butter

1¾ cups risotto (arborio) rice

⅔ cup dry white wine

1¼ quarts boiling stock (chicken,
     beef, or vegetable)

¾ cup grated Parmesan cheese

salt and pepper

1 Put the saffron in a small bowl, cover with 3–4 tablespoons of boiling water, and leave to soak while cooking the risotto.

2 Fry the onion and garlic in 4 tbsp of the butter until soft, but not colored. Add the rice and continue to cook for 2–3 minutes, or until all of the grains are coated in oil and just beginning to colour lightly.

3 Add the wine to the rice and simmer gently, stirring from time to time, until it is all absorbed.

4 Add the boiling stock a little at a time, about ⅔ cup, cooking until the liquid is fully absorbed before adding more, and stirring frequently.

5 When all the stock has been absorbed (this should take about 20 minutes), the rice should be tender, but not soft and soggy. Add the saffron liquid, Parmesan, remaining butter, and salt and pepper to taste. Leave to simmer for 2 minutes until piping hot and thoroughly mixed.

6 Cover the pan tightly and leave to stand for 5 minutes off the heat. Give a good stir and serve at once.

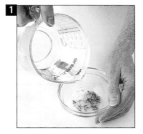

Green Risotto

A simple rice dish cooked with green vegetables and herbs. This recipe has been adapted for cooking in the microwave oven.

NUTRITIONAL INFORMATION

Calories 344	Sugars 4g	
Protein 13g	Fat 10g	
Carbohydrate ...54g	Saturates 4g	

15 MINS   20 MINS

SERVES 4

INGREDIENTS

1 onion, chopped

2 tbsp olive oil

generous 1 cup risotto rice

3 cups vegetable stock, hot

12 oz mixed green vegetables, such
   as asparagus, thin green beans,
   snow peas, zucchini, broccoli flowerets,
   and frozen peas

2 tbsp chopped fresh parsley

¼ cup thinly shaved fresh Parmesan
   cheese

salt and pepper

COOK'S TIP

For extra texture, stir in a
few toasted pine nuts or
coarsely chopped cashew
nuts at the end of
the cooking time.

1 Place the onion and oil in a large bowl. Cover and cook on HIGH power for 2 minutes.

2 Add the rice and stir until thoroughly coated in the oil. Pour in about ⅓ cup of the hot stock. Cook, uncovered, for 2 minutes, until the liquid has been absorbed. Pour in another ⅓ cup of the stock and cook, uncovered, on HIGH power for 2 minutes; repeat once more.

3 Chop or slice the vegetables into even-sized pieces. Stir into the rice with the remaining stock. Cover and cook on HIGH power for 8 minutes, stirring occasionally, until most of the liquid has been absorbed and the rice is just tender.

4 Stir in the parsley and season generously. Leave to stand, covered, for almost 5 minutes: the rice should be tender and creamy.

5 Scatter the Parmesan cheese over the risotto before serving.

Genoese Seafood Risotto

This is cooked in a different way from any of the other risottos. First, you cook the rice, then you prepare a sauce and mix the two together.

NUTRITIONAL INFORMATION

Calories	424	Sugars	.........0g
Protein	........23g	Fat	..........17g
Carbohydrate	...46g	Saturates	......10g

  10 MINS   25 MINS

SERVES 4

INGREDIENTS

1¼ cups fish or chicken stock, hot

1¾ cups risotto (arborio) rice, washed

3 tbsp butter

2 garlic cloves, chopped

9 oz mixed seafood, preferably raw,
    such as shrimp, squid, and mussels

2 tbsp chopped oregano, plus extra
    for garnishing

½ cup grated pecorino or Parmesan
    cheese

1 In a large saucepan, bring the stock to a boil. Add the rice and cook for about 12 minutes, stirring, or until the rice is tender. Drain thoroughly, reserving any excess liquid.

2 Melt the butter in a large skillet and add the garlic, stirring.

3 Add the raw mixed seafood to the skillet and cook for 5 minutes; if you are using cooked seafood, fry for 2–3 minutes.

4 Stir the oregano into the seafood mixture in the skillet.

5 Add the cooked rice to the pan and cook for 2–3 minutes, stirring, or until hot. Add the reserved stock if the mixture gets too sticky.

6 Add the pecorino or Parmesan cheese and mix well.

7 Transfer the risotto to warm serving dishes and serve immediately.

COOK'S TIP

The Genoese are excellent cooks, and they make particularly delicious fish dishes flavored with the local olive oil.

Chicken Risotto Milanese

This dish is known throughout the world, and it is perhaps the best known of all Italian risottos, although there are many variations.

NUTRITIONAL INFORMATION

Calories	857	Sugars	.........1g
Protein	........57g	Fat	..........38g
Carbohydrate	...72g	Saturates	......21g

 5 MINS   55 MINS

SERVES 4

INGREDIENTS

½ cup butter

6 cups thinly sliced chicken meat

1 large onion, chopped

2½ cups risotto rice

2½ cups chicken stock

⅔ cup white wine

1 tsp crumbled saffron threads

salt and pepper

½ cup grated Parmesan cheese,
  to serve

1 Melt 4 tbsp of butter in a deep skillet and fry the chicken and onion until golden brown.

2 Add the rice, stir well, and cook for 15 minutes.

3 Heat the stock until boiling and gradually add to the rice. Add the wine, saffron, and salt and pepper to taste and mix well. Simmer gently for 20 minutes, stirring occasionally, and adding more stock if the risotto becomes too dry.

4 Leave to stand for 2–3 minutes. Just before serving, add a little more stock and simmer for 10 minutes. Serve the risotto, sprinkled with the grated Parmesan cheese and the remaining butter.

Wild Mushroom Risotto

This creamy risotto is flavored with a mixture of wild and cultivated mushrooms and thyme.

NUTRITIONAL INFORMATION

Calories	364	Sugars	.........1g
Protein	........15g	Fat	..........16g
Carbohydrate	...44g	Saturates	.......6g

🍲 15 MINS   🕐 25 MINS

SERVES 4

I N G R E D I E N T S

2 tbsp olive oil

1 large onion, finely chopped

1 garlic clove, crushed

7 oz mixed wild and cultivated
  mushrooms, such as ceps, oyster, porcini,
  and button, wiped and sliced if large

9 oz risotto rice, washed

pinch of saffron threads

scant 3 cups hot vegetable stock

¾ cup white wine

3½ oz Parmesan cheese, grated,
  plus extra for serving

2 tbsp chopped thyme

salt and pepper

1 Heat the oil in a large skillet. Add the onions and garlic and sauté for 3–4 minutes, or until just softened.

2 Add the mushrooms to the pan and cook for 3 minutes, or until they are just beginning to brown.

3 Add the rice and saffron to the pan and stir to coat the rice in the oil.

4 Mix together the stock and the wine and add to the pan, a ladleful at a time. Stir the rice mixture and allow the liquid to be fully absorbed before adding more liquid, a ladleful at a time.

5 When all of the wine and stock is incorporated, the rice should be cooked. Test by tasting a grain – if it is still crunchy, add a little more water and continue cooking. It should take at least 15 minutes to cook.

6 Stir in the cheese and thyme, and season with pepper to taste.

7 Transfer the risotto to serving dishes and serve sprinkled with extra Parmesan cheese.

COOK'S TIP

Wild mushrooms each have their own distinctive flavors and make a change from button mushrooms. However, they can be quite expensive, so you can always use a mixture with crimini or button mushrooms instead.

Rice & Peas

If you can get fresh peas (and willing helpers to shell them), do use them: you will need 1¼ pounds. Add them to the pan with the stock.

NUTRITIONAL INFORMATION

Calories	409	Sugars	.........2g
Protein	........15g	Fat	..........23g
Carbohydrate	...38g	Saturates	......12g

🍲 10 MINS   🕐 50 MINS

SERVES 4

I N G R E D I E N T S

1 tbsp olive oil

4 tbsp butter

¼ cup chopped pancetta
   (Italian unsmoked bacon)

1 small onion, chopped

1½ quarts chicken stock, hot

1 cup arborio rice

3 tbsp chopped fresh parsley

1¼ cups frozen or canned petits pois

½ cup grated Parmesan cheese

pepper

1 Heat the oil and half of the butter in a saucepan.

2 Add the Italian unsmoked bacon and onion to the pan and fry for 5 minutes.

3 Add the stock (and fresh peas if using) to the pan and bring to a boil.

4 Stir in the rice and season to taste with pepper. Cook until the rice is tender, about 20–30 minutes, stirring occasionally.

5 Add the parsley and frozen or canned petits pois and cook for 8 minutes until the peas are thoroughly heated.

6 Stir in the remaining butter and the Parmesan. Serve immediately, with freshly ground black pepper.

Pesto Rice with Garlic Bread

Try this combination of two types of rice with the richness of pine nuts, basil, and freshly grated Parmesan cheese.

NUTRITIONAL INFORMATION

Calories 918   Sugars 2g
Protein . . . . .18g   Fat 64g
Carbohydrate . . .73g   Saturates 19g

🍞 20 MINS   🕐 40 MINS

SERVES 4

I N G R E D I E N T S

1½ cups mixed long-grain and
   wild rices

fresh basil sprigs, to garnish

tomato and orange salad, to serve

P E S T O   D R E S S I N G

½ cup fresh basil

1 cup pine nuts

2 garlic cloves, crushed

6 tbsp olive oil

½ cup freshly grated Parmesan cheese

salt and pepper

G A R L I C   B R E A D

2 small whole-wheat
   French bread sticks

6 tbsp butter or margarine, softened

2 garlic cloves, crushed

1 tsp Italian seasoning

1 Place the rice in a saucepan and cover with water. Bring to a boil and cook for 15–20 minutes; drain well and keep warm.

2 Meanwhile, make the pesto dressing. Remove the basil leaves from the stems and finely chop the leaves. Reserve ¼ cup of the pine nuts and finely chop the remainder. Mix with the chopped basil and dressing ingredients. Alternatively, put all the ingredients in a food processor or blender and blend for a few seconds until smooth; set aside.

3 To make the garlic bread, slice the bread at 1-inch intervals, taking care not to slice all the way through. Mix the butter or margarine with the garlic, herbs, and seasoning, then spread thickly between each slice.

4 Wrap the bread in foil and bake in a preheated oven at 400°F for 10–15 minutes.

5 To serve, toast the reserved pine nuts under a preheated medium broiler for 2–3 minutes until golden. Toss the pesto dressing into the hot rice and pile into a warmed serving dish. Sprinkle with toasted nuts and garnish with basil sprigs. Serve with the garlic bread and a tomato and orange salad.

Green Easter Pie

This traditional Easter risotto pie is from Piedmont in northern Italy.
Serve it warm or chilled in slices.

NUTRITIONAL INFORMATION

Calories 392	Sugars 3g
Protein 17g	Fat 17g
Carbohydrate ...41g	Saturates 5g

25 MINS   50 MINS

SERVES 4

INGREDIENTS

3 oz arugula

2 tbsp olive oil

1 onion, chopped

2 garlic cloves, chopped

1 cup arborio rice

scant 3 cups chicken or vegetable
  stock, hot

½ cup white wine

½ cup grated Parmesan cheese

¾ cup frozen peas, defrosted

2 tomatoes, diced

4 eggs, beaten

3 tbsp chopped fresh marjoram

1 cup bread crumbs

salt and pepper

1 Lightly grease and then line the
bottom of a 9-inch deep cake pan.

2 Using a sharp knife, roughly chop the
arugula.

3 Heat the oil in a large skillet. Add the
onion and garlic and cook for 4–5
minutes, or until softened.

4 Add the rice to the mixture in the
skillet. Mix well to combine, then

begin adding the stock a ladleful at a
time. Wait until all of the stock has been
absorbed before adding another ladleful
of liquid.

5 Continue to cook the mixture, adding
the wine, until the rice is tender. This
will take at least 15 minutes.

6 Stir in the Parmesan cheese, peas,
arugula, tomatoes, eggs, and
2 tablespoons of the marjoram. Season to
taste with salt and pepper.

7 Spoon the risotto into the pan and
level the surface by pressing down
with the back of a wooden spoon.

8 Top with the bread crumbs and the
remaining marjoram.

9 Bake in a preheated oven at 350°F for
30 minutes, or until set. Cut into
slices and serve immediately.

Chili Polenta Fries

Polenta is used in Italy as potatoes and rice are in other countries. It has little flavor, but it is transformed combined with butter, garlic, and herbs.

NUTRITIONAL INFORMATION

Calories 365	Sugars 1g
Protein 8g	Fat 12g
Carbohydrate ...54g	Saturates 5g

5 MINS 20 MINS

SERVES 4

INGREDIENTS

3 cups instant polenta

2 tsp ground red chilies

1 tbsp olive oil

⅔ cup sour cream

1 tbsp chopped fresh parsley

salt and pepper

1 Place 1½ quarts of water in a saucepan and bring to a boil. Add 2 teaspoons of salt and then add the polenta in a steady stream, stirring constantly.

2 Reduce the heat slightly and continue stirring for about 5 minutes: it is essential to stir the polenta, otherwise it will stick and burn. The polenta should have a thick consistency at this point and should be stiff enough to hold the spoon upright in the pan.

3 Add the ground red chilies to the polenta mixture and stir well. Season to taste with a little salt and pepper.

4 Spread the polenta out on a board or cookie sheet to about 1½ inch thick; leave to cool and set.

5 Cut the cooled polenta mixture into thin wedges.

6 Heat 1 tablespoon of oil in a skillet. Add the polenta wedges and fry for 3–4 minutes on each side or until golden and crispy. Alternatively, brush with melted butter and broil for 6–7 minutes until golden. Drain the cooked polenta on paper towels.

7 Mix the sour cream with parsley and place in a bowl.

8 Serve the polenta with the sour cream and parsley dip.

COOK'S TIP

Easy-cook instant polenta is sold in supermarkets and is quick to make. It will keep for up to 1 week in the refrigerator. The polenta can also be baked in a preheated oven at 400°F for 20 minutes.

Polenta Kabobs

Here, skewers of thyme-flavored polenta, wrapped in prosciutto, are broiled or barbecued.

NUTRITIONAL INFORMATION

Calories 212   Sugars 0g
Protein . . . . .8g   Fat 6g
Carbohydrate . . .32g   Saturates 1g

 20 MINS   45 MINS

SERVES 4

INGREDIENTS

1¼ cups instant polenta

3¼ cups water

2 tbsp fresh thyme, stems removed

8 slices prosciutto, 2¾ oz

1 tbsp olive oil

salt and pepper

fresh green salad, to serve

1 Cook the polenta in the water, stirring occasionally, for 30–35 minutes. Alternatively, follow the directions on the package.

2 Add the fresh thyme to the polenta mixture and season to taste with salt and pepper.

COOK'S TIP

Try flavoring the polenta with chopped oregano, basil, or marjoram instead of the thyme, if you prefer. Use 3 tablespoons chopped herbs to every 3 cups instant polenta.

3 Spread out the polenta, about 1 inch thick, on to a board; set aside to cool.

4 Using a sharp knife, cut the cooled polenta into 1-inch cubes.

5 Cut the prosciutto slices into 2 pieces lengthways. Wrap the prosciutto around the polenta cubes.

6 Thread the prosciutto wrapped polenta cubes onto skewers.

7 Brush the kabobs with a little oil and cook under a preheated broiler, turning frequently, for 7–8 minutes. Alternatively, grill the kabobs until golden. Transfer to serving plates and serve with a salad.

Gnocchi with Herb Sauce

These little potato dumplings are a traditional Italian appetizer, but, served with a salad and bread, they make a substantial main course.

NUTRITIONAL INFORMATION

Calories	.619	Sugars	.3g
Protein	.11g	Fat	.30g
Carbohydrate	.81g	Saturates	.9g

30 MINS   30 MINS

SERVES 6

INGREDIENTS

2 lb 4 oz floury potatoes, cut into
 ½-inch pieces

4 tbsp butter or margarine

1 egg, beaten

2½ cups all-purpose flour

salt

SAUCE

½ cup olive oil

2 garlic cloves, very finely chopped

1 tbsp chopped fresh oregano

1 tbsp chopped fresh basil

salt and pepper

TO SERVE

freshly grated Parmesan cheese (optional)

mixed salad (greens)

warm ciabatta

1 Cook the potatoes in a saucepan of boiling salted water for about 10 minutes or until tender; drain well.

2 Press the hot potatoes through a strainer into a large bowl. Add 1 teaspoon of salt, the butter or margarine, egg, and 1¼ cups of the flour; mix well to bind together.

3 Turn onto a lightly floured surface and knead, gradually adding the remaining flour, until a smooth, soft, slightly sticky dough is formed.

4 Flour your hands and roll the dough into ¾ inch thick rolls; cut into ½-inch pieces. Press the top of each piece with the floured prongs of a fork and spread out on a floured dish cloth.

5 Bring a large saucepan of salted water to a simmer. Add the gnocchi and cook in batches for 2–3 minutes, or until they rise to the surface.

6 Remove the gnocchi with a draining spoon and put in a warmed, greased serving dish; cover and keep warm.

7 To make the sauce, put the oil, garlic, and seasoning in a pan and cook, stirring, for 3–4 minutes until the garlic is golden. Remove from the heat and stir in the herbs. Pour over the gnocchi and serve, sprinkled with Parmesan, and accompanied by salad and warm ciabatta.

Spinach & Ricotta Gnocchi

Try not to handle the dough too much when making gnocchi, because this will make the gnocchi heavy.

NUTRITIONAL INFORMATION

Calories 712	Sugars 15g	
Protein 29g	Fat 59g	
Carbohydrate ...16g	Saturates 33g	

 20 MINS   15 MINS

SERVES 4

I N G R E D I E N T S

2 lb 4 oz spinach

1½ cups ricotta cheese

1 cup grated pecorino cheese

3 eggs, beaten

¼ tsp freshly grated nutmeg

all-purpose flour, to mix

½ cup unsalted butter

¼ cup pine nuts

⅓ cup raisins

salt and pepper

1 Wash and drain the spinach well and cook in a covered saucepan without any extra liquid until softened, about 8 minutes. Place the spinach in a colander and press well to remove as much juice as possible. Either rub the spinach through a strainer or purée in a blender.

2 Combine the spinach purée with the ricotta, half of the pecorino, the eggs, nutmeg, and seasoning to taste, mixing lightly but thoroughly. Work in enough flour, lightly and quickly, to make the mixture easy to handle.

3 Shape the dough quickly into small lozenge shapes and dust lightly with a little flour.

4 Add a dash of oil to a large saucepan of salted water and bring to a boil. Add the gnocchi carefully and boil for about 2 minutes, or until they float to the surface. Using a draining spoon, transfer the gnocchi to a buttered baking dish; keep warm.

5 Melt the butter in a skillet. Add the pine nuts and raisins and fry until the nuts start to brown slightly; do not allow the butter to burn. Pour the mixture over the gnocchi and serve sprinkled with the remaining grated pecorino cheese.

Potato & Spinach Gnocchi

These small potato dumplings are flavored with spinach, cooked in boiling water, and served with a simple tomato sauce.

NUTRITIONAL INFORMATION

Calories 315	Sugars 7g
Protein 8g	Fat 8g
Carbohydrate . . .56g	Saturates 1g

20 MINS 30 MINS

SERVES 4

INGREDIENTS

2 cups diced floury potatoes

6 oz spinach

1 egg yolk

1 tsp olive oil

1 cup all-purpose flour

salt and pepper

spinach leaves, to garnish

SAUCE

1 tbsp olive oil

2 shallots, chopped

1 garlic clove, crushed

1¼ cups strained puréed tomatoes

2 tsp soft brown sugar

1 Cook the diced potatoes in a saucepan of boiling water for 10 minutes, or until cooked through. Drain and mash the potatoes.

2 Meanwhile, in a separate pan, blanch the spinach in a little boiling water for 1-2 minutes. Drain the spinach and shred the leaves.

3 Transfer the mashed potato to a lightly floured chopping board and make a well in the center. Add the egg yolk, olive oil, spinach, and a little of the flour and quickly mix the ingredients into the potato, adding more flour as you go, until you have a firm dough. Divide the mixture into very small dumplings.

4 Cook the gnocchi, in batches, in a saucepan of boiling salted water for about 5 minutes, or until they rise to the surface.

5 Meanwhile, make the sauce. Put the oil, shallots, garlic, tomatoes, and sugar into a saucepan and cook over a low heat for 10-15 minutes, or until the sauce has thickened.

6 Drain the gnocchi using a draining spoon and transfer to warm serving dishes. Spoon the sauce over the gnocchi and garnish with the fresh spinach leaves.

VARIATION

Add chopped fresh herbs and cheese to the gnocchi dough instead of the spinach, if you prefer.

Baked Semolina Gnocchi

Semolina has a similar texture to polenta, but is slightly grainier. These gnocchi, which are flavoured with cheese and thyme, are easy to make.

NUTRITIONAL INFORMATION

Calories 259	Sugars 0g	
Protein 9g	Fat 16g	
Carbohydrate ...20g	Saturates 10g	

15 MINS   30 MINS

SERVES 4

INGREDIENTS

1¾ cups vegetable stock

scant 1 cup semolina

1 tbsp thyme, stems removed

1 egg, beaten

½ cup grated Parmesan cheese

3 tbsp butter

2 garlic cloves, crushed

salt and pepper

1 Place the stock in a large saucepan and bring to a boil. Add the semolina in a steady trickle, stirring continuously. Keep stirring for 3–4 minutes until the mixture is thick enough to hold a spoon upright; set aside and leave to cool slightly.

VARIATION

Try adding ½ tablespoon of sun-dried tomato paste or ⅔ cup finely chopped mushrooms, fried in butter, to the semolina mixture in step 2. Follow the same cooking method.

2 Add the thyme, egg, and half of the cheese to the semolina mixture, and season to taste with salt and pepper.

3 Spread the semolina mixture on a board to about ½ inch thick; set aside to cool and set.

4 When the semolina is cold, cut it into 1-inch squares, reserving any offcuts.

5 Grease a baking dish. Place the reserved offcuts in the bottom. Arrange the semolina squares on top and sprinkle with the remaining cheese.

6 Melt the butter in a pan, add the garlic and season with pepper to taste. Pour the butter mixture over the gnocchi. Bake in a preheated oven, at 425°F for 15–20 minutes until puffed up and golden. Serve hot.

Potato Noodles

Potatoes are used to make the "pasta" dough which is cut into thin noodles and boiled.

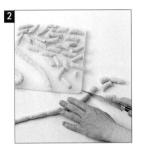

NUTRITIONAL INFORMATION

Calories 810	Sugars 5g	
Protein 21g	Fat 47g	
Carbohydrate . . .81g	Saturates 26g	

 30 MINS   25 MINS

SERVES 4

I N G R E D I E N T S

1 lb floury potatoes, diced

1½ cups plus 2 tbsp all-purpose flour

1 egg, beaten

1 tbsp milk

salt and pepper

parsley sprig, to garnish

S A U C E

1 tbsp vegetable oil

1 onion, chopped

1 garlic clove, crushed

1½ cups sliced open-cap
    mushrooms

3 smoked bacon slices, chopped

½ cup grated Parmesan cheese

1¼ cups heavy cream

2 tbsp chopped fresh parsley

1 Cook the diced potatoes in a saucepan of boiling water for 10 minutes, or until cooked through. Drain well. Mash the potatoes until smooth, then beat in the flour, egg, and milk. Season with salt and pepper to taste and bring together to form a stiff paste.

2 On a lightly floured surface, roll out the paste to form a thin rope shape.

Cut the rope into 1-inch pieces. Bring a large pan of salted water to a boil. Drop in the dough pieces and cook for 3-4 minutes: they will rise to the surface when cooked.

3 To make the sauce, heat the oil in a pan and sauté the onion and garlic for 2 minutes. Add the mushrooms and bacon and cook for 5 minutes. Stir in the cheese, cream and parsley, and season.

4 Drain the noodles and transfer to a warm pasta bowl. Spoon the sauce over the top and toss to mix. Garnish with a parsley sprig and serve.

COOK'S TIP

Make the dough in advance, then wrap and store the noodles in the refrigerator for up to 24 hours.

Desserts

For many people the favorite part of any meal is the dessert. The recipes that have been selected for this chapter will be a treat for all palates. Whether you are a chocolate-lover or are even on a diet, you will find a recipe to tempt you in this chapter. Choose from a light summer delicacy or a hearty hot winter treat, you will find desserts to indulge in all year around. If you are looking for a chilled sweet, choose the rich Vanilla Ice Cream, or if a warm dessert takes your fancy, Crispy-Topped Fruit Bake will do the trick.

Carrot & Ginger Cake

This melt-in-the-mouth version of a favorite cake has a fraction of the fat of the traditional cake.

NUTRITIONAL INFORMATION

Calories 249   Sugars 28g
Protein . . . . .7g   Fat 6g
Carbohydrate . . .46g   Saturates 1g

 15 MINS   1¼ HOURS

SERVES 10

I N G R E D I E N T S

1½ cups plus 2 tbsp all-purpose flour

1 tsp baking powder

1 tsp baking soda

2 tsp ground ginger

½ tsp salt

¾ cup packed light brown sugar

1½ cups grated carrots

2 pieces preserved ginger in syrup, drained and chopped

2 tbsp grated gingerroot

⅓ cup seedless raisins

2 medium eggs, beaten

3 tbsp corn oil

juice of 1 medium orange

F R O S T I N G

1 cup low-fat soft cheese

4 tbsp confectioners' sugar

1 tsp vanilla extract

T O   D E C O R A T E

grated carrot

preserved ginger

ground ginger

1 Preheat the oven to 350°F. Grease and line an 8-inch round deep cake pan with waxed paper.

2 Sift the flour, baking powder, baking soda, ground ginger, and salt into a bowl. Stir in the sugar, carrots, ginger, gingerroot, and raisins. Beat together the eggs, oil, and orange juice, then pour into the bowl. Mix the ingredients together well.

3 Spoon the batter into the pan and bake in the oven for 1–1¼ hours until firm to the touch, or until a skewer

inserted into the center of the cake comes out clean.

4 To make the frosting, place the soft cheese in a bowl and beat to soften. Sift in the confectioners' sugar and add the vanilla extract; mix well.

5 Remove the cake from the pan and leave to cool. Smooth the frosting over the top, decorate, and serve.

Crispy-Topped Fruit Bake

The sugar crystals give a lovely crunchy tasted to this easy-to-make dessert.

NUTRITIONAL INFORMATION

Calories 227	Sugars 30g
Protein 5g	Fat 1g
Carbohydrate ...53g	Saturates 0.2g

15 MINS   1 HOUR

SERVES 10

I N G R E D I E N T S

12 oz cooking apples

3 tbsp lemon juice

2½ cups plus 2 tbsp unsifted self-rising whole-wheat flour

½ tsp baking powder

1 tsp ground cinnamon, plus extra for dusting

6 oz blackberries, thawed if frozen, plus extra to decorate

¾ cup packed light brown sugar

1 large egg, beaten

¾ cup low-fat natural fromage blanc

½ cup lightly crushed white or brown sugar cubes, or sugar crystals

sliced dessert apple, to decorate

VARIATION

Replace the blackberries with blueberries. Use the canned or frozen variety if fresh blueberries are unavailable.

1 Preheat the oven to 375°F. Grease and line a 9- x 5-inch bread pan. Core, peel, and finely dice the apples. Place them in a saucepan with the lemon juice and bring to a boil. Cover and simmer for 10 minutes until soft and pulpy; beat well and set aside to cool.

2 Sift the flour, baking powder, and 1 tsp cinnamon into a bowl, adding any husks that remain in the strainer. Stir in 4 oz blackberries and the brown sugar.

3 Make a well in the center of the ingredients and add the egg, fromage blanc and cooled apple purée; mix well to incorporate thoroughly. Spoon the batter into the prepared pan and smooth the top.

4 Sprinkle with the remaining blackberries, pressing them down into the cake batter, and top with the crushed sugar cubes. Bake for 40–45 minutes; leave to cool in the pan on a wire rack.

5 Remove the cake from the pan and peel away the lining paper. Serve dusted with cinnamon and decorated with extra blackberries and apple slices.

Banana & Lime Cake

A substantial cake that is ideal for an afternoon snack. The bananas help to keep it moist, and the lime frosting adds extra zing and zest.

NUTRITIONAL INFORMATION

Calories ....235 Sugars 31g
Protein ....5g Fat 1g
Carbohydrate ...55g Saturates 0.3g

35 MINS   45 MINS

SERVES 10

INGREDIENTS

1½ cups all-purpose flour

1 tsp salt

1½ tsp baking powder

¾ cup packed light brown sugar

1 tsp grated lime peel

1 large egg, beaten

1 banana, mashed with 1 tbsp
   lime juice

⅔ cup low-fat plain fromage blanc

⅔ cup golden raisins

banana chips, to decorate

finely grated lime peel, to decorate

TOPPING

1 cup confectioners' sugar

1–2 tsp lime juice

½ tsp finely grated lime peel

1 Preheat the oven to 350°F. Grease and line a deep 7-inch round cake pan with waxed paper.

2 Sift the flour, salt, and baking powder into a mixing bowl and stir in the brown sugar and lime peel.

3 Make a well in the center of the dry ingredients and add the egg, banana, fromage blanc, and golden raisins; mix well until thoroughly incorporated.

4 Spoon the batter into the pan and smooth the surface. Bake for 40–45 minutes until firm to the touch, or until a skewer inserted in the center comes out clean. Leave to cool for 10 minutes, then turn out onto a wire rack.

5 To make the topping, sift the confectioners' sugar into a small bowl and stir in the lime juice to form a soft, but not too runny, frosting. Stir in the grated lime peel. Drizzle the frosting over the cake, letting it run down the sides.

6 Decorate the cake with banana chips and lime peel. Let the cake stand for 15 minutes so the icing sets.

VARIATION

For a delicious alternative, replace the lime peel and juice with orange, and the golden raisins with chopped apricots.

Potato & Nutmeg Biscuits

Making these scones with mashed potato gives them a slightly different texture from traditional biscuits, but they are just as delicious.

NUTRITIONAL INFORMATION

Calories 178	Sugars 8g	
Protein 4g	Fat 5g	
Carbohydrate ...30g	Saturates 3g	

15 MINS   30 MINS

MAKES 6

I N G R E D I E N T S

1½ cups diced floury potatoes

1 cup all-purpose flour

1½ tsp baking powder

½ tsp grated nutmeg

⅓ cup golden raisins

1 egg, beaten

¼ cup heavy cream

2 tsp light brown sugar

1 Line a cookie sheet with waxed paper.

2 Cook the diced potatoes in a saucepan of boiling water for 10 minutes, or until soft. Drain thoroughly and mash the potatoes.

3 Transfer the mashed potatoes to a large mixing bowl and stir in the flour, baking powder, and grated nutmeg, mixing well to combine.

4 Stir in the golden raisins, beaten egg, and cream and then beat the mixture thoroughly with a spoon until completely smooth.

5 Shape the mixture into 8 biscuits ¾ inch thick and put on the cookie sheet.

6 Cook in a preheated oven at 400°F for about 15 minutes, or until the biscuits have risen and are golden. Sprinkle with sugar and serve warm and spread with butter.

COOK'S TIP

For extra convenience, make a batch of biscuits in advance and open-freeze them. Thaw thoroughly and warm in a medium oven when ready to serve.

Panforte di Siena

This famous Tuscan honey and nut cake is a Christmas specialty. In Italy it is sold in pretty boxes, and served in very thin slices.

NUTRITIONAL INFORMATION

Calories	257	Sugars	........29g
Protein	.........5g	Fat	..........13g
Carbohydrate	...33g	Saturates	.......1g

🍞 🍞 🍞

10 MINS   1¼ HOURS

SERVES 12

INGREDIENTS

1 cup split whole blanched almonds

¾ cup hazelnuts

½ cup cut mixed peel

⅓ cup no-soak dried apricots

⅓ cup candied or crystallized pineapple

grated peel of 1 large orange

½ cup all-purpose flour

2 tbsp unsweetened cocoa powder

2 tsp ground cinnamon

½ cup sugar

½ cup honey

confectioners' sugar for dredging

1 Toast the almonds under the broiler until lightly browned; place in a bowl.

2 Toast the hazelnuts until the skins split. Place on a dry dish cloth and rub off the skins. Roughly chop the hazelnuts and add to the almonds with the mixed peel.

3 Chop the apricots and pineapple fairly finely and add to the nuts with the orange peel and stir well.

4 Sift the flour with the cocoa and cinnamon. Add to the nut mixture and mix.

5 Line a round 8-inch cake pan or deep loose-bottomed tart pan with waxed paper.

6 Put the sugar and honey into a saucepan and heat until the sugar dissolves, then boil gently for about 5 minutes, or until the mixture thickens and begins to turn a deeper shade of brown. Quickly add to the nut mixture and stir. Turn into the prepared pan and smooth the top using the back of a damp spoon.

7 Bake in a preheated oven at 300°F for 1 hour. Remove from the oven and leave in the pan until cold. Take out of the pan and carefully peel off the paper. Before serving, dredge the cake heavily with sifted confectioners' sugar. Serve in very thin slices.

Tuscan Puddings

These baked mini-ricotta puddings are delicious served warm or chilled and will keep in the refrigerator for three to four days.

NUTRITIONAL INFORMATION

Calories	293	Sugars	........28g
Protein	.........9g	Fat	..........17g
Carbohydrate	...28g	Saturates	.......9g

  20 MINS   15 MINS

SERVES 4

INGREDIENTS

1 tbsp butter

½ cup mixed dried fruit

1 cup plus 2 tbsp ricotta cheese

3 egg yolks

¼ cup superfine sugar

1 tsp ground cinnamon

finely grated peel of 1 orange,
   plus extra to decorate

crème fraîche or sour cream, to serve

1 Lightly grease 4 mini pudding basins or ramekin dishes with the butter.

2 Put the dried fruit in a bowl and cover with warm water; leave to soak for 10 minutes.

COOK'S TIP

Crème fraîche or sour cream has a slightly sour, nutty taste and is very thick. It is suitable for cooking, but has the same fat content as heavy cream. It can be made by stirring cultured buttermilk into heavy cream and refrigerating overnight.

3 Beat the ricotta cheese with the egg yolks in a bowl. Stir in the superfine sugar, cinnamon, and orange peel and mix to combine.

4 Drain the dried fruit in a strainer set over a bowl. Mix the drained fruit with the ricotta cheese batter.

5 Spoon the mixture into the basins or ramekin dishes.

6 Bake in a preheated oven at 350°F for 15 minutes: the tops should be firm to the touch but not brown.

7 Decorate the puddings with grated orange peel. Serve warm or chilled with a dollop of crème fraîche or sour cream, if liked.

Pear & Ginger Cake

This deliciously buttery pear and ginger cake is delicious with a cup of coffee or tea, or you can serve it with ice cream for a delicious dessert.

NUTRITIONAL INFORMATION

Calories 531   Sugars 41g
Protein . . . . .6g   Fat 30g
Carbohydrate . . .62g   Saturates 19g

 15 MINS   40 MINS

SERVES 6

INGREDIENTS

¾ cup plus 2 tbsp unsalted butter, softened

¾ cup plus 2 tbsp superfine sugar

1½ cups plus 2 tbsp unsifted self-rising flour

3 tsp ground ginger

3 eggs, beaten

1 lb eating pears, peeled, cored, and thinly sliced

1 tbsp moist brown sugar

1 Lightly grease and line the base of a deep 8 inch cake pan.

2 Using a whisk, combine 6 oz of the butter with the sugar, flour, ginger, and eggs and mix to make a smooth batter.

3 Spoon the cake batter into the prepared pan, leveling out the surface.

4 Arrange the pear slices over the cake batter. Sprinkle with the brown sugar and dot with the remaining butter.

5 Bake in a preheated oven at 350°F for 35–40 minutes, or until the cake is golden and feels springy to the touch.

6 Serve the pear and ginger cake warm, with ice cream or cream, if you wish.

COOK'S TIP

Moist brown sugar is often known as Barbados sugar. It is a darker form of light brown sugar.

Zabaglione

This traditional Italian dish is really a light but rich egg mousse flavored with Marsala wine.

NUTRITIONAL INFORMATION

Calories	158	Sugars	........29g
Protein	.........1g	Fat	...........1g
Carbohydrate	...29g	Saturates	.....0.2g

 5 MINS   🕐 15 MINS

SERVES 4

INGREDIENTS

5 egg yolks

½ cup superfine sugar

⅔ cup Marsala wine or sweet sherry

amaretti cookies, to serve (optional)

1 Place the egg yolks in a large mixing bowl.

2 Add the superfine sugar to the egg yolks and whisk until the mixture is thick and very pale and has doubled in volume.

3 Place the bowl containing the egg yolk and sugar mixture over a saucepan of gently simmering water.

4 Add the Marsala wine or sherry to the egg yolk and sugar mixture and continue whisking until the foam mixture becomes warm: this process may take as long as 10 minutes.

5 Pour the mixture, which should be frothy and light, into 4 glasses.

6 Serve the zabaglione warm with fresh fruit or amaretti cookies, if you wish.

Mascarpone Cheesecake

The mascarpone cheese gives this baked cheesecake a wonderfully tangy flavor. Ricotta cheese can be used as an alternative.

NUTRITIONAL INFORMATION

Calories 327   Sugars 25g
Protein ....9g   Fat 18g
Carbohydrate ...33g   Saturates 11g

15 MINS   50 MINS

SERVES 8

INGREDIENTS

½ tbsp unsalted butter

2 tbsp preserved ginger, chopped

2¼ cups mascarpone cheese

finely grated peel and juice of 2 lemons

½ cup superfine sugar

2 large eggs, separated

fruit coulis (see Cook's Tip), to serve

1 Grease and line the bottom of a 10 inch spring-form cake pan or loose-bottomed pan.

2 Melt the butter in a pan and stir in the crushed cookies and chopped ginger. Use the mixture to line the pan, pressing the mixture ½ inch up the sides.

COOK'S TIP

Fruit coulis can be made by cooking 14 oz fruit, such as blueberries, for 5 minutes with 2 tablespoons of water. Sieve the mixture, then stir in 1 tablespoon (or more to taste) of sifted confectioners' sugar. Leave to cool before serving.

3 Beat together the cheese, lemon peel and juice, sugar, and egg yolks until quite smooth.

4 Whisk the egg whites until they are stiff and fold into the cheese and lemon mixture.

5 Pour the batter into the pan and bake in a preheated oven, at 350°F for 35–45 minutes until just set. Don't worry

if it cracks or sinks – this is quite normal.

6 Leave the cheesecake in the pan to cool. Serve with fruit coulis (see Cook's Tip).

Chocolate Zabaglione

As this recipe only uses a little chocolate, choose one with a minimum of 70 percent cocoa solids for a good flavor.

NUTRITIONAL INFORMATION

Calories	224	Sugars	........23g
Protein	.........4g	Fat	..........10g
Carbohydrate	...23g	Saturates	.......4g

10 MINS   5 MINS

SERVES 4

I N G R E D I E N T S

4 egg yolks

4 tbsp superfine sugar

1¾ oz semisweet chocolate

1 cup Marsala wine

cocoa powder, to dust

1 In a large glass mixing bowl, whisk together the egg yolks and superfine sugar until you have a very pale mixture, using an electric mixer.

2 Grate the chocolate finely and fold it into the egg mixture.

3 Fold the Marsala wine into the chocolate mixture.

4 Place the mixing bowl over a saucepan of gently simmering water

and set the beaters on the lowest speed or swop to a balloon whisk. Cook gently, whisking continuously, until the batter thickens; take care not to overcook or the batter will curdle.

5 Spoon the hot batter into warmed individual glass dishes or coffecups (as here) and dust with cocoa powder. Serve the zabaglione as soon as possible so it is warm, light, and fluffy.

COOK'S TIP

Make the dessert just before serving because it will separate if left to stand. If it begins to separate, remove it from the heat immediately and place it in a bowl of cold water to stop the cooking. Whisk furiously until the mixture comes together.

Honey & Nut Nests

Pistachio nuts and honey are combined with crisp cooked angel-hair pasta in this unusual dessert.

NUTRITIONAL INFORMATION

Calories 802	Sugars 53g	
Protein 13g	Fat 48g	
Carbohydrate ...85g	Saturates 16g	

 10 MINS   1 HOUR

SERVES 4

INGREDIENTS

8 oz angel-hair pasta

½ cup butter

1½ cups chopped shelled pistachio nuts

½ cup sugar

⅓ cup honey

⅔ cup water

2 tsp lemon juice

salt

thick. plain yogurt, to serve

1 Bring a large saucepan of lightly salted water to a boil. Add the angel hair pasta and cook for 8–10 minutes or until tender, but still firm to the bite; drain the pasta and return to the pan. Add the butter and toss to coat the pasta thoroughly. Set aside to cool.

2 Arrange 4 small poaching rings on a cookie sheet. Divide the angel hair pasta into 8 equal quantities and spoon 4 of them into the rings. Press down lightly. Top the pasta with half of the nuts, then add the remaining pasta.

3 Bake in a preheated oven at 350°F for 45 minutes, or until golden brown.

4 Meanwhile, put the sugar, honey, and water in a saucepan and bring to a boil over a low heat, stirring constantly until the sugar has dissolved completely. Simmer for 10 minutes, add the lemon juice, and simmer for 5 minutes.

5 Using a spatula, carefully transfer the angel-hair nests to a serving dish. Pour the honey syrup over, sprinkle over the remaining nuts, and set aside to cool completely before serving. Serve the yogurt separately.

COOK'S TIP

Angel-hair pasta is also known as *capelli d'angelo*. Long and very fine, it is usually sold in small bunches that already resemble nests.

Quick Tiramisu

This quick version of one of the most popular Italian desserts is ready in minutes.

 15 MINS   0 MINS

SERVES 4

I N G R E D I E N T S

1 cup mascarpone or full-fat soft cheese

1 egg, separated

2 tbsp plain yogurt

2 tbsp superfine sugar

2 tbsp dark rum

2 tbsp strong black coffee

8 lady-fingers

2 tbsp grated semisweet chocolate

1 Put the cheese in a large bowl. Add the egg yolk and yogurt and beat until smooth.

2 Whisk the egg white until stiff, but not dry. Whisk in the sugar and carefully fold into the cheese mixture.

3 Spoon half of the mixture into 4 sundae glasses.

4 Mix together the rum and coffee in a shallow dish. Dip the lady-fingers into the rum mixture, break them in half, or into smaller pieces if necessary, and divide among the glasses.

5 Stir any remaining coffee mixture into the remaining cheese and spoon over the top.

6 Sprinkle with grated chocolate. Serve immediately or chill until required.

COOK'S TIP

Mascarpone is an Italian soft cream cheese made from cow's milk. It has a rich, silky smooth texture and a deliciously creamy flavor. It can be eaten with fresh fruits or flavored with coffee or chocolate.

Raspberry Fusilli

This is the ultimate in self-indulgence – a truly delicious dessert that tastes every bit as good as it looks.

NUTRITIONAL INFORMATION

Calories 235	Sugars 20g
Protein 7g	Fat 7g
Carbohydrate . . .36g	Saturates 1g

 5 MINS   20 MINS

SERVES 4

INGREDIENTS

½ cup dried fusilli

1 quart raspberries

2 tbsp superfine sugar

1 tbsp lemon juice

4 tbsp slivered almonds

3 tbsp raspberry liqueur

1 Bring a large saucepan of lightly salted water to a boil. Add the fusilli and cook for 8–10 minutes until tender, but still firm to the bite. Drain the fusilli thoroughly, return to the pan, and set aside to cool.

2 Using a spoon, firmly press ⅓ of the raspberries through a strainer set over a large mixing bowl to form a smooth purée.

3 Put the raspberry purée and sugar in a small saucepan and simmer over a low heat, stirring occasionally, for 5 minutes.

4 Stir in the lemon juice and set the sauce aside until required.

5 Add the remaining raspberries to the fusilli in the pan and mix together well. Transfer the raspberry and fusilli mixture to a serving dish.

6 Spread the almonds out on a cookie sheet and toast under the broiler until golden brown. Remove and set aside to cool slightly.

7 Stir the raspberry liqueur into the reserved raspberry sauce and mix together well until very smooth. Pour the raspberry sauce over the fusilli, sprinkle the toasted almonds over and serve.

VARIATION

You can use any sweet, ripe berry for making this dessert. Strawberries and blackberries are especially suitable, combined with the correspondingly flavored liqueur. Alternatively, you could use a different berry mixed with the fusilli, but still pour raspberry sauce over.

Peaches & Mascarpone

If you prepare these in advance, all you have to do is pop the peaches on the barbecue when you are ready to serve them.

NUTRITIONAL INFORMATION

Calories 301	Sugars 24g
Protein 6g	Fat 20g
Carbohydrate . . .24g	Saturates 9g

 10 MINS 10 MINS

SERVES 4

I N G R E D I E N T S

4 peaches

¾ cup mascarpone cheese

⅓ cup pecan or walnuts, chopped

1 tsp sunflower oil

4 tbsp maple syrup

1 Cut the peaches in half and remove the pits. If you are preparing this recipe in advance, press the peach halves together again and wrap in plastic wrap until required.

2 Mix the mascarpone and pecan or walnuts together in a small bowl until well combined: leave to chill in the refrigerator until required.

VARIATION

Use nectarines instead of peaches for this recipe. Remember to choose ripe but firm fruit that won't become soft and mushy when it is barbecued. Prepare the nectarines in the same way as the peaches and barbecue for 5–10 minutes.

3 To serve, brush the peaches with a little oil and place on a rack set over medium hot coals. Barbecue for 5–10 minutes, turning once, until hot.

4 Transfer the peaches to a serving dish and top with the mascarpone mixture.

5 Drizzle the maple syrup over the peaches and mascarpone filling and serve at once.

Vanilla Ice Cream

This homemade version of real vanilla ice cream is absolutely delicious and easy to make. A tutti-frutti variation is also provided.

NUTRITIONAL INFORMATION

Calories 626	Sugars 33g
Protein 7g	Fat 53g
Carbohydrate ...33g	Saturates 31g

5 MINS   15 MINS

SERVES 6

INGREDIENTS

2½ cups heavy cream

1 vanilla bean

pared peel of 1 lemon

4 eggs, beaten

2 egg yolks

¾ cup plus 2 tbsp superfine sugar

1 Place the cream in a heavy-bottomed saucepan and heat gently, whisking.

2 Add the vanilla bean, lemon rind, eggs, and egg yolks to the pan and heat until the mixture reaches just below boiling point.

3 Reduce the heat and cook for 8–10 minutes, whisking the mixture continuously, until thickened.

4 Stir the sugar into the cream mixture, set aside, and leave to cool.

5 Strain the cream mixture through a strainer.

6 Slit open the vanilla bean, scoop out the tiny black seeds, and stir them into the cream.

7 Pour the mixture into a shallow freezing container with a lid and freeze overnight until set. Serve the ice cream when required.

VARIATION

To make tutti frutti ice cream, soak ½ cup mixed dried fruit in 2 tbsp Marsala wine or sweet sherry for 20 minutes. Follow the method for vanilla ice cream, omitting the vanilla bean, and stir in the soaked fruit in step 6, just before freezing.

Florentines

These luxury cookies are a popular at any time of the year, but make particularly wonderful treats at Christmas.

NUTRITIONAL INFORMATION

Calories 186   Sugars 19g
Protein . . . . .2g   Fat 11g
Carbohydrate . . .22g   Saturates 5g

20 MINS   15 MINS

MAKES 10

INGREDIENTS

4 tsp butter

¼ cup superfine sugar

¼ cup all-purpose flour, sifted

⅓ cup almonds, chopped

⅓ cup chopped mixed peel

¼ cup raisins, chopped

2 tbsp candied cherries, chopped

finely grated peel of ½ lemon

4½ oz semisweet chocolate, melted

1 Line 2 large cookie sheets with baking parchment.

2 Heat the butter and superfine sugar in a small saucepan until the butter has just melted and the sugar dissolved. Remove the pan from the heat.

3 Stir in the flour and mix well. Stir in the chopped almonds, mixed peel, raisins, cherries, and lemon peel. Place teaspoonfuls of the mixture well apart on the cookie sheets.

4 Bake in a preheated oven at 350°F for 10 minutes or until lightly golden.

5 As soon as the florentines are removed from the oven, press the edges into neat shapes while still on the cookie sheets, using a round cookie cutter. Leave to cool on the cookie sheets until firm, then transfer to a wire rack to cool completely.

6 Spread the melted chocolate over the smooth side of each florentine. As the chocolate begins to set, mark wavy lines in it with a fork. Leave the florentines until set, chocolate side up.

VARIATION

Replace the semisweet chocolate with white chocolate. For a dramatic effect, cover half of the florentines in dark chocolate and half in white.

Summer Puddings

A wonderful mixture of summer fruits encased in slices of white bread that soak up all the deep red flavorsome juices.

NUTRITIONAL INFORMATION

Calories 250	Sugars 41g	
Protein 4g	Fat 4g	
Carbohydrate ...53g	Saturates 2g	

10 MINS   10 MINS

SERVES 6

INGREDIENTS

vegetable oil or butter, for greasing

6–8 thin slices white bread, crusts removed

¾ cup superfine sugar

1¼ cups water

½ pint strawberries

2½ cups raspberries

1¼ cups black- and/or redcurrants

¾ cup blackberries or loganberries

mint sprigs, to decorate

pouring cream, to serve

1 Grease six ⅔ cup molds with butter or oil.

2 Line the molds with the bread, cutting it so it fits snugly.

3 Place the sugar in a saucepan with the water and heat gently, stirring frequently until dissolved. Bring to the boil and boil for 2 minutes.

4 Reserve 6 large strawberries for decoration. Add half the raspberries and the rest of the fruits to the syrup, cutting the strawberries in half if large, and simmer gently for a few minutes, until

beginning to soften but still retaining their shapes.

5 Spoon the fruits and some of the liquid into molds. Cover with more slices of bread. Spoon a little juice around the sides of the molds so the bread is well soaked. Cover with a saucer and a heavy weight, leave to cool, and chill thoroughly, preferably overnight.

6 Process the remaining raspberries in a food processor or blender, or press through a nylon strainer. Add enough of the liquid from the fruits to give a coating consistency.

7 Turn out onto serving plates and spoon the raspberry sauce over. Decorate with the mint sprigs and reserved strawberries.

Chocolate Cheesecake

This cheesecake takes a little time to prepare and cook but is well worth the effort. It is very rich and is good served with a little fresh fruit.

NUTRITIONAL INFORMATION

Calories 471   Sugars 20g
Protein . . . . .10g   Fat 33g
Carbohydrate . . .28g   Saturates 5g

15 MINS   1¼ HOURS

SERVES 12

I N G R E D I E N T S

¾ cup all-purpose flour

¾ cup ground almonds

¾ cup brown crystal sugar

⅔ cup margarine

1½ lb firm tofu

¾ cup vegetable oil

½ cup orange juice

¾ cup brandy

6 tbsp unsweetened cocoa powder,
   plus extra to decorate

2 tsp almond extract

confectioners' sugar and ground cherries,
   to decorate

1 Put the flour, ground almonds, and 1 tablespoon of the sugar in a bowl and mix well. Rub the margarine into the mixture to form a dough.

2 Lightly grease and line the bottom of a 9-inch springform pan. Press the dough into the bottom of the pan to cover, pushing the dough right up to the edge of the pan.

3 Roughly chop the tofu and put in a food processor with the vegetable oil, orange juice, brandy, unsweetened cocoa powder, almond extract, and remaining sugar and process until smooth and creamy. Pour over the bottom in the pan and cook in a preheated oven 325°F for 1–1¼ hours, or until set.

4 Leave to cool in the pan for 5 minutes, then remove from the pan and chill in the refrigerator. Dust with confectioners' sugar and unsweetened cocoa powder. Decorate with ground cherries and serve.

COOK'S TIP

Ground cherries make an attractive decoration for many desserts. Peel open the papery husks to expose the orange fruits.

Char-Grilled Pineapple

Fresh pineapple slices are cooked on the barbecue, and brushed with a buttery gingerroot and brown sugar baste.

NUTRITIONAL INFORMATION

Calories 461	Sugars 44g	
Protein 5g	Fat 30g	
Carbohydrate . . .45g	Saturates 20g	

 10 MINS   10 MINS

SERVES 4

I N G R E D I E N T S

1 fresh pineapple

B U T T E R

½ cup butter

½ cup light muscovado sugar

1 tsp finely grated gingerroot

T O P P I N G

1 cup plain fromage blanc

½ tsp ground cinnamon

1 tbsp light brown sugar

1 Prepare the fresh pineapple by cutting off the spiky top. Peel the pineapple with a sharp knife, remove the eyes and cut the flesh into thick slices.

2 To make the ginger-flavored butter, put the butter, sugar, and gingerroot into a small saucepan and heat gently until melted. Transfer to a heatproof bowl and keep warm at the side of the barbecue, ready for basting the fruit.

3 To prepare the topping, mix together the fromage blanc, cinnamon, and sugar. Cover and chill until ready to serve.

4 Barbecue the pineapple slices for about 2 minutes on each side, brushing them well with the ginger-butter baste.

5 Serve the chargrilled pineapple with a little extra ginger-butter sauce poured over. Top with a spoonful of the spiced fromage blanc.

VARIATION

If you prefer, substitute ½ teaspoon ground ginger for the grated gingerroot. You can make this dessert indoors by cooking the pineapple under a hot broiler.

Italian Chocolate Truffles

These are flavoured with almonds and chocolate, and are simplicity itself to make. Served with coffee, they are the perfect end to a meal.

NUTRITIONAL INFORMATION

Calories 82	Sugars 7g
Protein 1g	Fat 5g
Carbohydrate 8g	Saturates 3g

 5 MINS   5 MINS

MAKES 24

I N G R E D I E N T S

6 oz semisweet chocolate

2 tbsp almond-flavored or
    orange-flavored liqueur

3 tbsp unsalted butter

1¾ oz confectioners' sugar

½ cup ground blanched almonds

1¾ oz grated milk chocolate

1 Melt the semisweet chocolate with the liqueur in a bowl set over a saucepan of hot water, stirring until well combined.

2 Add the butter and stir until it has melted. Stir in the confectioners' sugar and the ground almonds.

3 Leave the mixture in a cool place until firm enough to roll into 24 balls.

4 Place the grated chocolate on a plate and roll the truffles in the chocolate to coat them.

5 Place the truffles in paper candy cases and chill.

Index